Distributing Risk

Distributing Risk

INSURANCE, LEGAL THEORY, AND PUBLIC POLICY

KENNETH S. ABRAHAM

Yale University Press

New Haven and London

Designed by James J. Johnson
and set in Electra Roman.
Printed in the United States of America by
Halliday Lithograph, West Hanover, Massachusetts.

Library of Congress Cataloging-in-Publication Data

Abraham, Kenneth S., 1946–
    Distributing risk.

    Includes index
    1. Insurance law—United States.   2. Risk (Insurance)—
United States.   I. Title.
KF1164.A72   1986   346.73'086   85–22459
ISBN 0–300–03460–1 (alk. paper) 347.30686

THE PAPER IN THIS BOOK MEETS THE GUIDELINES FOR PERMA-
NENCE AND DURABILITY OF THE COMMITTEE ON PRODUCTION
GUIDELINES FOR BOOK LONGEVITY OF THE COUNCIL ON LIBRARY
RESOURCES.

10   9   8   7   6   5   4   3   2   1

8/7/89
LN

FOR SUSAN

Contents

Acknowledgments

Writing a book is very much an effort at self-education. In the course of that effort, however, an author inevitably is assisted and educated by others. I have been lucky enough to incur a number of debts, both intellectual and personal, while writing this book.

During 1982 and 1983 my work was generously supported by a grant from the Esther A. and Joseph Klingenstein Fund that freed me from teaching responsibilities. Supporting this kind of project was an experiment for the Fund, and I am grateful for its confidence in me. In addition, Dean Michael J. Kelly of the University of Maryland School of Law provided me with summer research support, a sabbatical leave, encouragement, and friendship during the several years the book was in preparation. When I took up residence at the University of Virginia School of Law, Dean Richard Merrill provided me with a summer stipend that enabled me to complete the project. I am grateful to both Dean Kelly and Dean Merrill for their support.

Several people read all or portions of a draft of the book, gave me comments and criticisms, and asked the kinds of questions that help put an author in touch with his potential audience. For this help I want to thank Charles Goetz, Paul Gewirtz, Henry Hansmann, David Luban, Jeffrey O'Connell, Samuel Rea, Robert Scott, Tony Waters, and Gordon Young. Guido Calabresi not only commented on the book; his teaching and scholarship have influenced me in countless ways over the years. Michael Tonry did more than simply read and comment. At every stage he was everything one hopes for in a colleague—inquisitive, helpful, dubious, and encouraging. Several others who have stimulated me and helped to

ix

create the intellectual background that I brought to the project also deserve thanks. These include Stanley Fish, Garrett Power, Walter Michaels, and Peter Quint.

I presented several chapters of the book at various workshops: before the Yale Law School Civil Liability Program; at the University of Maryland and University of Virginia Schools of Law; and at the Center for Philosophy and Public Policy of the University of Maryland. The participants in these workshops helped open my eyes to issues I had not seen before. Three chapters in the book appeared in somewhat different form in volumes 67 and 61 of the *Virginia Law Review* (chapters 4 and 5) and in volume 2 of the *Virginia Journal of Natural Resources Law* (chapter 3). I thank the editors of these journals for permission to use material from these chapters. I was lucky to have the aid of five research assistants who at various times helped me to mine the depths of insurance law: Deborah Clovis, Andrew Fried, Steven Meis, Elizabeth Osterman, and Neil Schechter. Their thoroughness and persistence was invaluable. I have also had the good fortune to work with two very capable and extraordinarily patient secretaries, Ann Garrett and Lisa Atwell. Both tolerated what must have seemed to be endless revisions with good cheer and the attention to detail that helps an author sleep at night.

Finally, to my wife, Susan, whose love and understanding throughout have helped me see the project to its completion, I dedicate the book.

1   The Relevance of Insurance to Public Policy

Americans spend well over two hundred billion dollars each year for private insurance. We insure to protect ourselves against fire, accidents, and other casualties and to soften the consequences of ill health, disability, and death.[1] Average citizens often are covered by Social Security, workers' compensation, and life, health, accident, disability, homeowner's, and automobile insurance. Insurance figures prominently in estate planning, in governmental activities, and in business ventures ranging from the local grocery store to the multinational corporation. Yet the intricacies of insurance and insurance law mystify both laypeople and most lawyers. This book attempts to demystify and to rethink the subject by examining the impact of private insurance on issues of legal and public policy and the relevance of public policy concerns to the law of insurance.

A body of rules so vast that it fills over twenty volumes of each of the two major treatises on insurance law has developed to deal with the legal issues related to insurance.[2] Together with the shorter and more analytical works on insurance law,[3] these treatises provide ready answers to specific legal problems. There is almost no writing, however, that moves beyond the rules of insurance law to inquire into the foundations of the subject. In subsequent chapters I want to uncover those foundations and trace their implications. But before embarking on that task, it will be useful to spend a few pages discussing why the subject of insurance is significant and examining the striking way in which contemporary scholarship has been nearly blind to that significance.

Insurance is a method of managing risk by distributing it among large numbers of individuals or enterprises. As I use the term, *risk* simply means the possi-

1

bility of injury or loss. By paying a relatively small sum—the insurance pre-mium—the insured policyholder receives a promise from an insurance company to pay the insured if he or she suffers a loss. The insured avoids the risk of suffering a large loss by substituting the certainty of suffering a small one. Assuming that the risks a company covers are largely independent of each other, the insurer pro-tects itself against the risk of suffering net losses by covering a large number of dif-ferent insureds. In effect, the insurer distributes risk among all of its insureds.

Two important points should be recognized at the outset, because they affect this relation between risk and insurance. First, risk is not entirely undesirable. A world without it would be intolerably dull. In such a world there would be no ad-venture, because nothing would be left to chance. Much of what makes life chal-lenging, complex, and satisfying would be missing. The right to take risks is very much a part of our political tradition and social compact. Indeed, the availability of a rich variety of risky endeavors is part of what is special about our culture. So we should not assume that more widespread or larger amounts of insurance are always desirable, though of course sometimes they are. The second point worth noting is that, even when risk is undesirable, insurance is not our only method of managing or avoiding it. There are many other devices for dealing with risk. We make contracts that allocate risks regarding the future price, supply, and safety of goods and services; we diversify our investments; we spend money on safety; and we engage in any number of other actions that manage risk.

Not only are there many ways of managing risk besides insuring; even insur-ance arrangements typically have elements of both individual risk bearing and collective risk sharing. Insurance can be made subject to deductible or coinsur-ance provisions* that require the insured to take partial responsibility for any loss suffered; and by definition the insured bears any loss above the stated policy limit. In addition, there is a less obvious yet very significant element of individual risk bearing that is incorporated in most forms of insurance. Insurers try to set the price of coverage in accordance with the insured's expected loss—the probability of a loss multiplied by the magnitude of the loss if it occurs. When such pricing is ac-curate, there is considerable individual risk bearing, for then the insured pays a premium based on the predictable risk that he or she will suffer a loss. The insurer simply pools the risk of unpredictable individual losses. However, since accurate prediction is difficult, considerable risk sharing actually occurs. Because of varia-tion in the predictability of losses, different kinds of insurance embody different proportions of individual responsibility for loss and collective risk sharing.

*A deductible provision specifies a sum to be deducted from the amount an insurer would otherwise be obligated to pay the insured; a coinsurance provision specifies the percentage of a loss an insurer must pay the insured.

A major function of the law governing insurance is to regulate these proportions of individual responsibility and collective risk sharing. Because legal regulation of insurance reflects the diversity of the insurance market and the mixed legal and economic system under which we live, neither a free market nor a collective approach predominates. Some features of the insurance market are left to individual choice, but others are regulated. Legal rules police the borderline between these realms by separating the issues that are subject to collective resolution through law from those that are left to individual decisions in the marketplace. Just as important, legal rules implement collective decisions about the scope, nature, price, and amount of insurance coverage that is desirable in different settings and about the appropriate influence of public policies and principles on these features of insurance coverage.

Regulation of this sort involves more than merely technical insurance issues; it involves fundamental questions of political and legal philosophy. On what bases shall we require individuals to bear risks? When is it legitimate to compel people to share risks that many of them would prefer to bear individually or to manage through other devices, such as investment in loss prevention? When should we use insurance to distribute risk, and when are other methods of risk management preferable? To what extent should what we try to accomplish with insurance, through law, depend on the effectiveness of and our attitudes toward other forms of risk taking and risk management?

Modern insurance law scholarship has paid little attention to these fundamental questions. Since most writing about insurance has occurred in the shadow of the treatise tradition, it has been concerned mainly with legal rules and their application rather than with the principles and policies that lie behind the rules. With a few important exceptions,[4] insurance law is the province of specialists focusing more on technical detail than on underlying structure and purpose.

Three themes important to a complete understanding of insurance and insurance law have been almost entirely ignored. These themes deal with economic and moral goals and with the nature of the legal process through which these goals are pursued. Throughout the book, I will try to show how these themes run through most of the problems of insurance law and how they should influence resolution of the fundamental questions I have just raised. Although the themes tend to operate simultaneously, it may be helpful to describe them here individually and to sketch some of the settings in which I shall examine them.

The first theme is economic. There is now a mature body of legal scholarship that uses economic analysis to generate a broad range of insights about law.[5] In field after legal field, economic analysis has directed the attention of legal thinkers to issues that had previously been ignored or incompletely understood. Economic analysis of insurance law is long overdue. In the chapters that follow I shall begin the task of bringing economic thought to bear on the problems of insurance and their relation to other fields of law. The first step is undertaken in chapter 2, which constructs a framework for analyzing these problems. Subsequent chapters then confront a series of different issues from an economic standpoint. In each of these chapters I try to show how economic ideas can clarify the aims of insurance law, and I recommend changes to help achieve these aims.

For example, many proposals for reform of accident law are designed to promote optimal deterrence—that combination of risk and safety which minimizes the social and economic costs of accidents and accident avoidance. The success of these reforms will depend in part on the availability of liability insurance that helps to promote, or at least does not impede, accurate calculation of the costs of accidents by those who are liable for them. Otherwise accurate optimization will not occur. Yet insurance that meets these requirements is not always available or feasible.

Chapter 3 pursues this insight in discussing the very different effects that liability insurance is likely to have on reform in such fields as medical malpractice, product liability, and environmental law. It then turns to a specific reform designed to deal with environmental damage: the publicly operated, privately financed toxic tort compensation fund. The analysis demonstrates that the deterrent effect of this approach is likely to be confounded by the inadequacies of the insurance devices on which it relies. The strong implication is that, in this field at least, the insurance system is not ready to serve as a surrogate for more traditional methods of governmental safety regulation. The chapter's broader message is that civil liability reforms must take account of the potential impact of insurance on their effectiveness if they are to succeed in achieving their goals.

A second example of the manner in which economic analysis can shed light on problems in insurance law is found in my effort to develop a theory of coordinated insurance coverage. The need for such a theory has arisen because of the proliferation of different kinds of insurance in recent years. The result has been that the coverage contained in different polices often overlaps. It is therefore increasingly common for insurance disputes to involve a single policyholder and not one, but several insurers. The methods by which the private market provides for coordination in the event of such potential duplication of coverage have never been fully appreciated. Nor have the judicial and legislative attempts to coordinate coverage when market methods fail realized all their potential. I argue in chapter 6 that one of the principal aims of coordination is, and should be, to create loss prevention incentives on the part of the policyholders to whose companies coverage responsibility is allocated when insurance policies overlap. In the course of that discussion I show how coordination can be used to promote this and other objectives.

The second theme that has been neglected in most contemporary studies of insurance is a philosophical one. Political and moral philosophy have long been concerned with the obligations of individuals to each other and with the proper role of government in redistributing resources among individuals.[6] Insurance law has implications for both these concerns. Insurance distributes risk among individuals, and insurance law regulates this process of risk distribution, sometimes working redistributions of its own. Yet there has been almost no examination or evaluation of the demands that can be made on insurance practices and insurance law in the name of moral principle.

These demands are by no means monolithic. Different moral philosophies yield very different conceptions of fairness in risk distribution. For instance, the philosophy known as libertarianism supports little if any legal adjustment of private risk distribution relations, but the cluster of views often termed egalitarianism suggests that requiring broad distribution of certain risks is sometimes morally appropriate. I first develop the general implications of several such philosophies in constructing the analytical framework that is the subject of chapter 2. The thematic studies in the remainder of the book apply the framework in an attempt to elucidate—among other things—the relation between the economic and moral values at work in insurance law.

A principal example of this approach is contained in chapter 4, where the tensions between economic efficiency and risk-distributional fairness are revealed through an analysis of insurance risk classification practices. These tensions produce compromises between comparatively efficient forms of classification and concerns about distributions of risk that burden recognizable groups or individuals in undesirable ways. For instance, the drive for efficiency may generate uneven distribution of the burdens of inaccurate loss prediction, classifications based on noncontrollable characteristics such as the sex of the insured, and the use of risk classes that are morally suspect for other reasons. The chapter explores the nature of these very different forms of risk-distributional unfairness and suggests methods of reconciling economic and risk-distributional values.

A final theme that has been largely ignored in the insurance literature concerns the nature of the legal process.[7] Different legal institutions make and apply insurance law, and these institutions have different strengths and weaknesses. Yet little has been written about the comparative competence of the three major insurance law-making institutions: the courts, state legislatures, and state insurance commissioners. Comparative institutional competence figures in almost every chapter in this book. This issue is of special importance in chapter 5, which examines what I call "judge-made insurance." The courts traditionally have used interpretive techniques to create insurance coverage even when the language of insurance policies does not appear to provide for coverage. But the justifications for this practice have not been recognized; nor have its proper limits been delineated. Chapter 5 explores the economic and risk-distributional justifications for the practice, assesses the competence of the courts as designers of insurance coverage, and isolates the features of this process that would be more sensibly allocated to other law-making institutions.

These three themes—economic, philosophical, and institutional—will guide my inquiry. The thesis the inquiry generates is that insurance law can be better understood and used more effectively if we become much more explicit about and attentive to its functions and capacities. We need to recognize more clearly the relation between insurance and other methods of managing risk and to examine closely the basic economic and philosophical questions posed by different approaches to the legal regulation of insurance. These are questions about trade-offs: between loss prevention and the broad spreading of risk, between present and future gains, and between different conceptions of fairness in the distribution of risk. Insurance is a powerful tool for managing risk, but its capacities are not unlimited. Isolating the trade-offs its use demands is an important aspect of this study.

The most important message I wish to transmit in this book is that the body of law governing insurance is not the obscure and insignificant field it is sometimes thought. Rather, legal regulation of insurance is an example of our approach to many important social problems, as well as a vehicle through which the abstractions at the heart of our political and economic system are translated into concrete policy. Insurance law is both a reflection of our views about the proper scope of risk sharing through private insurance and a principal means of affecting the balance between insurance and other methods of managing risk. It is time for its functions to be much better understood.

Because of this focus, none of the chapters that follow is concerned exclusively with any particular kind of insurance. Although there are many legal rules that pertain mainly to life or to health insurance, for example, the relation of insurance law to broader concerns about risk distribution can best be discovered by analyzing problems that cut across conventional insurance categories. I have chosen to study a variety of subjects: judicial, legislative, and administrative law problems; environmental issues of wide public interest; sexual and statistical discrimination in insurance; and a few matters, like the coordination of coverage, that until now have received very little publicity but are nevertheless of increasing importance. Each can be considered a case study designed to reveal the utility of the approach taken in this book and to encourage efforts to uncover still more in the field that is ripe for analysis. Although I take positions on the issues discussed in each chapter, my goal is not simply to persuade the reader that my views are correct, though of course I hope to do that. Rather, by discussing insurance issues in a new way, I want to open debate about questions that have not been previously understood and sometimes not even clearly recognized as questions.

Finally, a word about the audience to which this study is directed. A book on the minutiae of insurance law would be of interest to very few. Yet attention to technical detail is often necessary to rigorous analysis of this subject. Therefore, I have not avoided in-depth discussion of legal points when necessary. Instead, I have tried to strike a balance between legal analysis and the application of considerations of public policy to that analysis. Perhaps it is a measure of how complicated our world has become that basic issues like those I shall discuss are so often encumbered by technicality. However, that technicality cannot be stripped away without depriving issues of their richness. I believe that people who are not lawyers should be able to talk about and influence the directions the law takes. But nonlawyers cannot have this influence if they are exposed only to watered-down, oversimplified versions of law and legal analysis. They will have to roll up their sleeves and struggle amidst legal doctrine with the rest of us to have any real impact on what happens to insurance law. Those who are not lawyers will have to become comfortable with the language and operations of law in order to retain understanding and control of law.

But lawyers should not simply sit and watch while others struggle to understand how law works. New obligations have descended onto the professional side of the bar as well. Law has become increasingly (and properly) concerned with the economic and moral justifications for what it does. The old picture of the lawyer as a jack-of-all-trades who could learn any subject in enough detail to work with it may well be becoming obsolete; but lawyers, judges, and lawmakers certainly cannot afford to depend exclusively on experts in philosophy and economics for answers to legal problems. Lawyers trained mainly in legal analysis will have to become familiar with other disciplines or they will be left by the wayside. Insurance lawyers are no exception; they must become interdisciplinary professionals to be effective in shaping legal rules governing insurance.

In short, my hope is that this study will be of value not only to lawyers, judges, legal scholars, and insurance specialists. It is intended for anyone who is interested in the way modern ideas about public policy can illuminate legal issues and the ways in which even apparently specialized legal problems can raise important economic and philosophical questions.

2   The Purposes and Structure of Insurance Law

This chapter discusses the purposes and structure of insurance law, developing the tools for analyzing our subject. It constructs a framework for analyzing insurance law through examination of the purposes of this body of law and the different legal institutions that make it. This framework is not a substitute for traditional modes of analysis; it does not attempt to do the work of insurance law treatises in a new way. Rather, the goal here is to reveal something that treatises and similar studies could not, by their nature, aspire to reveal: an underlying structure that is less concerned with particular legal doctrines than with the principles and policies that justify the construction of legal doctrine in the first place.

Insurance law traditionally has been analyzed by considering the different kinds of insurance the rules of insurance law govern or the specific legal doctrines they implement.[1] More recent works have been organized according to patterns that cut across formal categories.[2] These works deal with such themes as the marketing of coverage, the claims process, and insurance regulation. But like so much in insurance law, both the traditional treatises and the thematic studies tend to be internally oriented. They focus primarily on the characteristics of each doctrine or theme, and they make little use of insights that have developed in fields outside insurance law. These approaches are very useful to the lawyer or student who desires a systematic overview of a particular legal doctrine or wants to locate the problem he or she faces within a well-conceived, logical structure.

Focus on substantive themes, however, tends to restrict the analyst's view of what links the themes together and, on occasion, transcends them. In order to see insurance law from a new perspective, a different approach is required. That approach, of course, should deal explicitly with insurance law doctrine; but it also should link insurance law with concerns that the field shares with other bodies of law, through the principles and policies that the law of insurance serves. This is the function of the framework developed below.

The framework is divided into two parts. The first part analyzes the principal purposes served by insurance law. These are economic efficiency, the fair distribution of risk, and promoting equitable relations between insurers and insureds.[3] The second part is devoted to the institutional context in which insurance law is made and applied. Three centers of authority—legislative, administrative, and judicial—play a role in furthering the purposes examined in the first part. It should be obvious that these purposes are not unique to insurance law and that the institutional context in which insurance law is developed is roughly the same one from which much of American law emerges. This familiar structure, however, is part of the point. It is time for insurance law to be recognized for what it is—not an exotic species that belongs in a legal zoo, but a system that is subject to and part of the same regime of principles and policies that constitutes the rest of the law. The value of the framework, then, is found not only in the framework itself, but also in the insights about insurance law that the framework can produce.

THE PURPOSES OF INSURANCE LAW

Any body of law must seek its ultimate justification within a political or moral theory that describes the proper role of law in promoting justice. However, I will not adopt a particular formal theory of justice for use in analyzing insurance law. In my view, insurance law—like most contemporary law—does not reflect any single notion of justice. An effort to link insurance law to such a notion would be an argument for that notion of justice, not a characterization of insurance law as it actually is. Instead, I will try to show that the three purposes of insurance law are derived from widely shared values and moral intuitions and that these values are reflected in the doctrines that constitute this body of law. In more general forms these values and intuitions often figure prominently in the different theories of justice I will be examining.

In recent years there has been much consternation in legal circles about the source and status of the values that drive the making and interpretation of law. Often the issue is addressed by questioning whether these values are objective and firm or subjective and arbitrary. I find this way of posing the issue misleading, however. Values—the purposes law serves—are not things in the same way as tables and chairs. For this reason they cannot be objective in the same way as physical facts. But neither, in my view, are values subjective in a way that necessarily makes them arbitrary. When values are shared—as they often are, even when individuals disagree at the margin as to the scope or implications of particular values—then they have as much objectivity as we have a right to ask for or ever need. Agreement on what is important creates objectivity in the realm of values. In discussing the purposes of insurance law, therefore, the issue is not whether the values served by this body of law are objectively grounded, but whether they are able to command agreement.

Almost every body of law serves a number of purposes. Even individual legal doctrines, statutes, or regulations are likely to have more than one purpose or justification. In the following sections I treat the purposes of insurance law separately so that each can be examined on its own. In practice, of course, purposes are not so easily isolated from each other. Sometimes they overlap; on occasions they collide. Conceiving of the purposes as analytically distinct, however, is a necessary part of the effort to understand insurance law and to use it effectively to serve these purposes.

Economic Efficiency

Economic efficiency is a measure of the degree to which particular allocations or uses of resources maximize their value. Efficiency has both technical and common sense meanings. Under one technical measure of efficiency, Pareto optimality, an allocation of resources is efficient if no one could be made better off by a reallocation without someone else's being made worse off. According to another measure, Kaldor-Hicks efficiency, an allocation is efficient if there is no reallocation under which those made better off could compensate those made worse off for their losses and still be better off after the reallocation.[4] In contrast, the view of efficiency commonly taken in the less technical legal literature translates these definitions into the notion that an allocation is efficient when resources are used in a manner that maximizes their value. In the discussions that follow I shall use the term *efficiency* in the nontechnical, popular sense. Although there are certain imprecisions entailed in employing the term this way, the popular notion of efficiency is nevertheless quite suitable for its primary purpose here: to distinguish concern with the productive and valuable allocation or use of resources from fairness in the distribution of those resources to particular individuals or enterprises.

Economic analysis of insurance and insurance law can serve two related purposes. Descriptive, or positive, analysis can describe and model the economic operation of legal rules and institutions. It can point out the incentive effects and distributional consequences of different insurance arrangements. Positive analysis should be of use to anyone who believes that the efficiency of a system is relevant to legal policy. On the other hand, normative analysis does not merely describe. It recommends, generally from the premise that economic efficiency is at least one goal and sometimes the primary goal that should be pursued by the legal system.

I believe that insurance law not only does reflect a concern with the efficient allocation of resources, but that it should reflect such a concern. As a result, my analysis often will be normative. The goal of even the normative analyses I undertake, however, is to show where the search for efficiency in insurance law may lead. Since my thesis is that insurance law serves a variety of purposes, of which economic efficiency is only one, my major objective will be to expose the economic implications of the problems being analyzed so that these implications may be considered along with the noneconomic concerns that also bear on these issues.

Insurance law promotes efficiency whenever it is structured to help reduce the sum of the costs of insurance and loss prevention.[5] The intuitive idea behind this formula is that resources are allocated inefficiently whenever more could be saved through loss prevention than can be protected through insurance. Money should be spent on loss prevention—safety precautions, reduction of production or activity levels, or both—rather than insurance so long as it promises to save more than the same expenditure on insurance would protect. In this way the sum of the two costs will be reduced.

For example, suppose that I own a building worth $1,000,000 and that the building is fully insured against fire. In order to simplify matters, let us assume that there is no deductible or coinsurance involved and that any fire would completely destroy the building. If the probability that the building will be totally destroyed by fire in any one year is 1 percent, then my expected loss (the probability of loss multiplied by the amount of the loss if it occurs) is $10,000. But suppose I can cut my expected loss in half by installing a sprinkler system at a cost of $2,000 per year. Whether I should install sprinklers depends on whether I can save more than $2,000 a year on fire insurance by doing so. Since in the absence of market imperfections my premiums will be slightly in excess of my expected loss ($10,000 before installation, $5,000 after), installation of sprinklers almost surely will make sense. By investing $2,000 in sprinklers, I can save about $5,000 on insurance, for a net saving of $3,000. Under these conditions, I should continue investing in loss prevention as long as one dollar spent on prevention reduces my expected loss by more than a dollar.

A second important feature of the relation between insurance and economic efficiency concerns the difference between risk neutrality and risk aversion. A person is risk neutral if he or she is indifferent in choosing between risks of different magnitude but of the same expected value—a 1 percent chance of losing $1,000,000 and a 100 percent chance of losing $10,000, for example. In contrast, a risk-averse individual is sensitive to magnitudes of risk. Such an individual would rather face the high probability of small losses than the low probability of large losses, even when each loss has the same expected value. Because of their risk aversion, such individuals tend to purchase insurance instead of taking risks. They are willing to pay more than their expected loss in order to reduce the risk of suffering an even larger loss. By satisfying risk-averse individuals' demand for protection against risk, insurance can enhance economic efficiency.

Notice, however, that a key to achieving an efficient allocation between the insurance and loss prevention methods of protecting against risk is the pricing of insurance coverage in accordance with expected loss. If pricing is inaccurate, then the allocation between these two methods will not be optimal. Even if I am risk neutral, I may purchase insurance if it is underpriced. And if I am risk averse—as most people are at some levels of risk—I may purchase more insurance than I would otherwise: I will underallocate to prevention and overallocate to insurance. On the other hand, if insurance is overpriced, then even risk-averse individuals may overallocate to prevention. They may install sprinklers, when sprinklers save less than their cost, because the insurance that is available would produce even less protection for the same investment. Of course, in practice people do not buy insurance and invest in loss prevention in sequence. They invest simultaneously in both, the combination depending on the cost of reducing the risk in question through loss prevention, the price of insurance, and the nature and degree of their risk aversion, among other things.[6]

A useful way of thinking about these allocational implications of different insurance arrangements is to focus on the trade-off between present loss distribution and future loss prevention. An insurance regime concerned exclusively with efficient risk allocation is future oriented. Such a regime is structured to create incentives for insureds to adopt optimal combinations of insurance and loss prevention. In contrast, a regime concerned with the distribution of losses in the present embodies distributional or equitable purposes that are likely to hinder the risk-allocational functions of insurance.

This is because any decision to distribute a loss when such distribution is not the result of an already determined risk allocation both disturbs a previous allocation and creates new incentives on the part of similarly situated insureds. If those incentives are not optimal, then the decision to favor present distribution over future allocation has been inefficient. In subsequent sections I will explore the reasons that such sacrifice may be warranted. In the remainder of this section, I examine the other factors that may impede efficient allocation of risk through insurance.

In a perfectly competitive market, the money available for insurance and loss prevention will be allocated efficiently without any legal assistance. Insurers will compete for the best risks by charging as nearly as possible in accordance with expected loss, and insureds will shop for optimal combinations of insurance and loss prevention. But a variety of factors may impede the insurance market's movement toward an efficient allocation. These are noncompetitive pricing, the cost of engaging in transactions that would bring about a more efficient allocation, and externalities.[7] Each of these phenomena suggests settings in which legal intervention may be appropriate.

Noncompetitive Pricing

Monopoly is the classic example of a market imperfection that prevents competitive pricing. When entry into the market by prospective sellers of insurance is restricted, through capital requirements, unfair competition, or regulatory standards, and prices are not adequately controlled, then the restricted output and excessive prices characteristic of a monopoly may be produced. People will be charged more than their expected loss (plus the administrative costs of providing insurance), and only the comparatively risk averse will purchase coverage. In such cases, an inefficiently low amount of insurance will be purchased, and there may be excessive investment in loss prevention.

Legal intervention to remedy such imperfections may be economically warranted if the benefits of intervention outweigh its costs. But we should also note that sometimes legal intervention causes rather than solves the problems arising from noncompetitive pricing. If through administrative regulation or other devices insurance prices are kept artificially low, then people may buy more insurance than they would if entry into the market by sellers were unrestricted and prices unregulated. Even in the face of such regulation, however, insurers can attempt to restrict output by decreasing the quality of the coverage and service they offer for the regulated price or (eventually) withdrawing from the market. Thus, when the right to sell insurance is limited, the level of premiums is controlled, the terms of coverage are regulated, or competition among insurers is otherwise inhibited, an inefficient allocation of risk-managing resources may result. Resources then will be under- or overallocated to insurance as compared to investment in loss prevention or other goods.

Transactions Costs

The second obstacle to the operation of efficient markets is the cost of the transactions that move resources to their most valued uses. In the frictionless world of economic theory, transactions that promote efficiency occur without cost. But in the real world efficient allocations may not occur because the cost of some transactions may exceed the additional value they would produce for the parties who would otherwise wish to engage in them.

Transactions costs frequently impede the efficiency of insurance markets in much the same way that they affect other markets. For instance, often potential insureds do not have complete information about the risks they face or the scope of the insurance coverage that is available to them. Unless they pay in time or money to inform themselves, they may make risk-related decisions that do not entirely serve their interests. Further, frequently individual preferences cannot be met by insurers because the cost of bargaining about and individualizing agreements on each preference would be excessive and because considerable uniformity in the nature of the insurer's undertakings is necessary to make actuarial calculations sound.

Insurers too are handicapped by having less-than-perfect information. One handicap in particular has significant effects on the allocation of resources between insurance and loss prevention. This is the problem of moral hazard. In order to compete for the lowest-risk insureds, insurers try to charge insureds based on their expected losses. In this way they avoid overcharging low-risk insureds and can attract their business. But insureds to some extent control the probability that losses will occur. Once an individual has purchased insurance, his or her incentive to control losses decreases. Moral hazard is the resulting tendency of an insured to underallocate to loss prevention after purchasing insurance.

For example, suppose that you purchase homeowner's insurance, protecting you (among other things) against loss due to fire and against liability to others for injuries they suffer while visiting you. You now have less incentive to be careful around the house than you did before you were insured because you will not bear the full cost of your carelessness. Probably you will still take many safety precautions after you are insured—you will not want your home damaged or your guests injured regardless of whether you will suffer a net economic loss if either of these events occurs. But other things being equal, insurance against loss will reduce your incentive to prevent the insured event from occurring, because you will have a tendency to treat your insurance coverage as though it were a good that can be consumed for free. Once you have paid a premium, you alone do not have to shoulder the cost of a loss. In effect the loss is borne by the other holders of homeowner's insurance, each of whom also has a reduced incentive to take loss prevention measures.[8] In this broad sense, the problem of moral hazard plagues all forms of insurance and tends to produce an underallocation of resources to loss prevention.

If it cost nothing to monitor an insured's behavior, the problem of moral hazard could be solved. The insured would simply be charged for coverage in accordance with the amount of care he had taken to avoid the loss in question. However, because loss predictions are imperfect and behavior cannot be monitored without cost, insurance may create incentive effects that are inefficient. To some extent these inefficiencies can be counteracted by contractual and legal devices that reduce the moral hazard of insurance. Exceptions to coverage for intentionally caused harm, both implied[9] and express,[10] and the requirement that the insured have an insurable interest in the person or property covered eliminate the most obvious moral hazard. Coinsurance[11] and deductible[12] provisions give the insured a stake in self-protection, as does the practice of limiting the dollar amount of coverage afforded by a policy. But in reducing moral hazard, these latter three devices also reduce the beneficial risk-spreading effects of insurance.

Perhaps the insurer's most important method of dealing with moral hazard is to create risk classes and to vary the prices charged for coverage, depending on the expected loss of each class of insureds. The more accurate and detailed this risk classification, the greater its influence on the allocation between loss prevention and insurance. For instance, by varying premiums with the loss experience of the insured—experience rating—the insurer can create loss prevention incentives and thereby mitigate moral hazard. An increase in the cost of insurance may indicate to the insured that he could more cheaply obtain the same total protection against loss by allocating more to prevention and less to insurance. A decrease in price may indicate the opposite—that too much has been allocated to prevention.

There is a point, however, at which the cost of acquiring and interpreting data to support further refinement of risk classifications is not worth the advantage to be gained from refinement. This point represents the limits of the insurer's capacity to reduce moral hazard and minimize the inefficient features of insurance through risk classification. Beyond this point risk is distributed among insureds with different expected losses, and prices only roughly reflect the riskiness of each insured's activities. As a result, insurers almost continually face the problem of adverse selection. This is the process by which low-risk insureds tend to purchase less coverage, and high-risk insureds tend to purchase more coverage than they would if prices were more accurate. Such individuals may then over- or underallocate resources to loss prevention.

Despite these limitations, in two ways insurance also can help to reduce certain transactions costs and thereby promote efficiency. First, the risk spreading embodied in insurance has allocational effects. A potential insured's uncertainty about future losses tends to inhibit the productive use of assets because some assets must be reserved or left liquid to cover potential losses. The purchase of insurance reduces these uncertainty costs by stabilizing the reserving process. Insurance fixes a sum—the insurance premium—that is automatically reserved to cover losses. Remaining assets (up to a point where policy limits are exhausted) can thereafter be used in more productive ways. Second, in its capacity as a risk pooler the insurer may acquire useful information more efficiently than individual insureds. Insurance prices or risk classifications can provide information about the riskiness of an insured's activities that the insured himself would have ignored or figured inaccurately. The insured may then be able to make more efficient decisions concerning the optimal combination of risk, insurance, and loss prevention to adopt in conducting his or her activities. Further, since the insurer pools a large number of similar risks, it will sometimes be better equipped than any individual insured—because of its superior access to loss experience statistics or greater ability to finance research into loss prevention methods—to discover more efficient courses of conduct than those its insureds currently follow. When this is so, and the insurer is able to have its suggestions for changes in behavior implemented, efficiency is enhanced.

Achieving these effects, however, also depends on the communication of useful information to the insured. The insured first must know the risks transferred by a policy to the insurer. If the policy is complex and convoluted, the insured may have only a rough idea of which risks he retains and which are transferred. The insured also must be able to understand the reasons for premium rates and the nature of the behavioral changes he or she can make to reduce future premium charges. Otherwise the insured will not be able to capitalize on the information that would make risk, insurance, and loss prevention decisions more efficient.

Externalities

The third phenomenon that may impede the efficient allocation of resources is what economists call "externalities." Externalities are social benefits or costs that are not translated into market signals. If I can avoid paying the full cost of a resource I consume, then I will consume an excessive amount of it. For example, a firm that pollutes a river when no liability attaches to its action externalizes the cost of pollution to others. If the firm is forced to internalize the cost of pollution by being held liable for pollution damage, it probably will "consume" less of the river.

In a sense externalities are simply one kind of transaction cost. The famous Coase theorem shows why, in the absence of transactions costs, externalities would not impede efficiency.[13] If downstream owners would benefit more from having a clean river than the polluter benefits from polluting, the former would pay the latter to refrain from polluting. If having a clean river were not worth its cost, no payment would be made and the pollution would continue. In either case, resources would be efficiently allocated. Similarly, even an otherwise inefficient legal rule could be circumvented contractually. If downstream owners had an absolute right to a clean river, then the polluter would buy this right from the downstream owners if the benefits of polluting warranted the cost of purchase. Because of transactions costs, however, externalities can result in inefficient allocations. Bargaining with downstream owners may be too costly, or collective action to buy out the polluter may not be feasible. Therefore, it often makes a critical difference what rule of legal liability is adopted.

Yet, even when legal rules are specifically designed to promote efficiency, the externalization of risk produced by insurance may confound the intended effects of the rules. For example, the influence of potential liability on behavior is a central feature of certain economic rationales for tort liability. Properly imposed, tort liability is supposed by these rationales to promote optimal deterrence, that is, the efficient combination of loss prevention and risk. However, insurance that is not priced precisely in accordance with potential defendants' expected losses may undercut the force of these rationales, as some of their proponents acknowledge.[14] To the extent that a potential defendant can externalize the costs of liability by purchasing insurance, its loss prevention incentives are reduced. If a firm's actual expected loss is high, but insurance premiums are only crudely rated, it may be economically irrational for the firm to conduct its activities more safely. It may be better off free riding on the loss prevention efforts of the other members of its risk class.

When there is much actuarial data and refined risk classification is inexpensive, liability insurance may not impede approaching optimal deterrence through the imposition of civil liability. Workers' compensation is sometimes thought to be an example of such a field. But when accurate data about expected losses are scarce or it is expensive for other reasons to apply available data, then the imposition of liability may simply cause defendants to purchase more insurance without having optimizing effects on behavior. Liability for some environmentally caused diseases whose etiology and effects are incompletely understood probably falls into this category. As I explain in the next chapter, until we can predict what forms of exposure to what kinds of chemicals will cause what kinds of disease, it will be very difficult to set accurate prices for insurance against toxic tort liability. It does not necessarily follow that the imposition of civil liability is inappropriate whenever insurance against such liability cannot be priced accurately. Rough allocation of costs to an entire industry, without regard to the actor that has caused any individual loss, may be a satisfactory goal. But we should recognize that it is this goal and not carefully individualized deterrence that is being achieved.

In short, the difference between the incentives produced by a refined as opposed to a very blunt insurance pricing system may be considerable. The law governing the devices that are used in combination with differential pricing to mitigate moral hazard in insurance—exceptions to coverage, coinsurance, and application screening, among others—should take the function of these devices into account if the effects of civil liability and insurance law are to work in tandem and not at cross purposes.

Fair Risk Distribution

Economic efficiency is by no means the only goal of our legal system. It certainly is not the only goal of insurance law. We care about avoiding waste and maximizing the productivity of resources, but not to the exclusion of other values. In the broadest sense the goal of any legal system is to achieve justice, and few would consider the single-minded pursuit of efficiency a sufficient prescription for reaching that goal.

The concept of efficiency ignores questions about the appropriate distribution of wealth and protection against risk, because the preferability of a given allocation of resources is measured by consumer willingness to pay for those resources. Consequently, the idea of efficiency assumes a given distribution of wealth. If wealth were differently distributed, other allocations of resources might be efficient because consumers would be willing to pay more or less for the same resources, depending on the wealth at their disposal. A natural consideration, therefore, is whether the distribution of risk produced by insurance and regulated or altered by insurance law is fair, regardless of whether the allocation involved is efficient.

This consideration arises in a special way. Few people in our society object, on grounds of fairness, that the amount of risk distribution people choose to have through private insurance is excessive. No one thinks it unfair or immoral that people do not have to bear all the risks of their activities. If we are ever concerned that people have chosen to share risk excessively, our concerns are grounded in reasons of efficiency and loss prevention. Our society worries little if at all that we tamper with fate by purchasing insurance coverage. The most obvious proof of this attitude is the opportunity to purchase large amounts of various forms of coverage. The controversial questions, then, concern how much *more* risk distribution than the private market provides, the law is justified in encouraging or requiring.

There are two legal approaches to altering the form and amount of risk distribution that the private market would arrive at in the absence of legal intervention. The first is by promoting additional risk spreading in general. If individuals do not purchase as much insurance as we believe, collectively, that they should, then legal rules promoting greater spreading—such as minimum insurance requirements or judicial decisions that interpret policy provisions expansively—may be in order.

The second method of rearranging risk is by redistributing it from one individual or group to another. For example, suppose that the members of a particular ethnic group—call them Claudians—are particularly prone to falling in bathtubs. Concern for efficiency alone would dictate that Claudians be charged more than other people for bathtub-fall insurance, if there were such a thing. Some might argue, however, that this extra risk should not be borne by Claudians because not all Claudians are prone to falling, those who do fall have no control over their falls, or singling out a specific ethnic group for such treatment unfairly discriminates against it. These are arguments for redistributing risk so that Claudians as a group do not bear all the risk that they actually pose.

However, unless arguments in favor of broader risk spreading or particular forms of risk redistribution are linked to principles or policies that have more general application, these implicit appeals to fairness as a ground for legal action will have an ad hoc quality that undermines their persuasiveness. Unfortunately, there is no consistent and developed theory of fair risk distribution now embodied in insurance law to supply such a link. Yet as I noted earlier, this is not the result of a weakness or confusion that originates in insurance law. Debate about the proper approach to distributive justice is a persistent preoccupation of political philosophy.[15] Consequently, there is no widely accepted theory of justice of which an approach to risk distribution could be a part.

It is possible, nevertheless, to sketch several of the leading theories of distributive justice and to tease out of them some important implications for insurance law. These theories are libertarianism, utilitarianism, and egalitarianism. Each theory has two features of special relevance to insurance law. The first is the designation of a value that occupies the place of highest importance within the theory. These values correspond to the names of the theories: individual liberty, social utility, and equality of concern and respect for individuals. The second feature of the theories is the role that each contends government should play, through law, in realizing these values.

Each theory represents a perspective that has a long history and can be identified with a distinct philosophical tradition. Yet the values they highlight also help
form our less abstract beliefs—reflected in a common-sense alternative to these
theories that I call "intuitive pragmatism"—about the proper relation between
collective risk sharing and individual responsibility for loss. The philosophical
systems that lie behind these beliefs do not resolve particular problems of insurance law. But understanding the moral foundations of different attitudes toward
risk distribution can help to clarify the choices that are available when concrete
issues arise.

The Libertarian View of Insurance Law

Libertarianism holds that individual liberty and freedom from restraint by
others is the principal social right. Under this view government has no business
involving itself in distributing (or redistributing) value, except to the extent necessary to protect against violence, coercion, theft, or infringement of individual
liberty.[16] All other actions by government improperly restrict individual liberty by
forcing individuals to pay for benefits accruing to others. Transactions among individuals for their mutual benefit will produce desired results without the coercion entailed in governmental action and regulation. Libertarianism yields the
obvious conclusion that most of insurance law, and certainly the features that have
deliberately risk-distributional effects, is illegitimate. Insurance itself will flourish
when and where it is desirable; any attempt by government, through law, to regulate the operation of insurance would diminish individual liberty. For example,
according to the libertarian view, even if Claudians are charged more than others
for bathtub-fall insurance, that is no business of insurance law. Claudians need
not purchase such insurance; and the rights of insurers to price coverage as they
desire may not be infringed in order to assist the Claudians.

Libertarianism expresses the strong emphasis in American political thought
on freedom from coercion by government. In its most extreme versions libertarianism sees the state as performing only night-watchman functions. In this sense
libertarianism is very conservative in its view of the role of government. Although
libertarians and proponents of economic efficiency often find themselves united
under the label "conservative," they hold very different positions. Conservative
proponents of efficiency usually oppose legal intervention in the market because
of their belief that such intervention is inefficient; but logically their position supports intervention when it would promote efficiency by remedying the imperfections in the market. In contrast, libertarians support the free market on grounds of
individual autonomy and liberty, not efficiency. This position leads the libertarian to oppose regulation of the market for any reason including the desire to fur-

ther efficiency or risk-distributional aims. In the libertarian view, any risk-distribution regime arrived at through the exercise of economic and political liberty is
just, precisely because it was arrived at in that fashion.

In short, libertarianism is not interested in maximizing wealth, utility, or
equality. It is concerned with protecting liberty, almost to the exclusion of other
aims. That is a message to which modern law, including insurance law, tends to
pay only limited attention. But in addition to the recognizable moral position it
reflects, libertarian thought can serve another function. It is a benchmark against
which more activist efforts at risk distribution can be measured.

Utilitarian Risk Shifting

Although individual liberty is central to the libertarian's concept of the moral
order, liberty and other rights are only means to a moral end for utilitarians. There
are many different forms of utilitarianism, but for each, morality demands action
that maximizes utility. The concept of utility is variously defined, sometimes as
pleasure, but often in terms of higher forms of satisfaction.[17] For some utilitarians
total happiness is to be maximized; for others the proper goal is to maximize average happiness. In either case utilitarianism calls for an attitude of generalized be-
nevolence in assessing the morality of individual or group conduct. Under this
view, one person's utility may not be valued above that of others. Because the effect of individual or government actions on social utility is the measure of their
morality, the satisfaction that might otherwise be achieved by one individual may
be sacrificed in order to achieve greater satisfaction by others.

Although utilitarianism and concern for economic efficiency have certain
similarities, they are different notions. Both use maximizing standards. Utilitarianism strives to maximize utility, and economic efficiency maximizes the value
of resources. But only to the extent that maximizing the value of resources maximizes utility is there a direct connection between efficiency and utility. There are
a number of reasons to suppose that the connection is at least not direct and that
in some ways the two notions contradict each other.[18]

Utilitarianism would support the use of insurance law to alter private risk arrangements if those arrangements did not maximize utility. But why might a utilitarian think that rearrangement of risk, either through greater risk spreading in
general or specific risk redistributions, would produce greater utility than a distribution arrived at through individual market choices? There are several possibilities.

Risk Spreading. There are a number of utilitarian justifications for legal devices designed to achieve greater risk spreading. Each is based on the proposition
that individual choices in the market do not always maximize utility. There are
four principal explanations for such a phenomenon, each with some force. First,

the logic of the market, including the market for protection against risk, assumes that people are rational: that they act in their own interest, accurately assessing information and making choices that are best for them. But this assumption does not always hold. Sometimes people do not know what is best for them or act as if they do not. They do not always succeed in maximizing their own satisfaction. It does not follow, however, that legal intervention always will improve this state of affairs. Less than perfectly rational decisions may nevertheless produce more utility than would intervention.

Second, people value not only their own security, but the security of others as well. This is at least part of the reason people contribute to charities, support publicly financed social welfare programs, and buy forms of insurance that protect others—family members, guests, passengers in a vehicle—as well as themselves. People feel better knowing that others are being taken care of, that catastrophe has not befallen others without the provision of assistance. But unless people cooperate in assuring that risk is more broadly spread, the market will not always provide as much of this protection as is collectively desired. Many of those who value other people's security will free ride on the efforts of a few philanthropists to provide it. A paternalistic approach is required to avoid this free riding so that each individual will contribute his share of protection for others. One way to obtain the extra risk distribution that people desire collectively but cannot cooperate to provide is through insurance law doctrines that spread risk beyond what people voluntarily would have purchased.

A third reason individual risk-spreading choices may not always maximize utility is that the ordinary statistical intuitions on which decisions to purchase insurance are based are sometimes inaccurate. As we have seen, rational decisions about insurance purchases rest in part on comparison of the cost of reducing a risk through investing in loss prevention with the cost of protecting against it through insurance. To the extent that comparisons made by individuals between these two expected values are statistically or logically faulty, utilitarianism could support legal efforts to promote the amount of spreading that would be desired in the absence of such misjudgments. And there is growing evidence that such judgments often are faulty. In at least some settings, people tend to overvalue risks with a high probability of occurrence but small potential severity and to undervalue low probability but high severity risks.[19] The result is a tendency in the aggregate for people to purchase too much low-limits coverage and not enough protection against catastrophic losses.

Of course, it does not follow that because a judgment is statistically faulty, it fails to maximize utility. An individual who is more concerned about relatively probable small losses than about unlikely large losses will spend his money on low-limits coverage without deductibles or coinsurance. A different individual might choose a deductible and spend the money saved on higher limits of coverage. Even when the latter judgment would minimize expected loss, however, it would not necessarily maximize the first individual's utility. His statistically unsound but nonetheless real concerns about security against small losses could render his insurance strategy optimal for him. The choice about whether and when the law should intervene to neutralize faulty statistical judgments of this sort is therefore a vexing one, even from a utilitarian standpoint.

Finally, the idea that individual choices serve individual interests has an unrealistically static quality to it. People change, sometimes in ways that cannot be taken into account in advance. The very act of consumption may cause a change in preferences. Goods or services may be valued less or more than anticipated because they now are possessed rather than merely desired.[20] This may be as true of the security provided by insurance coverage as it is of any other commodity. Because the time at which an individual's utility is measured may affect the measurement, there is reason not to be completely confident about individuals' utility-maximizing capacities.

The debate about whether individual choices in the marketplace—even a perfectly competitive marketplace—can maximize utility remains unresolved. Not everyone agrees that nonrational choices, desires for other people's security, misperceptions of risk, and the dynamic quality of preferences limit the capacity of individuals to maximize their own utility. But as Guido Calabresi has suggested, most people are likely to agree that one or more of these factors is sometimes influential.[21] Agreement on this much would lead to at least some willingness to regulate market choices in order to promote greater risk spreading. My own view is that in many contexts each of the points made above holds true and supplies a justification for legal promotion of greater risk spreading. However, that generalization does not help to evaluate individual issues. For our purposes the important task will be to see which of these points seem to underlie the risk-spreading devices we survey in subsequent chapters and to try to determine whether they justify the use of these devices in the contexts in which they operate.

Risk Redistribution. Utilitarian justification of legal efforts to redistribute risk also depends on the nature of utility-maximizing shortcomings or handicaps. For instance, if it were thought that more social utility could be produced by encouraging the use of public transportation, then the risks associated with train and bus riding could be partially redistributed so that they were shouldered by those who have automobiles. If coronary bypass surgery were thought to produce less utility than is widely supposed, then the risks associated with alternatives like dietary or drug therapy could be partially redistributed to those who decided to have the surgery. In each instance the method of redistribution would involve favoring the desirable activity with subsidies for below-market insurance premiums and increasing the cost of the disfavored activity by raising premiums for insurance coverage against the costs of that activity. A variety of subsidizing devices could be used, some more effectively than others. A number of these devices are discussed in chapter 4.

A very different kind of justification for risk redistribution is based on a postulate about the diminishing marginal utility of income. According to this postulate, if desires remain constant, then each additional dollar of income increases one's utility less than the previous dollar. To the extent that this postulate is true, overall utility might be increased by redistributing risk from those with more money to those with less.

It is fairly obvious that the postulate is not true in the way that this bold formulation suggests. But it also is difficult to deny that the postulate holds at some levels of income, as income increases or decreases. Some proof of this can be found, interestingly enough, in the existence of insurance itself. People are apparently willing to pay more than their expected loss for insurance against the loss. Otherwise insurance companies could not finance administrative expenses or earn profits.[22] This risk aversion may in part reflect the diminishing marginal utility of income. People pay a few of their last-earned dollars in order to avoid the risk of losing their first-earned dollars. Certain loss of the amount of an insurance premium reduces utility less than does the possibility of a larger loss, even when the risk of the larger loss has an expected value equal to the amount of the insurance premium.

Any effort to move from the limited truth of this postulate to the adoption of legal policy, however, is complicated by the difficulty of making interpersonal comparisons of utility. Even if loss of my latest dollar of income means less to me than loss of the dollar I earned before that one, the utility I lose by surrendering my latest dollar may not be the same as what you lose when your latest dollar is surrendered. This is even more likely to be the case if we have different incomes to begin with. So transferring money from me to you, even if I have more income than you, will not necessarily increase our aggregate utility. Nevertheless, it seems very likely that transferring money from the very wealthy to the very poor would often increase aggregate utility, even if it is not possible to determine the amount of that increase.

However, even if there is a directly proportional relation between wealth and utility levels, using the insurance system to spread or redistribute risk will not necessarily transfer money from the wealthy to the poor. It will transfer money from those whose activities are comparatively safe to those whose activities are comparatively risky and, generally, from the lucky to the unlucky. Thus, encouraging or requiring people to buy bathtub-fall insurance and charging uniform premiums may benefit the Claudians in our continuing example, since they tend to fall in bathtubs more often than others. But only if both Claudians and all others start with the same amount of wealth will such a requirement increase social utility. If this assumption about the wealth equality of these two groups is unwarranted, then redistributing risk between them will not necessarily increase utility because it will not necessarily transfer funds from the rich to the poor.

Notwithstanding these caveats, something like the diminishing marginal utility of income theory seems to lie behind a variety of legal doctrines and statutory devices that extend insurance coverage beyond what is purchased voluntarily.[23] The notion commonly supporting these devices is that it is generally better for a large group of people each to bear a small loss than for one individual to bear a large loss himself. Of course, this attitude tells decision makers little about where to stop spreading or redistributing—the point at which any additional utility lost by those sharing the burden would exceed the utility gained by the party whose loss is covered.

Utilitarian justifications are not the only ones available to support these and other forms of risk redistribution. Many risk-redistributional arguments depend instead on the kinds of claims about equality that are discussed in the next section. Before ending our examination of utilitarianism, however, we need to address a final question. Even if increased risk spreading or specific redistributions of risk would produce more social utility, is insurance law an effective means for achieving this goal? Is insurance law one of the devices for promoting risk spreading or redistribution that is most likely to help maximize utility, or are other devices—such as taxation—likely to be more suitable? Abstract questions about aggregate social utility are not easy to answer conclusively. But a preliminary answer can be given.

The following chapters suggest that the use of insurance as a wealth redistribution device is subject to many difficulties. Large-scale, global redistribution of wealth certainly cannot be accomplished well using insurance alone. Insurance can spread or redistribute risk and in so doing accomplish a certain amount of wealth redistribution. But insurance law and insurance are unwieldy devices for achieving wholesale shifts in wealth. Too many other phenomena besides risk relations affect the distribution of wealth, and too many social forces may confound the limited effects that insurance could have on the distribution of wealth. Local rather than global risk rearrangement—especially involving greater risk spreading rather than risk redistribution—may be accomplished in more satisfactory fashion. And risk redistribution itself is likely to be much more successful when risk is redistributed across activities rather than from the poor to the wealthy. Thus, while the redistributional issue cannot be resolved definitively, it is in the direction of the more local forms of risk rearrangement that prospects for use of private insurance as a tool of social policy look best.

Egalitarian Insurance Principles

Equality is a concern of almost all theories of distributive justice. Libertarianism stresses the equal liberty of all; utilitarianism holds that each individual should count for one and none for more than one. Egalitarian theories, however, place equality at the center of concern instead of valuing it as a by-product of liberty or one aspect of the utilitarian calculus. For egalitarians the equal worth of all is a first principle from which other principles follow.

Merely stating equality as a first principle, unfortunately, does not yield concrete policies. Equality in all respects is an impossibility; equality of some kinds is incompatible with equality along other dimensions.[24] So the question for egalitarians becomes: in what sense is equality to be given priority and how is that determination to be made? One problem the egalitarian faces is that our society does not at present meet strict egalitarian standards. Therefore, an egalitarian might ask how to move into full compliance with these standards. Can forms of inequality that would be intolerable in an already egalitarian setting be permitted if they would promote eventual equality? This possibility of reverse discrimination poses a serious dilemma for the egalitarian, and it is a dilemma for insurance law in much the same way that it is for other areas of law and social policy. We will look a bit more closely at the problem of reverse discrimination in insurance in chapter 4, when we discuss redistribution through risk classification. For present purposes the important question is, what do egalitarian principles require of insurance on its own terms rather than as a means of achieving broader social equality?

To begin answering this question we must first recognize that egalitarianism is not a monolithic notion, but a cluster of somewhat similar views. Different egalitarian premises would require different forms of legal regulation of insurance arrangements. For example, a straightforward belief in equality of wealth probably would lead to legal devices encouraging risk spreading in general and risk redistribution from rich to poor. On the other hand, egalitarian theories less concerned with equality of results than with equality of means would lead to different standards. Both John Rawls[25] and Ronald Dworkin,[26] two philosophers of justice taking the latter view, consider the results of the natural lottery of skills, talents, and other endowments to be morally irrelevant to the distribution of wealth. In their view an individual's life prospects should not be affected by contingencies of birth or accidental endowment with superior abilities. Differences in these endowments produce inequality in the means by which individual can pursue their own aims. But eliminate this inequality of means, and at least some of the inequality that results from the ensuing pursuit of individual aims may be tolerable under their systems. Rawls, for example, would allow inequalities in the initial distribution of wealth if they would work to the advantage of the least advantaged members of society.

Rawls means his theory to apply to the basic structure of society rather than to subsystems such as private insurance transactions. Nevertheless, means-oriented egalitarianism captures a value that may guide an egalitarian analysis of insurance and risk relations.[27] The natural lottery blindness reflected by this kind of egalitarianism would recommend at a minimum that such immutable characteristics as sex, race, nationality, and genetic handicaps be ruled out of consideration in setting insurance premiums. A legal rule requiring that all such characteristics be ignored in setting premium rates would help to equalize the resources required for different individuals to obtain insurance coverage. The result would be greater spreading of the risk that these characteristics increase or decrease any individual's expected loss.

A strong belief in natural lottery blindness not only would render such immutable characteristics as age and sex morally irrelevant to the appropriate distribution of risk; any other factors with roots in the natural lottery probably also would be at least prima facie suspect. Foremost among these would seem to be the insured's ability to control the risk in question. If an insured has no means of controlling a risk he poses because of inherent weakness or lack of skill, it would deny him equality of means to charge him more for insurance coverage than those with the strength or skill he lacks. Of course, the risks posed by almost every activity can be controlled by reducing the level of participation or by avoiding the activity entirely. Therefore, an egalitarian scheme of risk distribution would also need to distinguish between socially optional and unavoidable activities. Although the results of the natural lottery in skills and talents might legitimately affect the cost of engaging in optional activities, skills and talents should have little or at least less effect on the cost of engaging in activities that for practical purposes are mandatory in our society.

These two criteria, the degree to which a risk is controllable and the degree to which the activity producing it is socially optional, would form the basis of an egalitarian standard of fair risk distribution in insurance. To return to our continuing example of the Claudians who fall in bathtubs, we can see that both factors would influence legal regulation of the insurance arrangements available to this group. To the extent that the risk of bathtub falls is uncontrollable, Claudians should not be charged more for fall insurance. And to the extent that use of bath-tubs standing up is thought to be unavoidable, the price of coverage should be blind to Claudians' tendency to have more than an average number of falls.

Controllability and optionality, however, are not self-defining notions. They direct attention to a problem rather than solving it. If it is not asking too much of Claudians that they install handholds in their bathtubs, then the risk in question is controllable. Thus, an egalitarian must decide which risks equality demands be shared and which accidents and contingencies may be allowed to burden or ben-efit people individually without sacrificing the form of equality to which the egal-itarian adheres. In this sense controllability and optionality are normative conclusions about the risks for which individuals can properly be asked to bear insurance responsibility.

As Michael Sandel has shown, normative conclusions of this sort are derived from premises about the personal characteristics that are properly considered in-dividual assets and those that are properly considered the collective property of so-ciety.[28] At first glance this may appear to be a strange notion. Personal characteristics seem inherently to be individual assets. But in fact many personal characteristics are treated in part as collective assets. Whenever we provide special benefits that neutralize particular handicaps—by building wheel chair ramps, for example—we are treating the health of the nonhandicapped as a collective asset rather than allowing the burdens of being handicapped to rest only on those who have suffered them. Since not all the benefits or burdens that fall initially on in-dividuals are automatically shifted to the body politic, however, there is a certain arbitrariness to any line drawn between individual and collective assets. For this reason the egalitarian must justify the line he draws by giving reasons for his con-clusions regarding the controllability and optionality of insured activities and the risks attendant to them.

To a limited extent, insurance law already mandates risk redistribution in ac-cordance with the controllability and optionality criteria. The only truly immut-able trait that plays a major role in insurance risk classification is sex, and its use is under attack on several fronts.[29] There is also more effort to assure the affordability of insurance for socially unavoidable activities like driving than for such optional pursuits as boating or such entrepreneurial ones as conducting a business. Still, a system more powerfully influenced by egalitarian values might pay greater atten-tion to these criteria, perhaps by calibrating the effects of risk classification in ac-cordance with the controllability and optionality of the risks and activities being insured. Territorial classification of residential fire and automobile insurance, for example, might have to be tempered to account for the semidetermined character of people's choices about where they live. And there might have to be much more analysis of the characteristics—such as alcoholism—that cause other kinds of accidents before we could be confident that these could be altered by individual acts of will, changes in habits, or practice.[30] Hard decisions about the force of the egalitarian ideal that these criteria implement still would be required to resolve individual issues. But the criteria can provide guidance that is lacking in the bare notion of equality.

One final point is worth noting about means-oriented egalitarianism. A system concerned with efficiency makes use of a market as its central allocation device. Yet an egalitarian system that allows some scope for ambitions, tastes, and risk taking is likely to rely heavily on markets as well. In a system concerned with the fair distribution of means for achieving individually chosen ends and not the ends themselves, a market approach not only may be a compatible feature, but also a necessary one. Otherwise it may be impossible for people to satisfy their ambitions, tastes, and preferences for or against risk.[31]

But there are also important differences between economic and egalitarian values. Often it makes economic sense to charge insureds their expected loss even if they have no control over losses and the activity insured is socially unavoidable. For then activities will be charged their true social costs, and resources may gravitate toward other activities where losses are more controllable. By contrast, in an egalitarian system the controllability and optionality criteria are not means to a utility or wealth-maximizing end, but reflections of the end itself: the principle that because individuals are of equal worth, they should be treated as equals. This principle requires that we all bear certain risks beyond some individuals' control even though this risk sharing may increase the costs of some activities. Controllability and optionality are relevant here not becuase of their relation to efficiency, but because a preference for equality requires that they be considered in fashioning a risk-sharing system.

Intuitive Pragmatism

Libertarianism, utilitarianism, and egalitarianism are formal and sytematic theories. But few people, even those with rigorous philosophical training, adopt views that embrace only one of these theories and exclude the values emphasized by the others. There is something greatly appealing about each. We all care about the preservation of political and religious liberties; few are willing to ignore altogether the aggregate social utility or disutility of alternative public policies; and the appeal of equality, of various sorts, is also strong.

The central values in the three major theories of distributional justice each play a role in a different approach, which I earlier called "intuitive pragmatism."[32] The approach is pragmatic because it values liberty, utility, and equality, but it is willing to sacrifice one or more of these values for significant gains in the others. The approach is intuitive because its determinations are made through a weighting of values that cannot be articulated in the form of a mechanical calculus. For example, most people agree that liberty may be sacrificed to assure the minimum conditions of survival for all members of society. And most would be willing to sacrifice equality when large gains in welfare for many could be achieved at the expense of small losses in equality by a few. In these cases the pragmatist has a provisional preference for liberty or equality that can be displaced by strong gains in the other realms. He cannot say in general what level of benefit in these other realms would overcome that preference; rather, decisions are made in individual cases on the basis of intuitive judgment.

Intuitive pragmatism thus is not a combination or mixture of the other three theories. It is a theory in which none of the values pursued by the other theories is superior in general to other values. No value trumps the others; a first-order weighing takes place on every occasion when there is conflict. In practice, each value may have certain favored cases in which it is likely to be very influential—egalitarianism in the field of race relations, libertarianism when political rights are at stake, and so forth. But this is the product of a first-order weighing in each instance rather than the consequence of a preexisting scale that determines outcomes in advance. The facts of the issue at hand are considered in light of the complex of values held important by the analyst. In short, pragmatism, as I am defining it, is not a little bit of each other theory; it denies all of them.

Further, although pragmatism's decision procedure is intuitive, it is not private. Pragmatism appeals not to secret intuitions, but to those that can be made publicly available and assessable. Reliance on intuitive judgment, then, rejects both the relatively mechanical decision procedure of the three formal theories of justice and the use of private tastes as the basis of value preferences. Pragmatic judgments do not rely on some special mental faculty. The arguments that may be made in favor of a pragmatic judgment about risk-distributional justice are the standards by which that judgment must be evaluated since there are no higher standards. This does not mean that there are no right answers; the pragmatist can expect that his right answer will command agreement through the force of his arguments in its favor.

In general my own brand of pragmatism often leads to the view that insurance law does not pay quite enough attention to egalitarian values. I value liberty and utility, but I believe that they exercise a bit more influence on insurance law than would be ideal. Consequently, when I analyze particular insurance law issues in subsequent chapters, I frequently ask whether greater risk sharing or a more egalitarian redistribution of the set of risks under study would be warranted. The only way an intuitive pragmatist can refute the charge that this attitude is arbitrary is by attempting to articulate, in the context of particular judgments made about specific sets of facts, the principles that have guided those judgments. Critics will then be able to determine whether the set of judgments in question can be ascribed to a consistent attitude toward distributive justice or merely to a set of ad hoc preferences.

Because insurance law—whether legislative, judicial, or administrative—is not often explicitly philosophical about its premises, this method of analysis is an important one. As we examine the different problems in insurance law in subsequent chapters, it will be necessary to search for the libertarian, utilitarian, and egalitarian premises that lie behind different resolutions of these problems. Yet because no single theory dominates, it is a pragmatic vision that we will be examining.

Equity Between Insurers and Insureds

The third purpose of insurance law is a kind of residual category. A fully developed theory of justice might completely describe the relations that ought to exist between business entities and individuals, including insurers and insureds. Most theories of justice, however, are not worked out in the detail necessary to guide specific fields of law. In addition, rights and obligations derive not only from abstract moral relations, but also from concrete interactions. Not only social structures, but also individual relationships may create moral or legal responsibilities. Many legal rules governing relations between insurers and insureds reflect this fact. They seem designed as much to promote fair dealings in individual cases as to structure a systematically just set of relations among insurers and insureds. To distinguish this purpose from overall fairness in the distribution of risk, I describe it as achieving equity between insurers and insureds.

One important difference between equity and the other purposes of insurance law is that equity tends to focus on relations between present parties and to pay less attention to the impact of current legal actions on future risk relations. Although many legal doctrines that have roots in equitable concerns can be interpreted so that they speak to future parties, their justification generally must be sought elsewhere. Indeed, the impact of many equitable principles on future efficiency and risk-distributional fairness is negative. These principles should therefore be conceived as deliberately designed to remedy current inequities rather than to regulate future conduct.

The factors that trigger legal intervention into insurer-insured relations in order to promote equity are varied. They are not necessarily unique to insurance law, but often are characteristic of the problems of contract fairness in general. I shall describe and assess the significance of these factors in this section, leaving criticism of their influence in particular settings for later chapters. For convenience, they may be divided into four categories, though the categories sometimes overlap and combine to support legal intervention. The first three factors lead to rules that restrain the insurer from denying coverage (or some other benefit) to the insured after a loss occurs. These involve information imbalance, bargaining power disparity, and action by the insurer that creates detrimental reliance by the insured.[33] In contrast, a fourth factor supports the restriction of coverage because of the moral hazard of insurance.

Information Imbalance

Insurers are almost always in possession of more information that is relevant to an insurance transaction than are insureds. This is certainly true in dealings with ordinary consumers and is often true in commercial transactions as well. Insurers not only have statistics on the incidence of the risks in question; their advertising and the marketing conduct of their agents may create the impression that the coverage offered is broader than the policies sold actually provide. Further, insurers know precisely the scope of coverage they offer. Yet they draft policies in language (even the simplified, plain language of new consumer-oriented policies) that is often dense, complex, difficult to understand, and sometimes ambiguous. Admittedly it is sometimes law and lawyers who force this complexity into insurance policies. But not only are insurance policies difficult to understand; they normally are not furnished to the insured until sometime after he has agreed to purchase coverage. The typical insured therefore does not have the opportunity to scrutinize the product he is offered before deciding whether to purchase it.

The result is a series of legal doctrines that promote disclosure of information or extend coverage even when insurance policies deny it. In these situations, the ordinary rules of contract offer and acceptance—which do not always honor an insured's expectations—are suspended, and an insurance rule that makes the insured's reasonable expectations the touchstone of the contract is substituted. Whether the insured was informed about what he purchased thus serves as one of the tests for legal intervention to promote equity. If insureds are informed, then the market for insurance will function more efficiently because insureds will be better equipped to make choices that serve their interests. But concern with information imbalance also represents the law's commitment to the value of informed decision making in itself. Promoting informed assent furthers the freedom of contract ideal of individuals who bargain at arm's length and fashion an agreement that suits their mutual needs. It does this by limiting the insurer's right to stand on the terms of the insurance policy as written unless those terms are fully disclosed.[34]

Disparity of Bargaining Power

The insurer's power to dictate policy terms is itself sometimes sufficient to influence legal determination of the rights of insurer and insured. A great deal of administrative regulation seeks its justification in the insurer's power to dictate the terms of coverage, especially when the coverage sold is statutorily mandated or a practical necessity. The courts, on the other hand, rarely upset the terms of an insurance arrangement solely because of a disparity in the bargaining power of the parties. Yet if the insurer's power to dictate policy terms is used not only for the purpose of gaining a special economic advantage, but also to dictate onerous or unnecessarily restrictive terms, then the courts are likely to scrutinize what is dictated much more carefully than they would in situations where bargaining power is equal.[35]

Defining the difference between a policy provision that simply gives the insurer an advantage and one that is unduly onerous or restrictive is no easy task. Many commentators argue that the distinction cannot be drawn: one person's legitimate advantage is another's overreaching. Further, some argue that if the stronger party is prohibited from extracting an advantage in one way, probably it will extract it in another, perhaps simply by increasing prices.[36] And in any event in a truly competitive market, even an economically powerful actor, like an insurance company, will not be able to extract such an advantage from weak actors, like insureds, because competitors will offer better terms and will effectively foreclose that possibility. But there are answers to these arguments against distinguishing between legitimate profit taking and overreaching: insurance markets are not always perfectly competitive, and different policy provisions with identical economic impacts may not necessarily have identical equitable implications.

In addition, in my view the law in this field has begun implicitly to recognize a difference between an onerous and uniformly applied term and a term that is invoked by the insurer only selectively. The evil of the latter approach is that it allows the insurer to function lawlessly, sometimes rigidly relying on an onerous term, but on other occasions waiving a policy defense. Of course, all insurance policy provisions can be used in this way. But some seem deliberately designed to protect against only a portion of the situations to which they explicitly refer. To deal with the dangers of such overinclusive policy provisions, legal rules designed to deprive insurers of discretion to treat some insureds differently from others have developed. Rules governing warranties by the insured,[37] access to duplicate coverage,[38] and substantive unconscionability,[39] for example, all place limits on the scope of otherwise very restrictive policy provisions. In so doing these rules help assure that the insurer does not adopt the most onerous means available to protect itself against unwarranted claims or dishonesty by insureds.

Slightly different but related dangers are regulated by other doctrines that temper the insurer's bargaining power during the claims process. These doctrines work to counterbalance the strategic advantage possessed by insurers because of their control over the manner in which performance of policy obligations occurs. One doctrine imposes extracontract liability on the insurer for bad-faith failure to settle legitimate first-party claims;[40] another allocates responsibility for avoiding conflicts between the insurer's own interest and that of its insured regarding offers to settle liability claims;[41] and a third defines the insurer's responsibility for avoiding similar conflicts when providing the insured with a defense against liability claims.[42] Each doctrine emphasizes that insureds have a right to equitable dealing by insurers that transcends specific provisions in their insurance policies. All three of these doctrines are explored at length in chapter 7.

Finally, equitable principles come into play when the insurer's behavior misleads the insured about the content of a policy. Because the insurer controls the terms of coverage, this phenomenon also seems in part to turn on a disparity in the bargaining power of the parties. Traditional legal doctrines governing misrepresentation conform to these principles. So also do newer doctrines, unique to insurance, which honor an insured's expectations about coverage when those expectations have been created by conduct of the insurer. These are examined in chapter 5.

Detrimental Reliance

The third factor that prompts legal intervention to promote equity between insurers and insureds is the insured's reliance, to his detriment, on the assumption that he is insured against the loss in question. Because of such reliance, the insured fails to obtain from some other source the coverage he assumes is provided by his own insurer. The circumstances in which detrimental reliance may occur are governed by very different rules of law and statutory provisions—estoppel, negligence liability for the insurer's delay in processing applications, the obligation to provide notice of changes in the terms of group coverage, the incontestability of life insurance coverage after the expiration of a specific period—and are therefore subject to different legal tests. But each seems closely linked to the principle that an insured who justifiably relies on an assumption that he has coverage, especially when the insurer is responsible for that assumption or is at least aware of it, is entitled to coverage.

Sometimes these doctrines assume detriment or damages without requiring that it be proved; incontestability statutes are an example. Often it is sensible not to require proof of detriment since proof may be difficult and expensive even when possible. However, it should be recognized that not only equitable but also risk-distributional values are often influential in the formation of such doctrines. When the claim that the insured detrimentally relied is doubtful—that is, when it is unlikely that he could have obtained the coverage in question elsewhere—then promoting broader risk spreading rather than encouraging equitable dealing appears to be the goal underlying the legal doctrine that creates the coverage in question. Otherwise, concern with actual proof of both detrimental reliance and the insurer's responsibility for it probably would be more pronounced.

When detriment is proved, or there is at least justification for presuming its existence in the majority of similar cases, the principle underlying the extension of coverage has recognizable equitable roots in the law of torts. The insured has suffered a loss that (given the validity of the presumption) would have been compensated (by some other insurer) but for the insurer's representation or conduct implying that there was coverage. When the presumption of detrimental reliance is unwarranted, however—for example, when there is no reason to believe that the insured could have obtained coverage elsewhere had he known it had not been provided to him—tort principles would deny recovery. Under these circumstances no causal connection between the insurer's wrong and the insured's loss could be proved. The extension of coverage must then be justified, if at all, by contract or contract-like principles. In effect, decisions holding that coverage attaches, even absent detriment, award expectation damages for breach of contract and must seek justification in considerations that transcend concern with equitable dealing between the parties.

Moral Hazard

The three preceding reasons for equitable intervention all work in the insured's favor. In contrast, the desirability of avoiding moral hazard results in protection of the insurer rather than the insured. Moral hazard exists because insureds sometimes have more information about their expected losses than insurers. Certainly because insureds can control their own behavior, they have it within their power to act inconsistently with insurers' interests by taking less care than they would were they not insured. Both sorts of imbalance disadvantage the insurer.

In this sense doctrines guarding against moral hazard not only reflect the economically sound policy against inducing the destruction of life or property and the taking of unwarranted risks. They also arise out of equitable considerations. Over the long run, insurers distribute risk, and legal rules that protect insurers therefore redound to the benefit of the community of insureds. In the short run, however, the insurer occupies the same position as any other contracting party with its own interests at stake. Legal doctrines protecting insurers against moral hazard, or allowing them to protect themselves, recognize the insurer's position as an ordinary contracting party subject to advantage taking by insureds.

The requirement that the insured have an insurable interest in the subject matter of coverage, implied exceptions to coverage that operate in the insurer's favor, limitations of coverage to losses caused unintentionally or by accident, rights of subrogation, and risk classification practices all recognize the possibility of moral hazard. These doctrines certainly do not eliminate moral hazard; they attempt to reduce it in a fashion that reconciles the benefits of coverage against loss with concern for loss prevention. The insurer's pricing practices are based on the assumption that, before loss, its interests and those of the insured largely coincide. Some legal protection is necessary to assure that this is so. Otherwise much more extensive limitations on the sale of coverage might be required.

THE INSTITUTIONAL CONTEXT

I now turn from the purposes of insurance law to the structure within which it is made and applied. It is easy to underplay the differences among legal institutions, since in modern jurisprudence their functions overlap, and lines of demarcation are not entirely clear. But underplaying differences can be dangerous. These institutions have different strengths and they fashion different kinds of rules. The purposes of insurance law analyzed in the preceding pages can be affected significantly by these differences.

The legal institutions that help to accomplish these purposes are familiar. Legislatures enact statutory provisions governing insurance. Administrative agencies enforce these provisions and, acting under authority granted to them by legislative enactment, both promulgate additional rules and enforce them in the course of regulatory activities. In their capacity as law enforcers the courts oversee the exercise of regulatory authority, but they also regulate relations between insurers and insureds pursuant to independent judicial authority.

This allocation of responsibilities is unremarkable; it parallels the allocation that exists in body after body of American law. Consequently, we may dispense with discussion of many of the general insights that have been established about modern legal administration.[43] What concerns us here is not the general, but the particular: how the legal institutions that create and apply insurance law go about their task, and how this activity produces rules and decisions designed to achieve the objectives examined in the preceding sections of this chapter.

Legislatures

Insurance law is largely a creature of state rather than federal law-making institutions. For many years insurance was considered immune to federal regulation under the commerce clause of the U.S. Constitution.[44] In 1944, however, the Supreme Court held that federal antitrust law applied to the business of insurance,[45] and a scramble culminating in enactment of the McCarran-Ferguson Act ensued.[46] In McCarran-Ferguson, Congress declared that insurance should continue to be subject to state law, but that federal antitrust legislation would be applicable to it to the extent that the business of insurance was not regulated by the states by 1948.[47] Every state responded with regulatory legislation.[48]

Although this allocation of authority has its detractors,[49] it has been largely satisfactory to the principals. The states have retained both regulatory authority and the power to levy taxes on the business of insurance. The insurance industry has been able to pursue a divide-and-conquer strategy that has left state regulation weaker than it generally is at the federal level in other fields. In part as a consequence, state legislation governing insurance is disorganized in two senses.[50] First, the substance of legislation varies a good deal from state to state. There is nothing like the semblance of national uniformity that has resulted from the widespread state adoption of the Uniform Commercial Code. Second, the typical state insurance code is hardly a code at all, but an unsystematic compilation of separately enacted individual provisions: Professor Spencer Kimball once referred to American insurance codes as a "rubbish heap."[51] Although a good deal of generalization about insurance legislation is possible, individual questions must be resolved through state-by-state and statute-by-statute examination.

State insurance legislation takes two forms: (1) direct action through prescription of entire policies[52] or specific provisions,[53] prohibition of particular provisions,[54] promulgation of solvency standards, specification of mandatory coverage requirements and the like; and (2) delegation of regulatory authority to an administrative agency, usually an insurance commissioner. Direct legislative action comes in a variety of forms. First, there is considerable state legislation governing the terms of insurance policies. Second, legislation controls marketing and claims procedures. It not only regulates agents, brokers, marketing, and claims handling in general, but also prescribes certain detailed rules regarding the marketing of particular kinds of insurance. Third, mandatory coverage legislation attempts to assure that insurance is afforded all or most individuals affected by certain activities—operation of motor vehicles, for example. Such legislation often establishes substitute or residual insurance markets when the private market cannot or will not provide all the required coverage. Last, a sizable portion of most state insurance codes is devoted to assuring the solvency of insurance companies. Provision for periodic audits, capital requirements, and investment limitations all are designed to protect policyholders by assuring the existence of a fund out of which insurance proceeds will be paid.

Direct legislative action tends to be relatively specific. It usually contains standards against which compliance can be measured and delegates (even by implication) little interpretive authority to insurance commissioners or courts. In contrast to such fields as commercial law, where there is little administrative regulation, legislatures dealing with insurance law have no need to delegate indirectly through promulgation of broad standards requiring elaboration. When legislatures create insurance law, they can do so specifically and with precision. When precision is not feasible but action is desired, explicit delegation of rule-making authority to the administrative regulator can do the job. It is in the latter realm that many of the crucial actions in the regulatory process occur.

Insurance Commissioners

The vast preponderance of insurance regulation in the United States takes place under the authority of insurance commissioners to whom legislatures in each state have delegated regulatory powers. Just as the scope of direct legislative regulation varies from state to state, the scope of the insurance commissioners' delegated authority also varies. In general, however, the breadth of the insurance commissioner's formal authority is immense. Insurance commissioners have authority to regulate policy terms and premium rates, and they can influence matters outside their express authority with indirect pressure. Not all policy types and terms are subject to direct regulation, but many are. In addition, commissioners often have authority to issue regulations governing marketing methods and company solvency. Thus, the commissioner formally possesses authority to affect and sometimes to dictate policy provisions, rates, marketing, and other procedures in many lines of insurance. A variety of enforcement techniques also is available.[55]

In fact, however, this authority is exercised sparingly. Insurance regulation in practice often is inconsistent and unsystematic. There are a number of explanations for this phenomenon. First, much administrative regulation has a tendency to evolve toward an accommodation between the regulator and the regulated industry. This may be described pejoratively as the capture of the regulator by those regulated or may be seen more neutrally as the almost inevitable result of interaction between two bureaucracies that deal more with each other than with the putative beneficiaries of regulation.[56] In either case, the more cooperative and less adversarial the resulting relationship, the less outright regulation there is likely to be. Insurance regulation is especially subject to this tendency. Because state rather than federal regulation is involved, local consumer groups are likely to be less organized and more poorly financed than the national insurance industry.[57] And insurance itself is an obscure subject, which normally engenders fewer emotions and hence less organized public interest than other subjects of regulation—the location of hazardous waste dumps, for instance.

Second, a strong case can be made that some regulation works in favor of existing enterprises and to the disadvantage of potential competitors and the public.[58] For example, most insurance codes provide commissioners with authority to regulate rates to assure that they are not excessive, inadequate, or unfairly discriminatory.[59] Assurance that rates are not inadequate is designed as a solvency protection device, but it can also be used to inhibit competition and thereby encourage noncompetitive pricing and reduced output. The move toward open competition in insurance rate making over the past decade has been designed in part to reduce this possibility.[60]

A third reason for the unsystematic character of insurance regulation has been the inadequacy of resources available for regulation. Insurance commissioners' staffs are notoriously overburdened. The sheer number of requests for approval of rate and policy provision changes often has overwhelmed staff capacity to review these filings effectively. Most such submissions therefore are approved without exacting review. Given these limitations, the commissioner's most effective weapon is the power not to stay his hand and to single out particular proposals for intense scrutiny.[61] But this power is only as strong as the threat that backs it up, and such a threat can be carried out infrequently if resources are limited.

An often repeated generalization about this state of affairs is that there is no consistent or developed theory underlying American insurance regulation.[62] The generalization is inaccurate in one sense. There are certainly standard phrases that define the objectives of regulation: assuring the availability, affordability, and quality of coverage and assuring the solvency of insurers. But the charge is quite accurate in a different sense. There is no dominant organizing notion in insurance regulation that is equivalent to those that have been adopted in certain other fields of business law: the goal of assuring fair disclosure and an unmanipulated market in securities law, or the need for a legal backdrop of clear but contractually displaceable rules in commercial law. However, if we step back and locate the insurance commissioner's place within the institutional context of insurance law, we can obtain a better idea of both the potential for growth in that role and the inevitable limits upon it. As in many other fields of administrative regulation, the insurance commissioner is neither a legislator nor a judge, although he or she is a bit of both; and the legislative mandate with which the commissioner works has limitations of its own.

Though the characterization is something of a caricature, it can hardly be denied that the essence of the legislative process is the reconciliation and compromise of conflicting interests. Contending interests are sometimes those of principle; and individual legislators often take positions based on principle. But on the whole, the process is not and is not expected to be juridical. Legislatures tend to respond to interest primarily and to reason secondarily. The precise shape of legislation never can be entirely accounted for by reference to principle, since legislation is the product of compromise and, moreover, of compromise within a group rather than an individual judgment balancing contending considerations. It is a rare body of statutory law that reflects a thoroughgoing consistency of method and purpose. To the extent that they are intentionally consistent and systematic, securities and commercial law statutes are notable exceptions, not typical models. Even a code enacted on one occasion is normally composed of many compromises among competing approaches.

So the body of legislation that insurance commissioners work with is not entirely susceptible to systematic rationalization. The contrast between the insurance commissioner's task and that of an agency like the Securities and Exchange Commission is thus at least partly a product of differences between the legislation they administer. It would not be realistic to expect insurance regulation to reflect a completely consistent theory of regulation since the legislation being administered does not reflect such a theory. Equally inappropriate would be an analogy between the regulatory role of the insurance commissioner and the judicial role of the courts. The traditional role of the courts is to respond mainly to reason and principle; the commissioner must respond not only to reason, but, much more than the courts, also to partisan interest and the demands of expediency.

In the face of these constraints it is unlikely that a systematic and consistent substantive rationale for all of an insurance commissioner's decisions will be available. Rather, many decisions will seem incremental, and much of the regulatory product will appear to be pragmatic muddling through. Moreover, given resource limitations, even deliberate attempts to impose consistency and order will be imperfect, since it will be impossible to scrutinize all possible subjects of regulation. Some will emerge unregulated; their treatment will appear inconsistent with those matters that have been affected by the commissioner's influence or authority.

Nevertheless, there are at least two respects in which insurance regulation stands to gain through more consciously attending to the theory behind it. First, a more developed sense of the goals of regulation could aid decision.[63] Traditionally regulation has been conceived mainly as a remedy for market imperfections that impede economic efficiency. But regulation can serve distributional and equitable goals as well. As the insurance market becomes more competitive and traditional justifications for regulation fade away, these two goals may gain importance.

To the extent that a commissioner sees himself as a quasi-legislator, as a responder to interests that must be compromised, a consistent pattern of regulatory goals is unlikely to emerge from his actions. And where knowledge sufficient to help predict the impact of regulatory action is unavailable, prudent regulation may have to be incremental rather than comprehensive.[64] But many features of the regulatory enterprise can be responsive to principle and subject to rational justification. Even when compromises are necessary, they can be interpreted in light of their effectiveness at achieving previously set objectives. In short, by articulating a regulatory program, an insurance commissioner's goals can be understood, and the pattern of compromises he or she must make in order to implement parts of the design can be evaluated within that articulated scheme. The tension between the democratic and legislative features of the process, on the one hand, and the rational and principled features, on the other, may not be entirely reconcilable. But the tension between them can be brought into the open by attending to the latter features and carving out the space within which they may operate.

A second common weakness of insurance regulation in many states is that it has tended to be reactive, leaving legislatures and courts to fashion creative approaches to new problems. The impression is often left that regulators see themselves as umpires of a game whose rules are set by others rather than as participants in the formulation of those rules. Yet as discussions in several of the chapters to follow reveal, many problems could be solved best at the administrative level. The absence of such solutions has prompted legislatures and courts to take actions that are less effective than they might have been had they been taken by insurance commissioners.

Courts

In many respects the courts are likely to be less effective regulators of insurance transactions than insurance commissioners. The courts have limited technical expertise and fact-finding capacity. They are constrained by the issues raised in the cases that come before them. They are bound to have difficulty coordinating enforcement of different decisions. And administrative agencies, like insurance commissioners and their staffs, often have more public accountability than courts.

Nevertheless, the courts perform two important functions in helping to shape insurance law. First, they act as supervisors of the lawfulness of actions taken by other branches of government. This power to scrutinize other governmental actions is significant, but infrequently exercised. For example, it is uncommon for a court exercising its powers of judicial review to declare an insurance statute unconstitutional.[65] It is more common, but still unusual, for courts to invalidate administrative actions regulating insurance.

Of greater importance is the courts' second and more frequently exercised power to regulate relations between insurers and insureds. Courts are well equipped to conduct inquiries into the contractual history of individual transactions and to alter paper rights so that they conform to equitable demands. The history of insurance law is replete with examples of judicial regulation of this sort. Legislative policy regarding insurance transactions is sometimes expressed in statutory schemes that require judicial interpretation and reasoned elaboration to effectuate their purposes, although this happens less in insurance than in fields where a regulatory structure does not exist. The courts often use this opportunity to protect the interests of insurance consumers. In addition, in the face of weak administrative regulation, the courts perform a separate consumer protection function through formulation of legal doctrines giving policyholders rights at variance with policy provisions.[66] Judicial regulation of this sort is much more likely to be concerned with policy provisions and other relations between insurers and insureds than with the price of coverage or the solvency of insurers.

Finally, if history is any guide, some version of the private right of action that is increasingly recognized in other fields as a check on the performance of administrative agencies may be created by the courts in this field as well.[67] It is too soon to say whether that right will provide only for judicial review of administrative action under stricter standards than previously have applied, or whether damages for violation of statutory standards normally enforced administratively will also be available. But the growth of such rights in parallel fields makes it likely that they will eventually be created in insurance law, as the courts continue their traditional attempt to maintain equitable relations between insurers and insureds. A few decisions creating such private rights already have appeared.[68]

Any scheme of classification necessarily oversimplifies its subject. Ordering all insurance law in accordance with the framework developed in this chapter is obviously no exception. The framework seems a serviceable way, however, to systematize this body of law into a form that permits generalization and yields the insights that come from seeing the common properties of seemingly disparate phenomena. Of course, not every feature of insurance law fits comfortably within the categories carved out here. For one thing, legal rules in our system often serve many purposes. In addition, legislatures, administrative agencies, and courts are complex institutions, and no single characterization ever will capture the full complexity of their behavior. As we proceed to study more concrete problems, therefore, it will pay to remember that the categories through which these analyses take place are intended to clarify and not to obscure. Because analytical categories are only guides to understanding and not truths in themselves, insights may also be generated by testing the explanatory value of these categories at the same time that we employ them.

3 Insurance, Deterrence, and Special Compensation Funds: The Problem of Toxic Torts

With an understanding of the purposes and structure of insurance law at hand, we are now in a position to address the relations among insurance, legal theory, and public policy in specific terms. A good place to start is by looking at the interaction between insurance and the deterrence of unsafe conduct through the threat of civil liability. As we saw in general terms in the preceding pages, liability insurance may have either efficient or inefficient effects on deterrence. Accurate insurance pricing and risk classification can encourage the insured to invest in a more efficient combination of loss prevention and insurance, but inaccurate pricing or classification can allow insureds to externalize the risk of liability and to ignore the benefits of possible loss prevention efforts. The deterrent properties of liability insurance therefore depend on the way premiums are set and risks are classified. Not all forms of liability insurance are capable of inducing efficient behavior by their insureds. Some are likely to be much more successful in this endeavor than others.

These differences in the capacity of different kinds of insurance to promote optimal deterrence are, consequently, of critical importance in fashioning injury compensation systems. Yet many proposals for the adoption of such systems or for other modifications in the law of torts—accident law, for our purposes here—do not adequately consider the potential impact of insurance on their effectiveness.[1] This chapter will examine that impact by focusing mainly on a single prominent problem: liability for injuries caused by exposure to toxic chemicals.

We will first explore the relation between insurance and deterrence in the tort field with particular emphasis on toxic torts. We will next consider the impact of insurance on a much-proposed alternative to toxic tort liability: the creation of

44

special compensation funds that would provide compensation to victims on a nonfault basis in administrative proceedings. Finally, we will isolate and analyze the demands that are beginning to be made on the insurance industry as a surrogate regulator of the dangers of toxic substances. My conclusion is that the deterrent effects of special compensation funds, even when linked with surrogate regulation by the insurance industry, cannot effectively replace direct governmental regulation of environmental hazards. The principal goal of special compensation funds should be exactly what their name implies—compensation, not deterrence. And the insurance industry's regulatory responsibilities, even if expanded, should stand in the same relation to governmental controls as they always have—they should be secondary, not primary. These fundamental limitations need to be recognized before further reform occurs.

The discussion focuses on toxic torts because they have been and will continue to be so much in the public eye. The dangers of dioxin, benzene, asbestos, and other toxic chemicals are in the news almost every day; the discovery of storage dumps of hazardous waste is the cause of continuing alarm. In recent years we have seen mass disasters so frightening that the places they occurred have come to signify the events themselves: Love Canal, Times Beach, Bhopal. But the analysis I undertake can be generalized beyond the problems of exposure to toxic chemicals and the special compensation funds being created to deal with these problems. This field is only one of many that depend heavily on insurance to help the law achieve its objectives. Few reforms will be successful if they make overly optimistic or uninformed assumptions about how insurance will influence them. Taking a careful look at the potential effectiveness and limitations of toxic tort reform is a good way to see how unwarranted assumptions about the nature and capacities of insurance may confound hopes for law reform.

INSURANCE AND DETERRENCE

The old world in which those who caused accidents paid their victims out of their own pockets was a comparatively simple one. In that world, the deterrent effect of tort liability seemed straightforward. In theory at least, a potential defendant could calculate the cost of liability, discounted by the probability of its imposition, and thereby determine whether the benefit to be derived from a hazardous activity was worth seeking.[2] Private law thus could realistically strive to promote optimal levels of safety and risk.

That world has been eclipsed by the advent of widespread liability insurance. The deterrence of risky conduct is no longer simply a matter of imposing liability under the right circumstances. Individuals and business enterprises now may be protected by prepaid liability insurance that protects them against the risk of liability for injuries caused by their activities. Under these circumstances, only if liability insurance premiums are feature rated (to reflect the safety level of an activity's operations) or experience rated (to reflect the insured's actual liability record) will something approaching optimal deterrence be achieved. Absent such risk classification, insured enterprises may be able to evade some of the costs of their activities and to avoid adjusting their risky activities to appropriate levels.

The Problem of Predicting Costs

In order to achieve the economic goals underlying the imposition of tort liability, a potentially liable enterprise must be able to predict the costs that it will eventually have to pay because of today's (or this month's or this year's) activities. This cost internalization fostered by tort liability is desirable because it encourages choice of the lesser of either loss prevention costs or future liability costs. When both of these costs are predictable, enterprises whose activities are hazardous should be able to make this choice with reasonable accuracy. On the other hand, when the cost of future liability is highly speculative, enterprises may inaccurately calculate the comparative costs and benefits of investment in loss prevention and the risk of liability for failing to prevent losses. The threat of tort liability under these circumstances will under- or overdeter, depending on the nature of an enterprise's miscalculation.

The crucial point to note about this predicament is that the predictability of liability varies a great deal from activity to activity. For instance, the number and severity of automobile accidents (and the liability losses they produce) are relatively predictable because the factors on which these numbers depend change slowly. In addition, most law suits arising out of automobile accidents are instituted within a few years of an accident's occurrence. Ordinary economic inflation and legal inflation (in the form of changes in legal doctrine supporting greater recovery), therefore, do not have much impact on the predictability of claims or claim severity.

In contrast, liability for injuries caused by defective products or by medical care is considerably more difficult to predict. New products and medical procedures are continually being introduced. The number and severity of injuries that will be associated with such products or procedures cannot be predicted with accuracy until experience accumulates. Nor are lawsuits claiming liability for product-related or medical injuries resolved as quickly as the lion's share of automobile claims. Product-related injuries do not occur immediately upon sale, and the results of medical malpractice may not be discovered for years after treatment. Legal and economic change in the interim, therefore, may have effects on claims experience that render previous predictions wildly inaccurate.

Even greater inaccuracies plague the toxics field today. For many reasons, the amount of damage that current and past uses of toxic substances ultimately will cause cannot be predicted. Scientific uncertainty is one reason; knowledge of the hazardous properties of toxic chemicals is in its infancy.[3] The synergistic effect of chemicals that have been mixed together during storage in waste dumps are even less clear. The ways in which hazardous waste migrates from storage facilities into contiguous property and water supplies are not completely predictable. And toxic tort disasters tend to be catastrophic in scope and sporadic in occurrence. All this makes it very difficult to predict the ultimate riskiness of activities involving toxic substances.

Compounding the difficulty of prediction is the extraordinarily long tail on toxic tort claims. Because of the very long latency period between exposure to a toxic substance and manifestation of disease caused by exposure—twenty years is not unusual[4]—a large portion of the claims arising out of current exposures will not be made for many years. Even if the frequency and severity of future claims were predictable in current dollars, economic and legal inflation over such a long period would make assessment of ultimate financial exposure extremely speculative. Attempts to promote cost internalization by handlers of toxic substances, therefore, promise only limited success for some time. There are two ways to approach the task: to prohibit or limit liability insurance against damage caused by toxic substances or to try to tailor the price of liability insurance to the actual riskiness of an enterprise's activities.

Prohibiting or Limiting Insurance Coverage

One way to encourage cost internalization would be to prohibit or, more realistically, to limit the amount of liability insurance available to the handlers of toxic substances. Such an approach would produce an *in terrorem* prospect of uncertain but possibly great future liability. This threat might induce more cautious behavior by the affected enterprises. Of course, the threat might also overdeter, producing more safety than its cost would be worth. The argument for this approach also is weakened by the fact that many of the largest chemical manufacturers already voluntarily operate under such a scheme. Their liability insurance frequently is subject to enormous deductibles: in the millions annually. Yet they do not know and will not know for some time whether their predictions about potential future liability, and the optimal amount of precautions necessary to avoid liability, have been economically sensible.

In addition, in the case of small enterprises—the ma-and-pa hazardous waste dump or the small business handling modest amounts of various toxic substances and operating at the margin of profitability—prohibition or limitation of permissible insurance could have catastrophic consequences. Such firms would be encouraged to externalize to the future, so to speak, by minimizing loss prevention efforts that would optimize costs, if at all, only in the long run. At some point in the future, perhaps after these businesses had ceased operating, injuries caused by their failure to take safety precautions would begin to show themselves.[5]

In a world of economically rational firms with perfect information this notion of externalization to the future would make no sense. Firms would discount to present value any potential future liability and take that value into account in assessing the costs and benefits of alternative actions. In point of fact, however, managers do not always behave in a manner that will be economically rational over the long term. In large firms managers often have a strong incentive to maximize short-term results so that their leadership appears to be successful.[6] In small firms, long-term prospects probably demand even less consideration. Often cash must be generated in the present to put children through college, purchase homes, replace automobiles, and so forth.

These pressures make it likely that the need for protection against an uncertain and distant future often will be subordinated to more immediate demands. Limiting permissible insurance may produce deterrence when the threat of liability looms large and near. But when that threat is beyond the horizon, the absence of insurance may have quite the opposite effect. A firm that does not face annual increases in liability insurance premiums unless it increases the safety of its operations may simply ignore the long term.

Risk Classification and Insurance Pricing

The second and more attractive way to promote cost internalization and safety in this field—through risk classification of liability insurance—is at present a less promising alternative than might be hoped. When insuring is permitted, effective cost internalization depends on accurate insurance pricing. The insurance industry, however, suffers from the same acute lack of quantitative information about the dangers of toxic chemicals that troubles the rest of us. The plight of the insurance industry is similar to that of firms that would have to self-insure if liability insurance were prohibited or limited. The absence of detailed, reliable data makes it difficult to evaluate risk and, accordingly, to price premiums for insurance against liability for claims to be filed in the distant future.[7] Under these circumstances there is certainly no reason to be confident that liability insurance pricing will result in accurate cost internalization.

Recent developments in tort law, some expressly applicable to toxic exposures and others relevant mainly by analogy, may also hinder accurate insurance pricing. Such doctrinal innovations as shifting burdens of proof as to causation[8] and apportionment of damages,[9] the market share liability concept,[10] and joint and several liability by independent tortfeasors[11] are not merely alterations in the traditional burdens of proof. In practice, the doctrines enable some plaintiffs to recover damages from defendants who have not actually caused the loss (or the entire loss) in question. Minimally culpable defendants, for example, may be held liable for damages suffered by a victim when, in fact, the injuries resulted from the combined activities of many other actors.[12] Insurance premiums will have to take account of this quasi-vicarious liability exposure.

Some of the factors that support shifting evidentiary burdens and imposing market share or joint and several liability may be fairly accurate proxies for the loss-causing potential of an enterprise. A firm that has produced 20 percent of a particular chemical may be responsible, in some sense, for 20 percent of all the injuries caused by exposure to the chemical. But the causal connection between potential liability and the riskiness of an activity may not always be this closely correlated. For instance, a small contributor to a waste dump might be held liable for all exposures to all the chemicals in the dump under a joint and several liability approach. Under such circumstances, the potential imposition of liability on some firms and the concomitant evasion of liability by otherwise culpable firms may tend to distort the premium-setting process. In fact, the premiums charged all members of the industry may gravitate toward the same level, notwithstanding significant differences in the safety precautions or operating procedures of different firms. Thus, although innovative legal doctrines may facilitate victim compensation, to the extent that they impose liability out of proportion to the loss-causing potential of each insured, they may distort the desired effects of insurance pricing.[13]

The Informational Function of Premiums and the Move to Claims-Made Coverage

One solution to difficulties in risk prediction faced by the insurance industry is to market a form of insurance that does not rely heavily on long-term prediction in order to set premiums. Insurers of enterprises that handle toxic substances increasingly have adopted this strategy by replacing the conventional form of pollution liability insurance—occurrence coverage—with claims-made coverage.[14] The differences between the two forms of coverage can be significant.

Occurrence policies cover liability for activities that take place during the policy period, regardless of when a suit that seeks to impose liability for these activities is filed. The insurer's obligation to indemnify the insured for activities occurring during the policy period, therefore, may extend to claims filed years after the expiration of that period.[15] Occurrence policies thus attempt to charge in the present for all the eventual results of present activities. Consequently, this form of policy is very difficult to price with confidence, especially when claim frequency and severity seem likely to increase in the future at unpredictable rates.

In contrast, claims-made policies insure against liability for claims that are filed during the policy year, regardless of when the allegedly tortious activity took place. A claims-made policy provides coverage during the policy year for injuries caused by activities occurring in the past.[16] Therefore, an insurer selling claims-made coverage need predict only the extent of its insured's exposure to claims that actually will be made during the forthcoming policy period. Because the insurer need not predict long-term claim exposure, claims-made policies can be priced more confidently than occurrence policies.

Although the shift from occurrence to claims-made coverage solves many of the insurance industry's prediction problems, it does little to remove the obstacles to thorough cost internalization. If anything, such a shift may be a step in the opposite direction. A claims-made pricing system forces insured enterprises to internalize some costs. But they are mainly not the future costs of today's activities; they are the costs incurred this year as a result of activities that took place in the past. In effect, claims-made premiums are installment payments for coverage against losses caused by past activities. So a claims-made premium increase reflects only the additional costs anticipated this year as a result of past activities. Such an increase may induce the insured to recalculate the costs and benefits of possible safety precautions now occurring. But that recalculation is likely to be crude since it is based on the incomplete information conveyed by the claims-made premium increase. In contrast, an increase in occurrence premiums is a message about the future costs of this year's activities, not those of the past; and it is a message not only about next year's costs. Such an increase is an estimate of all the liability costs ultimately to be expected from current activities.

Thus, a disadvantage of claims-made coverage is that it can send incomplete and imprecise messages to insureds. An enterprise desiring to calculate the aggregate liability that today's activities will produce over the next twenty years receives little guidance by looking at the amount of this year's claims-made premium. Therefore, a claims-made pricing system may induce an enterprise to underestimate the cost of prospective liability as compared to the cost of an investment in loss prevention that would avoid some of that liability. In turn this may mislead the insured to favor insurance over loss prevention. The magnitude of this tendency is difficult to estimate. But in a period of steeply increasing claims, it is at least fair to suggest that a claims-made system probably will be less effective than occurrence pricing in helping to optimize the combination of insurance and loss prevention adopted by risky enterprises.

In sum, the capacity of any system of liability to promote optimal deterrence depends on how predictable liability is. At present, accurate prediction of liability for damages caused by toxic substances is more difficult than prediction of many other forms of civil liability. Individual firms that bear financial responsibility for such damage will be able to assess accurately the costs and benefits of their operations only if they can predict the ultimate cost of liability for damages caused by those operations. Barring such predictability, insurance premiums and the costs of self-insurance protection will, at best, only roughly reflect the cost side of the cost-benefit calculation.

However, these weaknesses do not necessarily mean that the move to claims-made coverage has been inappropriate. A claims-made insured is always at risk that its coverage will not be renewed because of unsafe operations, and that it will be exposed thereafter to claims that have not yet been reported. This threat creates incentives for safety that occurrence coverage does not produce. Further, the accuracy and fairness of claims-made rates are easier to evaluate and police since they are based on more reliable data. And if pricing occurrence premiums is highly speculative, then some movement to claims-made may be unavoidable. Certainly current market activity suggests that this is the case.

SPECIAL COMPENSATION FUNDS, INSURANCE, AND SUBROGATION

Bringing a toxic tort lawsuit is a complex and costly undertaking. Identifying the party responsible for one's exposure, specifying the chemical or chemicals to which one was exposed, and proving a causal connection between that exposure and the injury or disease complained of is often extremely difficult. The latency period between exposure and manifestation of disease may be long, and scientific knowledge about the disease-causing properties of toxic chemicals in many cases still is primitive. As a consequence, there has been movement to replace or complement tort liability with compensation schemes that would circumvent the difficulties of proving a tort claim and thereby provide a quicker and simpler method of compensating victims. I call these schemes "special compensation funds."

Some compensation funds typically are created or proposed to deal with a particular type of environmental hazard. The much-publicized federal Superfund for leaning up hazardous waste storage sites is only the most prominent example.

The funds are financed, at least in part, by assessments against firms engaged in the industry that poses the hazard.[17] The funds pay for cleanup operations,[18] provide compensation to the victims of the industry's operations,[19] or both.[20] Some funds are also empowered to obtain reimbursement for their expenditures from offending firms.[21]

These governmentally operated, privately financed compensation funds are curious hybrids. A traditional public system of controlling toxic substances and compensating their victims would pay victims out of general revenues[22] and control behavior through direct regulation.[23] A purely private approach would rely on civil liability rather than general revenues to provide compensation and on the incentive effects of the threat of liability to deter unsafe activity. The distinction between these pure types, of course, has never been sharp.

Special compensation funds tend to blur the public-private law distinction even further by borrowing very liberally from both realms. Compensation for specific environmental injuries traditionally has been obtained through legal action between private parties. Now compensation can also often be obtained from a governmentally operated fund. In the past, when governments intervened directly to alleviate an environmental problem, as in the cleanup of waste discharges or oil spills, such activities were financed with general revenues. Although governments may continue to carry out cleanup operations, such activities now can be financed not by broad-based taxation, but by specific surcharges on the industries against whose activities the funds protect.

One important feature of many of these funds is the way their goals parallel those of the traditional tort liability system that they partially replace. Not only are the funds designed to compensate those injured by exposure to toxic substances; many also seem intended to promote appropriate levels of care and safety by the generators, handlers, transporters, and users (hereafter referred to collectively as handlers) of such substances. The funds attempt to achieve this deterrence goal mainly through a device called "subrogation"—the transfer to the fund of a victim's rights against the polluting enterprise in exchange for the payment of compensation by the fund. Such a system is designed to encourage cost internalization by making responsible firms liable to the fund even after their victims have received compensation from the fund.

There is nothing theoretically objectionable about pursuing optimal deterrence in this way. Indeed, other things being equal, a system that promotes optimal deterrence is preferable to one that does not, for it will be more efficient. But if special compensation funds are to promote deterrence, the constraints under which such funds labor must be recognized. Two principal constraints deserve special consideration: first, the effects described earlier through which liability insurance may encourage inefficient behavior by the enterprises in question; and second, the limits in the capacity of insurance mechanisms to adjust to a regime that relies on a single device—a compensation fund—to fulfill the ideal of both providing compensation and promoting optimal levels of deterrence.

The ability of compensation funds to perform these mixed public and private law functions depends on the seemingly obscure but, in fact, critical factor we have just noted: whether they are granted subrogation rights. Nonsubrogated funds relieve a responsible party of liability once the victim has received compensation from the fund for injuries caused by that party, because the fund has no subrogation rights. Subrogated funds do not relieve the responsible party of liability. Instead the fund acquires the victim's rights against that party (to the extent of payment out of the fund) once the fund has paid the victim. Thus, a subrogated fund can sue the responsible party to obtain reimbursement for the fund's payments.[24]

Whether a fund is granted subrogation rights should depend very much on the goals that the designers of the fund seek to achieve. The predominant goal of nonsubrogated funds should be to assure that the victims they serve receive compensation. Such funds are a relatively simple and straightforward method of assuring compensation. In contrast, subrogated funds not only provide compensation; they also attempt to promote deterrence through exercise of their rights of subrogation against responsible parties. In practice, a fund that seeks primarily to compensate victims will achieve its goal much more easily than a fund that seeks both to compensate victims and to deter risky conduct through subrogation actions. The differences between the two types of funds hinge on this crucial point.

Nonsubrogated Funds

A nonsubrogated fund can pursue its goal of assuring compensation with at least theoretical ease. Enterprises engaging in the activities posing the risks covered by the fund are assessed surcharges to finance the fund. Victims receive compensation in accordance with fund procedures. After payment, the claimant's cause of action against the responsible enterprise or enterprises is extinguished. A nonsubrogated fund operating in this way accomplishes inter-enterprise risk spreading in something of the same way as private liability insurance: potentially liable parties share risk by contributing to a fund out of which payments to victims are made. But there are also important differences between the way insurance premiums and fund surcharges are calculated. Unlike most private liability insurance schemes, compensation funds usually set their "premiums" in the form of surcharges that bear no close relation to the amount of risk posed by the enterprise charged. Since the amount of a surcharge does not depend on an individual enterprise's riskiness, nonsubrogated funds produce much less deterrence than more precisely calibrated insurance charges can achieve.

The surcharges of a nonsubrogated fund may have some deterrent impact on activity levels by raising the costs of producing certain substances more than others. But a nonsubrogated fund's impact on safety levels is likely to be minimal because such funds cannot use much risk classification. Surcharges can be assessed according to the volume or toxicity of the chemicals produced or some combination of these and other proxies for the loss-causing potential of each enterprise. However, surcharges based on the volume or toxicity of an enterprise's product ingnore differences in the safety precautions taken by individual enterprises. And even basing surcharges on the observable safety features of an enterprise's operations would not incorporate actual loss experience into surcharge rates. In short, differentiation between the surcharges assessed against relatively safe and relatively unsafe enterprises cannot be very precise. As a result, the deterrent effects produced by nonsubrogated funds are minimal. Almost inevitably, such funds must remain primarily concerned with compensation rather than deterrence.

Subrogated Funds

Subrogated funds ideally have the potential to produce much greater deterrence of risky activities than nonsubrogated funds. In theory, they might even have more influence on safety than the tort system they would partially replace. Once freed from many of the obstacles inherent in the traditional adversary system, claimants could receive speedy compensation for their losses from the fund. The fund could then bring a subrogation action unencumbered by the difficulties faced by the small claimant suing a large enterprise. With financing of investigation and other litigation costs readily available, the pressure to settle would be reduced.[25] A body of experts could be retained to deal with recurring scientific issues. A fund would be a powerful plaintiff, capable of vigorous pursuit of its aims in a legal action.

This picture of a fund optimizing deterrence through the exercise of its subrogation rights unfortunately is heavily idealized. The same factors that hinder the pricing of insurance against toxic tort liability would undermine a subrogated fund's capacity to promote optimal deterrence. A fund's subrogation rights can help to optimize deterrence only if the threat of liability to the fund forces handlers of toxic substances to compare the ultimate liability costs of today's activities with the cost of loss prevention efforts that would reduce liability costs. Whether the liability threatened is conventional liability in tort or subrogation liability to a fund, the enterprise's cost-benefit calculation will be similar. It will have to compare the cost of insurance against liability, whether to an ordinary plaintiff or to a fund, with the cost of precautions that would help reduce future liability.

Yet, for the reasons enumerated earlier, estimates of the total cost of future liability for current activities will remain unreliable for some time to come. Neither the risky enterprises themselves nor the companies insuring them against liability to a subrogated fund could have justifiable confidence in the accuracy of their estimates of the relevant costs. Under such conditions, claims-made insurance against liability to the fund will predominate, and the new burden-shifting and liability-sharing doctrines described earlier will further confound efforts to optimize deterrence.

The impliction of this predicament are worth underscoring. Except when subrogation actions are necessary simply to finance the fund—an objective that can be achieved much more easily by increasing surcharge rates—the result could be a good deal of unnecessary administrative expense. A subrogated fund already will have surcharged potential defendants in order to finance itself, perhaps in very rough proportion to the perceived riskiness of each enterprise's operations or the product it produces. By pursuing subrogation actions, a fund then would end up double charging legally responsible enterprises without obtaining much additional deterrence for the effort. Remember that as a defendant in a subrogation action, each such enterprise could be protected by liability insurance. Yet unless that insurance were priced quite differently from the fund's surcharges, insurance premiums would simply spread the cost of subrogation liability to the same pool of firms and on much the same basis as did the surcharges that had already been paid by these firms.

Therefore, until the pricing of liability insurance advances to a more refined state, it is worth asking whether this approach of cost internalization through subrogation is worth the administrative costs it would entail.[26] Nearly the same degree of cost internalization and concomitant deterrence might be achieved by a nonsubrogated fund that classifies and revises its surcharges in accordance with risk estimates *ex ante* and disregards the *ex post* fine-tuning of subrogation actions. Until the state of the art permits refined risk classification of insurance coverage against subrogation liability to a fund, subrogation suits will have little deterrent effect. Because premiums charged individual insureds will not depend very much on individual subrogation liability experience, the money the suits would generate may as well be collected by the less cumbersome and less expensive method of increasing surcharges.

Enough may be known eventually, however, about certain industries, activities, or chemicals to warrant much more refined experience rating of the insurance associated with them. At this point, different funds might be created for each class of industry, activity, or chemical, and subrogation rights granted or withheld depending on the nature of the insurance available to the actors involved. Alternatively, administrators of subrogated funds could be granted authority not to institute subrogation actions when the overall costs entailed would exceed the estimated benefits of bringing such actions.

A different distinction might be drawn for reasons of distributional fairness rather than economic efficiency. Since the goal of subrogation liability is optimal deterrence of unsafe activity, exposures occurring before the enactment of the fund and before the dangers of the chemical in question were recognized might be treated differently from all other exposures.[27] Permitting subrogation actions for the latter set of exposures—especially as liability insurance pricing becomes more refined—would emphasize a fund's concern with deterrence by focusing liability on the individual enterprises responsible for losses paid by the fund.

But subrogation liability for exposures that occurred before a chemical's dangers were or should have been recognized may be a different story. Once a fund is in place, the entire industry it covers will be financially responsible to its victims through contributions to the fund which compensates them. Disallowing subrogation would distribute the burden of compensation to the industry as an whole. Tracing responsibility on an enterprise-by-enterprise basis for exposures occurring prior to the danger-recognition point would produce no additional deterrence.

We need to tread carefully here because the point at which the dangers of a particular chemical were (or should have been) recognized will not be easy to mark—we are learning now that some dangers were recognized by certain firms some years before they were publicly disclosed. There certainly is a strong distributional argument that there should be no immunity from subrogation claims for almost any exposures to almost any chemicals occurring after the mid–1970s. The possibility that nearly any chemical might pose hidden dangers became so well known at that time that enterprise immunity for exposures occurring subsequently could be considered inequitable, even if it were no less efficient than the alternative.

Aside from these considerations, other factors may legitimately influence the decision whether to seek marginally more precise deterrence by granting subrogation rights to a fund. First, a finding of liability to a fund has punitive overtones that surcharge assessments possessing equivalent cost-internalization effects would lack. The high visibility of a lawsuit, therefore, may have more symbolic effect than a low-visibility decision about surcharge pricing.[28] Second, in order to promote deterrence, all tort law relies on delayed imposition of liability and on a very rough measure of the costs imposed by tortious activity. Liability to a subrogated fund may merely be slightly more delayed and a bit more roughly measured.

Perhaps most important, the advisability of granting funds rights of subrogation should be assessed in light of alternative methods of deterring and controlling risky activities involving toxic substances. Inspection of chemical facilities, levying of fines for violations of safety standards, and other forms of exacting regulation represent such an alternative.[29] If these controls are both feasible and effective, creating a nonsubrogated fund and focusing mainly on the fund's compensation objectives until insurance pricing becomes more refined may be a sensible approach. The weaker these regulatory activities—and their strength has varied over the past few years, as the 1983 controversy at the Environmental Protection Agency indicated—the more persuasive the argument for using subrogation to promote safer operations. Undoubtedly the restrained regulatory involvement at the federal level during the 1980s—for budgetary and ideological reasons—at least partially explains the strength of support for using compensation funds not only to compensate victims but also to promote deterrence.

SURROGATE REGULATION: SOLUTION OR DISASTER?

For the reasons discussed above, special compensation funds are at present unlikely vehicles for promoting optimal deterrence in the toxics field. Nevertheless, the funds that have adopted this goal probably will maintain it, and newly created funds probably will be granted subrogation rights in order to promote cost internalization. I have several reasons for this prediction. First, relieving handlers of toxic substances of direct financial responsibility for their actions would in all likelihood be politically unpalatable even though the net benefits of subrogation might not warrant its use. In addition, as knowledge of the effects of exposure to toxic substances increases, as insurers perfect their inspection and risk-management techniques, and as the number of claims arising out of past exposures stabilizes or becomes more predictable, the feasibility of achieving more precise deterrence through liability insurance pricing may increase.

All of this, however, might require insurers to play a much more active role than they now do in managing the risks of handling toxic substances. This role as surrogate regulator would be a new one and would place unconventional demands on insurers. I am not necessarily advocating such a role for the insurance industry, but it is important to understand what that role would entail and to assess the validity of the insurance industry's traditional opposition to it. Some of the industry's opposition to its evolving status undoubtedly stems from institutional inertia. But industry opposition to the growing demands placed upon it is not necessarily irrational or exclusively self-interested. An expansion of its role could create serious difficulties.

Any attempt to constitute the insurance industry a surrogate regulator could change three features of its conventional role: (1) the industry's right to make the choice between claims-made and occurrence coverage; (2) the possible shift in its position as a relatively passive risk spreader to more active risk manager; and (3) limitation on the industry's traditional right to reject uninsurable risks and to fashion policy provisions that exclude coverage of deliberately unsafe activities. Each of these changes would present problems that could not be overcome without significant sacrifices in the private management of private enterprises.

Claims-Made or Occurrence Coverage?

As long as toxic tort claims and damages increase at unpredictable rates, neither claims-made nor occurrence coverage will be terribly effective at promoting precise cost internalization. As we saw earlier, however, occurrence coverage at least attempts to estimate the long-term costs that should be internalized, while claims-made pricing requires predicting exposure only during the year an insurance policy is in effect. The disappearance of occurrence coverage would mean that attempts to calculate aggregate future exposure would occur even less intensively than they do now. The insurance industry, strategically positioned to encourage research and experimentation that would eventually yield data on which to calculate long-term risk, has begun to abdicate this potentially key responsibility. The natural tendency of the handlers of toxic substances to externalize to the future—a reaction that occurrence coverage partially checks—now may proceed unimpeded. In a period of increasing claims this could prove to be a dangerous trend. If we were serious about using the insurance industry as a surrogate regulator, then its reliance on claims-made coverage might have to be prohibited.

Even if policy makers could legally force or strongly encourage insurers to write occurrence coverage, however, such action could be unwise. Market forces are not now preventing the disappearance of occurrence coverage. This may well indicate that the allocation of responsibility between insurers and the handlers of toxics by claims-made coverage is economically optimal at present. On the other hand, the shift may in part reflect the handlers' ability to externalize to the future and thereby to shift the risk of ultimate insolvency to their potential victims. Nevertheless, requiring the insurance industry to bear the risk of a very uncertain toxics future merely because it may be strategically positioned to encourage research in the area may place the burden on the wrong party. From an ethical and distributional perspective, placing that risk on the shoulders of chemical manufacturers and handlers seems more appropriate.

Further, until insurers develop a sufficient statistical base to support refined price differentiation, pricing occurrence coverage will remain highly speculative. As such data accumulate, the natural desire of insured enterprises for security of future expectations may counteract their tendency to externalize to the future and encourage insurers to begin offering occurrence coverage again. The risk that future claims may be far more numerous and severe than expected is one that the insurance industry should not have to bear alone. Insurers are risk spreaders, not speculators. Yet forcing them to write occurrence coverage in their present state of comparative ignorance of the claims future would place them in the latter role.

Risk Spreader or Risk Manager?

At times when budgetary and other constraints reduce the scope of direct governmental involvement in managing the dangers of toxic substances, special compensation funds are likely to be an increasingly attractive method of filling the breach. Yet a fund's effectiveness in promoting deterrence depends on refinement of the insurance mechanisms that can be used to protect handlers from liability to subrogated funds. If compensation funds are to become an integral part of surrogate regulation, still other devices besides pricing refinement will have to be developed to promote careful operations by insureds. But moving toward surrogate regulation in this way could begin to transform the insurance industry from a relatively passive risk spreader to a more active risk manager.[30] Although this move may be warranted, it appears to be a second-best way of controlling dangerous conduct.

In some contexts, insurers may well be better placed than insureds to make risk management decisions or to hire independent consultants for this purpose. When insurers are in fact strategically positioned to be the cheapest cost avoiders, they will have to emphasize preinsurance inspections, periodic regulatory compliance audits, subjective evaluation of the applicant's operations, and continuing involvement in risk management. Although insurers traditionally have participated in the assessment and management of their insureds' risks,[31] such involvement generally has been a secondary insurance function. Given the potentially enormous risk that insurers of toxics liability may bear, however, their interest in having risks properly managed could elevate risk management from a lesser to a principal insurance function. Moreover, coaxing insurers into active risk management—something that their prevailing use of outside chemical safety and engineering consultants indicates they are not now equipped to handle—would leave surrogate regulation incomplete. At least one additional set of devices would be required.

Policy Defenses and Financial Responsibility Requirements

The insurance industry would be handicapped in its role as surrogate regulator unless it possessed some means of directly influencing its clients' behaviors. Insurers need several tools to encourage compliance with safety standards in order to reduce the incidence and severity of accidents. As we saw earlier, one effective device, refined classification and experience rating of premiums, will not be generally available for some time. Direct risk management activities of the sort described in the preceding section, on the other hand, require some form of sanction for noncompliance in order to be effective. For example, preinsurance inspections can carry a strict sanction: failure to pass an inspection can result in the denial of coverage. When liability insurance or other proof of financial responsibility is a prerequisite to the right to handle toxic substances, insurers then have considerable leverage over their prospective insureds. Once coverage has been provided, a different approach is required. Here policy defenses are perhaps the most workable tool for enforcing compliance with the insurer's risk management standards. For example, coverage against liability resulting from breach of regulatory requirements or the insurer's own safety standards can be excluded specifically from the scope of a policy's protections.

Although giving insurers the tools they would need to act as surrogate regulators may assist them in promoting deterrence, this may undermine the coordinate goal of assuring compensation to the victims of their insured's activities. This problem and a possible solution are described below.

The Conflict between Compensation and Deterrence. Coverage exclusions are a fairly standard means of protecting against the moral hazard that arises when a dangerous activity is covered by insurance. Insureds who continually breach safety requirements are denied coverage for losses arising out of the breach and, in addition, find that their coverage is not renewed. The fact that the threat of nonrenewal may be more effective under a claims-made than under an occurrence policy system may well be the most notable advantage possessed by claims-made coverage, at least when cancellation and nonrenewal are not restricted. However, to the extent that assuring compensation to victims remains a principal goal of the system, denying coverage for losses caused by breach of safety standards could be viewed as undesirable. This is because compensation would be unavailable whenever the responsible enterprise was judgment-proof—that is, insolvent or otherwise unable to pay—and its insurance policy excluded coverage.

This should not be a significant danger normally. The chances that defendants in most cases will turn out to be judgment-proof are modest. The vast majority of the toxic chemicals in use today are manufactured and handled by very large enterprises. Such enterprises would usually experience no difficulty in paying judgments; in effect they often pay them now because their insurance is subject to enormous deductibles. Nevertheless, even some of these manufacturers and users might not survive the crushing burden of liability posed by a major environmental catastrophe on a scale greater than Love Canal, or a toxic-damage epidemic comparable to the now-burgeoning asbestos litigation.[32] And while most enterprises manufacturing or using hazardous substances are large, those that are small would surely be bankrupt long before their liability to all the victims of such mishaps could be satisfied. As a consequence, allowing insurers to put teeth into the standards they set as surrogate regulators could threaten the system's goal of assuring victims compensation. The great advantage of special compensation funds is that they reduce this threat by spreading the burdens of compensation and, in effect, the risk that any particular responsible enterprise may become insolvent.

A different problem is that placing financial responsibility or mandatory insurance requirements on handlers of toxic substances renders the insurer's position as a surrogate regulator even more significant. Unless legal requirements force insurers to extend coverage to all applicants who meet predetermined qualifications, insurers often will have the power to put individual handlers out of business. That power has not been lightly surrendered to the insurance industry in other contexts. In the field of automobile liability coverage, for example, governmentally operated substitute insurance markets have been instituted to assure that insurance coverage is available to those who are denied it in the private market.[33] But establishing such a market in the toxics field would both defeat part of the purpose of financial responsibility requirements and bring government back into a field that it had been trying to abdicate in part to the insurance industry.

An Alternative. The purpose of financial responsibility requirements and an insurer's policy defenses are thus essentially at odds with each other. If insurers are permitted to act as surrogate regulators by invoking exclusion provisions in their liability policies, the compensation goals of financial responsibility requirements may be frustrated. A rough compromise is available though it has the natural deficiencies of any compromise: invalidate policy exclusions as between the insurer and its insured's victims, but allow such exclusions to be effective as between the insurer and the insured.[34] In effect, when the insured has violated safety standards that are conditions of coverage, the insurer would serve only as a guarantor of its insured's liability rather than as an indemnifier. This approach assures victims their compensation and reduces the moral hazard at which such policy conditions are directed by requiring careless insureds to reimburse insurers the sums paid victims. But the approach does not fully eliminate moral hazard, and it places the risk of the insured's insolvency on the insurer. This risk could be more real than fanciful, since those operations with the greatest incentive to take safety shortcuts, which would otherwise invalidate coverage, would probably be the smaller firms operating closest to the margin of solvency.

The Insurer's New Role

The three possible developments canvassed here threaten to cast the insurance industry in a role quite different from that which it traditionally has occupied. First, requiring the industry to offer occurrence coverage would force insurers to underwrite currently unpredictable risks. In effect, the insurance industry would be the vehicle for pooling a highly speculative risk. Yet insurers' investments normally are regulated in order to protect the community of insureds against that very sort of speculation. It would be ironic if in this case underwriting activity turned out to be even more speculative than investment activity. Second, appointing the industry as a frontline risk manager would require it to play an authoritative role—perhaps even an authoritarian one—in making decisions about the way other businesses conduct their operations. This role more typically belongs to a corporate parent or major creditor than to an insurer. Third, making insurers guarantors of the financial responsibility of their insureds even when the latter have violated express conditions of coverage would be almost unprecedented. A firm having a major stake in the solvency of another normally is an investor or creditor whose downside risk is counterbalanced by a speculative position in the risky firm's profitability. Yet insurers in such cases usually would have no significant equity investment in their insureds. Their risk would be large, but their profit-making potential in any individual case would be actuarially small.

The insurance industry will obviously prefer not to assume the risks associated with any of these new roles. Insurers are not risk takers but risk spreaders. In most situations they avoid excessive risk by relying on the statistical certainty of the law of large numbers, by charging very high premiums for coverage against uncertain exposure, or by declining to offer coverage at all. But these devices would be unavailable to them in the new roles discussed above. Charging high occurrence premiums is not really a useful option because the present unpredictability of future claims renders even high-priced occurrence coverage very speculative. Declining to cover an applicant at all might be difficult in cases where securing a license to handle toxic substances depends upon proof of financial responsibility. And new surrogate regulatory responsibilities might even expand the liability that insurers traditionally bear by exposing the insurers to liability for their own faulty risk management decisions.[35] In this instance the burdens of the industry's new role would outweigh the benefits to it.

Some might argue that the extra business generated from the need for insurance against toxic tort liability could provide adequate returns to the industry even in the face of these additional risks. But if it is thought advisable to cast the industry into a new role, the traditional methods of paying insurers for their services may be inadequate. Insurers might justifiably demand new methods of compensation for taking risks they would prefer to avoid entirely. None of the methods available at present, however, seems satisfactory.[36] With the proliferation of toxic tort litigation, providing insurers extraordinary compensation may be the only way to justify requiring them to bear extraordinary obligations. Until satisfactory forms of compensation are developed, the process of surrogate regulation may not proceed very far.

Understanding the relation between insurance and deterrence is indispensable to any effective reform of accident law, including reform that deals with the consequences of exposure to toxic substances. The role insurance plays should not be taken for granted when fashioning new ways to control and compensate for environmental injury. Indeed, our survey of the problems entailed in structuring special compensation funds suggests how important a factor insurance is in any attempt at tort law reform. The key is that tort liability, compensation alternatives, and insurance mechanisms should be considered in conjunction and adjusted so that they can work together rather than in opposition. Because of present limitations, the main purpose of special compensation funds should be exactly what their name implies: to compensate victims. Deterrence of excessively risky activities should be relegated to a secondary position in a fund's hierarchy of goals. Direct governmental regulation still should be considered the most effective device for controlling unwarranted risk in this field. In the meantime, we should recognize the drawbacks of placing the insurance industry in the role of surrogate for this more desirable method of deterring unsafe conduct.

The advent of special compensation funds is an important event in the evolution of our tort and compensation systems. The intricacy of these systems demands that we recognize the impact of this change on their other features. As we respond to emerging environmental problems by fashioning new ways to achieve the old goals of compensation and optimal deterrence, we will do well not to lose sight of the limitations under which the system labors.

4 Efficiency and Fairness in Risk Classification

We saw in the preceding chapter how difficult it is to achieve the goals of insurance law when accurate pricing of insurance is not feasible. In this chapter we examine in detail the different effects that can be achieved when accurate insurance risk classification is a more realistic possibility.

The heart of any insurance system is its method of classifying risks and setting prices. Different methods of classification can produce very different safety incentives, distributions of risk, and protection against loss. Classification practices have enormous economic significance, but they also have moral implications since risk classification is a method of distributing risk. Yet the nature of risk classification and the economic and moral purposes it serves have not been adequately analyzed. Scholarly studies have tended to focus on specific forms of classification without sufficiently linking their analyses to principles of more general application.[1] And debate by the public at large has often seemed beset by contradiction.

The result has been a series of unresolved and, in the view of some, unresolvable controversies concerning the risk classification practices of the insurance industry. On one hand, differences in the predictability of loss from insured to insured and in the actual loss experience of different insureds seem highly relevant to the price each insured should be charged for coverage. On the other hand, insurance is seen as a method of risk sharing in which groups of insureds bear the risk that others will suffer a loss. A particularly intense conflict arises when losses are associated with the age or sex of the insured since classification based on these characteristics is likely to be especially suspect.

In short, attitudes toward insurance always seem to be pulling in two directions—one that highlights the risk-assessment or efficiency-promoting features of insurance classification and the other that stresses the risk-distributional function of insurance. The decision of the Supreme Court in *Arizona Governing Committee v. Norris*[2] and the debate that has accompanied it provide only the latest example of the tension between the risk-assessment and risk-distributional aims of insurance and insurance law. Congress has considered the problem in recent years and may well act on it at some point in the future.[3] This chapter explores the ways in which this tension can be resolved, by analyzing in detail the competing principles in this field. But before embarking on this task, it will be useful to place the problem in context.

Insurance operates best in the face of a very special sort of uncertainty. In fact, the tension between risk assessment and risk distribution is so characteristic of the operation of insurance under uncertainty that risk-sharing schemes from which the tension is missing seem only to resemble what we think of as the real thing. For example, if we knew precisely how many losses of a certain sort would occur but nothing at all about who would suffer them, then insurance against such losses would be feasible. But it would be insurance embodying only the distribution of risk among those insured and no assessment of the extent of each individual's risk: each insured would pay exactly the same premium. Similarly, if we knew who was at risk of suffering a loss if it occurred but nothing about how many of those at risk would suffer a loss, something like insurance would also be feasible: insureds would be charged retroactively for their proportionate share of whatever losses ultimately occurred. Again, this arrangement would embody risk distribution but no individualized risk assessment. Although both of these schemes involve risk sharing, each is simpler than the standard insurance arrangement because neither involves any individual risk assessment.

Insurers, however, typically know something about individual risks. Because in such instances it is possible both to assess and to distribute risk, the tension between assessment and distribution is inevitable. Risk assessment through classification of insureds into groups posing similar risks necessarily limits the amount of risk distribution achieved by any insurance arrangement, because it uses knowledge about risk expectancies to set different prices for members of different groups. But no risk classification system ever can classify and price individual risks with anything near complete accuracy. The future is too uncertain for that. Nevertheless, when even reasonably accurate risk assessment is feasible, insurance classification can promote economically efficient behavior by encouraging insureds to compare the cost of insurance with the cost of investment in loss prevention that would reduce the sum of these two costs. In contrast, when risk assessment is not accurate but insurance is still available, inefficient behavior is a likely result: this is the moral hazard of insurance described in the preceding chapters.

Often a classification scheme can be made more accurate and therefore more efficient. But as we shall shortly see, promoting efficiency through risk classification sometimes requires sacrificing other values. The burdens of inaccuracy may be unevenly distributed; risk classes may have to be based on variables not within the control of insureds; and certain variables—for example, race or sex—may have social or moral connotations that are unacceptable. For convenience I describe these concerns as sacrifices in risk-distributional fairness. Although these concerns are similar in that each sometimes demands inefficient forms of risk classification, risk-distributional fairness is by no means a monolithic notion. An important part of my argument is that we need to be more careful to isolate the different kinds of risk-distributional concerns that different approaches to insurance classification raise. Without attention to details of this sort, remedies will be proposed that are overbroad, undereffective, or both.

A variety of legal tools is available for addressing these issues and regulating the combination of efficiency and risk distribution reflected in the insurance market's classification practices. Legislative control can be exercised through statutory provisions governing insurance classification[4] or through more general prohibitions against various forms of discrimination. The decisions of the Supreme Court in the *Manhart*[5] and *Norris*[6] cases, for example, applied antidiscrimination provisions of the Civil Rights Act of 1964 to employer-sponsored pension plans. Legislation in every state also delegates to insurance commissioners considerable authority to regulate risk classification and premium rates. Most often the delegations include a statutory obligation that the commissioner assure that premium rates not be excessive, inadequate, or unfairly discriminatory.[7] This mandate affords the commissioner broad discretion to fashion compromises between the twin goals of efficiency and risk-distributional fairness. Finally, the courts also play a role through judicial enforcement of statutory standards and through oversight of administrative action.[8]

The remainder of this chapter looks carefully at the factors these institutions should consider in fashioning legal policy to govern the risk classification process. First comes an analysis of the economic forces that affect risk classification and the techniques that are available to deal with these forces. I explain why classification and differential pricing have developed in response to these forces, examine the criteria that may be used to dissect the notions of efficiency and risk-distributional fairness in this context, and analyze the problems insurers encounter in setting prices. Then I explore in detail the efficiency concerns that are relevant to classification and pricing systems and scrutinize the differing demands that may be made on classification systems in the name of fairness. Finally, having dealt with the unfairness of efficiency, I address the coordinate question of the costs of fairness.

THE NATURE OF INSURANCE CLASSIFICATION AND PRICING

The Emergence of Risk Classification

The starting point for any analysis of the nature of insurance classification should be an obvious but fundamental fact: insurance is only one of a number of ways of satisfying the demand for protection against risk. With few exceptions, insurance need not be purchased at all. People can do without insurance if it is too expensive. Indeed, as the price of coverage rises, the amount purchased and the number of people purchasing will decline. Instead of buying insurance people will self-insure, by accumulating savings against the risk of loss, self-protect, by spending more on loss prevention, or simply use the money saved to purchase other goods and services.[9] An insurer must compete against these alternatives even in the absence of competition from other insurers.

One method of competing for protection dollars is to divide potential purchasers into groups, classifying them according to their probability of loss and the potential magnitude of losses if they occur. Different risk classes then may be charged different premiums, depending on that expected loss. Were it not for this need to compete for protection dollars, an insurer could simply charge each individual a premium based on the average expected loss of all its insureds (plus a margin for profit and expenses) without incurring the costs of classification.

Insurers often can capture more protection dollars by classifying because through classification they can offer low-risk individuals lower prices. Two costs are incurred, however, by classification. First, the process of classification itself is costly. Data must be gathered, statistical operations performed on it, and marketing may be more costly when prices are not uniform. Second, classification necessarily raises premiums for poor risks, who then purchase less coverage as a result. In the aggregate, classification is worthwhile to an insurer when the gains produced from extra sales and lower payouts outweight the costs of classification plus the costs of lost sales.[10] Even in the absence of competition from other insurers, engaging in at least some classification is likely to enable an insurer to capture more protection dollars than it loses.

When there is not only competition for available protection dollars, but competition among insurers for premium dollars, the value of risk classification to insurers becomes even clearer. The more refined (and accurate) an insurer's risk classifications, the more capable an insurer is of skimming good risks away from insurers whose classifications are less refined. If other insurers do not respond, either by refining their own classifications or raising prices and catering mainly to high risks, then their book of risks will contain a higher mixture of poor risks who are still being charged premiums calculated for average risks. Additional poor risks will gravitate toward these insurers whose classifications have not isolated and charged poor risks higher premiums. The resulting adverse selection will further disadvantage these insurers' competitive positions.

This prospect tends to explain the proliferation of risk classifications in insurance markets. Depending on the line of insurance involved, there may be hundreds of separate classifications into which insureds are placed. Different insurers sometimes may classify in different ways in the hope of capturing a different slice of the universe of good risks. However, up to the point where the cost of refining classifications is not worth the competitive benefit derived, all insurers will classify at roughly the same level of refinement. Otherwise they will lose good business to other insurers and find as well that the busines they retain is less and less profitable.

How to Evaluate a Classification System

The central concept in the construction of risk classification systems is the notion of expected loss—the predicted probability that an insured will suffer a loss multiplied by the predicted severity of the loss if it occurs, as previously stated. In constructing risk classes, the insurer's goal is to determine the expected loss of each insured and to place insureds with similar expected losses into the same class, so that each may be charged the same rate.[11]

Expected loss is a prediction of an insured's actual losses. For two reasons, however, actual losses vary from expected loss. First, calculations of expected loss normally do not and cannot be based on all relevant variables. A classification based on one or a few variables is likely to be at best a rough estimate of any individual insured's actual loss. Calculations of expected loss make use of statistical facts about group probabilities of loss. If different variables were considered, an individual's expected loss might be entirely different. Second, expected loss is only the predictable component of any individual's actual loss. For practical purposes a large component of most individuals' and enterprises' actual losses must be considered to occur by chance. Such random losses are either impossible to predict at all given current knowledge or too costly to predict. This is especially true of the severity of losses, as distinguished from the frequency of losses, that may occur. Even very refined risk classification systems consequently predict only imperfectly. Their accuracy depends on the proportion of losses that are due to chance, understood in the way just described.

The tension between risk assessment and risk distribution in classification can best be comprehended by examining the role that expected loss plays in the five different features of classification schemes. The first three features—the separation, reliability, and incentive value of risk classes—are associated with risk assessment and its concomitant impact on economic efficiency. Two additional features of risk classes—their homogeneity and admissibility—bear on the risk-distributional fairness of the system that uses the classes.[12] These five features reflect the different aspects of economic efficiency and risk-distributional fairness that are relevant in evaluating risk classification systems.

Separation

The first key to accurate risk assessment is achieving separation of risk classes. Separation is a measure of the degree to which insureds in different risk classes have different expected losses. The greater the separation between classes, the greater the statistical support for charging members of the classes different premiums, and the lower the risk of misclassification.

To achieve separation, the difference between the mean expected losses of any two classes should be significant enough to warrant charging them different premiums. Separation will not be pursued, however, beyond the point where the costs of gathering data needed for further refinement exceed the competitive benefit that can be derived from that refinement. A class must be large enough, moreover, for the inferences that are drawn from its loss experience to be statistically sound, or credible.

For example, suppose that age and sex correlate with driver accident rates, and that both are used in constructing risk classes. If male and female drivers ages nineteen to twenty-six are placed in separate classes, and if the males are rated higher, there may not be complete separation. Some twenty-six-year-old males may have lower expected losses than some nineteen-year-old females.[13] The less overlap of this sort that occurs, the greater the separation between the two classes. In some classification schemes, however, the demands of separation have been sacrificed to assure credibility. Statistical techniques for reducing credibility concerns are available, but they pose accuracy problems of their own.[14]

Figures 1 and 2 illustrate two different degrees of separation. The vertical axis measures the distribution of expected loss (the number of insureds with a given expected loss) and the horizontal axis measures the amount of expected loss. The difference between the mean expected losses of classes A and B is greater in figure

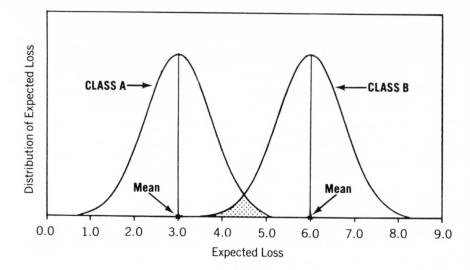

Figure 1

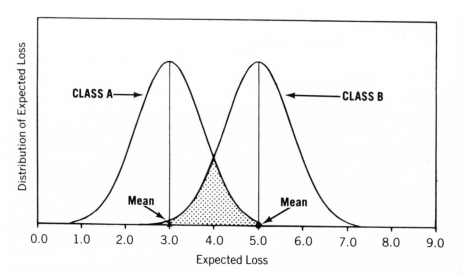

Figure 2

1 than in figure 2. Thus, the separation between the classes in figure 1 is greater than in figure 2. The shaded area of overlap between the two classes indicates the portion of all insureds who have similar expected losses but who are charged different premiums. The smaller overlap in figure 1 reflects the greater separation between the two classes.

Reliability

A second aspect of accurate risk assessment (and therefore of efficient classification) is the reliability of the variables on which risk classes are based. Not only is the separation of risk classes desirable in theory; in practice the classes should be susceptible to as little administrative error and fraud as possible. Otherwise, assignments of individuals to different classes may be unreliable, and the classes will tend to be heterogeneous and to overlap.

The main cause of unreliability is the difficulty of verifying data furnished by the applicant herself or himself. When verification is feasible and relatively inexpensive, reliability is not undermined. Medical examinations can be given before accepting life insurance applications, driver's licenses used to prove age, and data banks relied upon to verify accident experience. But when verification is difficult, then the insurer must choose between disregarding a potentially predictive variable and undermining the reliability of its classifications. For example, mileage driven is a comparatively good predictor of driver accident rates, but it is often thought too difficult to verify to warrant its use. Smoking apparently accounts for a sizable minority of residential fires,[15] but a nonsmoker's discount for purchasers of homeowner's insurance is rare. In both these instances the demands of reliability prevent the use of a potentially powerful classification variable.

Incentive Value

Not only should risk classes reflect differences in expected losses among classes of insureds; ideally they also should create loss prevention incentives on the part of insureds. To achieve this goal, insofar as possible classes should be based on variables within the insured's control. In this context as elsewhere the notion of control encompasses not only the ability to conduct activities more safely, but also the capacity to vary levels of production or activity, since such variation also may affect the reduction or prevention of losses. Periodic reclassification of insureds also should be feasible, to take account of the effects on expected loss of loss prevention efforts by insureds.

There are two major ways to use classifications to create incentive effects: feature rating and experience rating.[16] Feature rating relies on observable features of the insured or the insured's operations to calculate expected losses and construct risk classes. The features used as variables may be levels of safety or levels of activity. Basing fire insurance rates on building characteristics (size, materials used in construction, and presence or absence of sprinkler systems) and basing product liability insurance rates on sales volume are both examples of feature rating. Data collected over the years and intuitive hunches[17] by insurers suggest which features are correlated with loss rates and therefore should be used as classification variables.

Experience rating, on the other hand, uses the loss experience of the insured during one period to help set the premiums charged in the following period. Experience rating is usually used in combination with feature rating. For example, drivers may be classified initially according to their sex, age and marital status; their rates then may be revised upward or downward in subsequent policy periods, depending on their claims experience.

Feature and experience rating affect loss prevention incentives in different ways. Over a given policy period, feature rating creates no loss prevention incentives, but in the long run this form of rating can have incentive effects. If the insured has not made large, fixed investments in the features in question, he may be able to modify these features of his activities during later policy periods. Conversely, feature rating will have little incentive effect when the risk insured against depends mainly on features that are fixed over the long term.

The long-term effects of feature rating, therefore, depend on the kind of control the insured can exercise over the features used as classification variables. Some forms of feature rating may affect activity levels but not the safety of given activities. A family that decides not to purchase a second car may effectively limit its level of teenage driving but not the safety of the teenage driving that it still allows. Similarly, over the long term, fire insurance rating based on building materials may have a marginal effect on the number or kinds of houses that are built, but it cannot directly affect residential fire safety activities.

Some feature rating schemes unfortunately have little incentive value even when they are based on controllable variables. A product manufacturer has control over its sales volume, but feature rating based on volume is likely to have little effect on safety because the insured has no incentive to lower sales in order to reduce premiums. Other forms of feature rating, however, can affect levels of safety if they are based on features of an activity that can be modified—the use of a comparatively safe kind of equipment or vehicle, for example, or the installation of sprinkler or alarm systems.

Both safety levels and activity levels can be indirectly affected even when noncontrollable features are used as classification variables. Feature rating based on noncontrollable characteristics, such as age or sex, can affect activity levels by encouraging insureds to reduce the level of involvement in the insured activity.

So long as other features of the insured's operations affecting risk are controllable, safety levels also may change: under such rating insureds are encouraged to reduce their reliance on insurance and to shift instead to safety measures for protection against the risk in question. Ideally, of course, it might be preferable to move to experience rating under these circumstances, although such a move may not always be feasible.

Experience rating also has both advantages and shortcomings. The insured who is subject to experience rating has a decided incentive to reduce his claims or liability experience because his future premiums will be affected by that experience. But unlike feature rating based on controllable variables, experience rating does not indicate which behavior the insured should alter in order to modify his expected loss. He knows that more care will probably reduce risk, but he is given no information about effective ways to take more care. The insured is only given an incentive to discover and modify these variables himself. Further, when past loss experience is not a good predictor of future experience, experience rating may create incentives to alter behavior that in fact is not closely related to losses.

In terms of incentive value, therefore, feature rating is probably preferable when the effect of particular variables on expected loss is relatively predictable and changes in other conduct probably will not alter loss experience significantly. Experience rating, on the other hand, probably is preferable when the effect of different variables on loss varies from insured to insured or when insureds are in a better position than the insurer to determine what features of their activities can be most effectively varied to affect loss experience.[18] Feature rating provides insureds with the insurer's conclusions about the best way to reduce losses; experience rating reflects the conclusion that the insured, not the insurer, is in the best position to make this determination.[19]

The incentive value of both feature and experience rating also depends, however, on the information that rates and rate changes communicate to insureds. Even otherwise-appropriate feature rating categories and finely tuned adjustments in premiums through experience rating can have little effect on safety incentives if insureds do not know the amount of insurance savings available from changes in their operations or reductions in their loss experience. In this sense the incentive value of rate structures depends not only on pricing in accord with expected loss, but also on the simplicity and explainability of rating variables and price adjustments.[20]

Much products liability insurance, for example, is provided by comprehensive general liability policies that afford the insured coverage against a variety of risks. Because in the past the price of the products liability component often was not separately indicated, it was difficult for insureds to determine what portion of

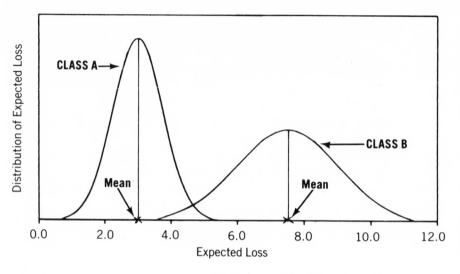

Figure 3

any premium adjustment could be ascribed to changes in expected products liability losses.[21] In short, not only are there costs involved in generating the information on which rate classes are based and communicating it to insureds; there is
also a cost to the insured of consuming that information.[22] The more complicated
or confusing the information, the greater the cost of consumption, and the less
incentive value any form of rating is likely to have.

Homogeneity

A fourth feature of any risk classification system is the homogeneity of its risk
classes. Social concerns instead of economic incentives operate here. Since all the
members of a class are charged the same rate, it is desirable that they have similar
expected losses. The more homogenous the members of a class in this respect, the
stronger the argument for charging each the same rate. Like insureds then are
treated alike. On the other hand, the more heterogeneous the expected losses of
the insureds in a class, the weaker the argument for the classification.

Figure 3 illustrates two different degrees of homogeneity. Class A is more homogeneous than class B because the expected losses of its members are more similar than those in class B. To put it another way, the average deviation from the
mean expected loss in class B is greater than in class A.

Like separation, homogeneity is a relative notion. No risk class is completely homogeneous because a class must be large enough to support statistically sound predictions about its claims experience. Moreover, even in an apparently homogeneous class insureds might have very different expect losses if a different variable were used for classification. For example, suppose that a twenty-year-old male driver is twice as likely as a forty-year-old male driver to be involved in an accident in any given year. Then separate rate classes based on age might be worthwhile. Yet data on additional characteristics—annual mileage driven or the tendency to drive while drunk, for example—could be unavailable, unreliable, or prohibitively expensive to obtain. The variable used to distinguish the classes therefore would explain only a portion of the losses of those classified. The remainder of their expected loss would have to be considered uncertain.

Nevertheless, for several reasons variables that explain only a portion of the expected losses of members of the same risk class are not automatically objectionable. Because of the absence of knowledge about the causes of losses, classifications that explain only a portion of expected loss nevertheless may approach the practical limits of predictive capacity. And when several factors are combined into multivariable classes, their predictive value is higher and classes are more homogeneous. Further, objections to seemingly heterogeneous classifications may be based as much on the nature of the variables used or ignored in the classification as on the heterogeneity they create. Life insurance and annuity rates, for instance, are based largely on the life expectancies of individuals at a certain age. Yet this heavy reliance on age as a classifying factor in life insurance is rarely subjected to objections as strong as those levelled against heavy reliance on age in classifying automobile insurance risks.[23] The difference in attitudes may be related more to the belief that actual loss experience or some specific characteristic within the insured's control would be a preferable variable for use in automobile insurance than to any perceived difference in the predictive power of age in the two settings. In short, the demands made in the name of homogeneity may depend on whether the available alternatives are superior in other respects, such as incentive value or admissiblity.

Finally, homogeneity should be understood not only as a relative notion, but also as a comparative notion. The homogeneity of risk classes can be assessed not only in relation to an ideal, but also in comparison with each other. An otherwise acceptable degree of heterogeneity in one class could become objectionable because of the greater homogeneity of other classes. This difference in homogeneity would place a greater risk-sharing burden on members of the more heterogeneous class than on those in other classes. As I will explain when I address risk-distributional issues more explicitly, this possibility may lead to classification schemes designed to avoid uneven distribution of such burdens.

Admissibility

Some variables with predictive power may be socially, legally, or morally inadmissible for use in constructing risk classes. Race, sex, or age, for example, may be good predictors of certain kinds of loss experience. But race is almost always an inadmissible consideration, and both sex and age are sometimes objectionable, depending on the kind of insurance involved.[24] In addition, characteristics that are admissible on their face but that have a disparate impact on the members of one race or sex also may be suspect. Most automobile insurance classification uses not only age and sex as variables, but also the insured's territory of residence. Because inner cities are high-risk areas, young black males tend to be charged very high rates. Even when the impact of these variables is not so pronounced, the use of territorial variables tends to have income-regressive effects because a higher proportion of the poor live in high-risk urban areas.

The point to underscore here is that admissibility concerns can veto, or at least call into question, variables that otherwise might satisfy one or more of the four other classification criteria discussed above. In this sense admissibility is not simply a separate dimension of assessment, but a conclusion about the validity of a particular form of classification in light of standards external to the classification system itself.

No system of classification can simultaneously maximize satisfaction of all five classification criteria. Variables that on paper appear to produce homogeneity and separation may not be reliable in practice. Yet those that are reliable may produce less homogeneous or less separated classes. Variables not within the control of insureds may produce the most homogeneous classes but may sacrifice incentive value. Finally, inadmissible characteristics may occasionally produce the greatest separation or homogeneity. As a result, all systems leave themselves open to the criticism that any particular goal is not being achieved to the greatest extent possible. In a system of mixed goals, however, this is not a prescription for unresolvable conflict or unprincipled compromise. Instead, it is an invitation to weigh the strength of each goal and to fashion a system that most closely reflects this weighting. We now turn to examine directly the risk-assessment and risk-distribution goals of insurance classification.

RISK ASSESSMENT AND ECONOMIC EFFICIENCY

Here I shall consider the cluster of economic values that tend to be seen in the legal literature as efficiency concerns. As we saw in chapter 2, there are imprecisions entailed in speaking this way since efficiency is not a monolithic notion, especially in the technical literature.[25] Nevertheless, it is useful to rely on the general notion of efficiency in the production of economic value and to distinguish that notion from concern with the fair distribution of value. To understand the nature of efficient risk classification, we need to use the criteria developed in the preceding pages in order to isolate both the positive effects of classification and the limits on their complete achievement.

The Nature of Efficient Classification

Other things being equal, insurers strive to charge insureds in accord with their expected costs,* which equal their expected losses plus a portion of the other costs of providing them coverage.[26] To the extent that risk classes and prices conform to this standard, a number of results follow. First, insureds share the risk of random losses but pay premiums on an individual basis for expected losses.[27] Because the members of each class are charged in accord with their expected costs, total premiums are designed to cover the aggregate losses of the class. No subsidies run from one risk class to another. The only subsidy under this ideal flows from the lucky to the unlucky.

This formulation is more than just a way of saying that efficient classification entails intertemporal risk spreading—coverage against the concentration of losses in a given period—but no interpersonal or interenterprise spreading. Insureds are unlikely to suffer the exact amount of their expected losses over the course of their insuring lives. Only large enterprises suffering frequent losses approach this expectation. Therefore, even efficiently classified insurance coverage provides more than simple intertemporal protection. Because insurance protects against the risk of greater than expected losses, in general, the distinction between expected and random losses is central to the notion of efficient classification. An efficient system has elements of both risk assessment and risk distribution, but the scope of each is distinct. Individual insureds are assessed the risk of suffering expected losses and are charged accordingly; the risk of suffering random losses is distributed among all insureds.

The second effect of an efficient classification system is that it does not discourage allocation of an optimal amount of resources to loss prevention. Because insurance is priced in accord with expected cost, insureds have the incentive to compare the cost of protecting against risk by insuring with the cost of reducing

---

*In the pages that follow, I shall refer to charging in accord with expected loss and expected cost interchangeably, except where the difference is significant.

risk through loss prevention. Efficient classification discourages insureds from purchasing insurance when they can more cheaply protect against risk by investing in loss prevention.* In contrast, inefficient classification may produce suboptimal loss prevention incentives. When coverage is priced below expected cost, for example, insureds may not take safety precautions that would otherwise be worthwhile because they may be able to obtain equivalent protection against risk by purchasing insurance at a lesser cost than the precautions.

Finally—and this is a vital point—an efficient classification system does not strive to make its premiums equal expected cost beyond the point where that goal is worth achieving. Information about risk is accumulated and risk classes are refined only so long as the competitive benefits of refinement are worth their cost. Consequently, all individual differences are not recognized by a classification system. When an insurer can no longer attract or make enough profit from additional low-risk insureds to justify discovering and classifying them, an equilibrium is reached, and no further refinement occurs. Some groups may then seem to subsidize or be subsidized by others.

For example, suppose that people raised on farms are especially poor drivers, or that obstetricians trained in Ohio are unusually immune to malpractice suits. Because classification systems are unlikely to have the information necessary to make these variables the basis of risk classes, neither farm-born drivers nor Ohio-trained obstetricians will be charged exactly in accord with their true expected costs. From the standpoint of one in possession of this unavailable information, the former may seem to be subsidized by other drivers, and the latter may seem to have subsidies extracted from them by other insured physicians. But it is a bit misleading to say that these situations involve subsidies since it would be inefficient to make the investment necessary to discover and eliminate them.

This example makes it plain that there is nothing special or preordained about the classifications that turn out to be efficient. Had insurers begun decades ago to maintain data about farm-born drivers or the birthplaces of obstetricians, then using these variables for classification might now be efficient. But in many cases the

---

*The description here actually is a bit oversimplified, although it is sufficiently accurate for our purposes. Insurance can provide coverage against a specified amount of loss or it can include deductibles or coinsurance that protect against only a portion of any loss. Similarly, some loss prevention activities reduce risk across-the-board, whereas others may reduce the risk of large loss but have little effect on the risk of small losses, or vice versa. Therefore, the combination of insurance and loss prevention adopted by any insured will depend not only on the comparative costs of each kind of investment in protection against risk, but also on the nature of that protection and the nature of the risk aversion that demands it.

clock cannot be turned back nor a new approach taken without sacrificing real economies. Moreover, even if restructuring a classification system would otherwise be efficient, in all likelihood no individual insurer would have an incentive to restructure. The reason is that competitors would take advantage of the classifications introduced by the innovating insurer and compete on an equal basis for the newly discovered low-risk insureds without having made the investment required of the innovator. Therefore, some form of collective action would be required for the innovation to occur.

To sum up the implications of our discussion thus far, insurance relies upon group rather than individual estimates of expected loss in order to function. With very few exceptions—large enterprises with detailed loss histories and frequent current losses—estimating expected loss individually is impossible. Most individual loss experience is not statistically credible enough to warrant individual rating, though a few insurers occasionally do gamble on unique risks—the well-being of John McEnroe's left arm is an example. Group probabilities provide the credibility necessary to the predictions that are at the heart of the system. Until an individual insured is treated as a member of a group, it is impossible to know his expected loss, because for practical purposes that concept is a statistical one based on group probabilities. Without relying on such probabilities, it would be impossible to set a price for insurance coverage at all. In this sense there is risk sharing even within the risk-assessment component of insurance classification. No one has a true expected loss. Rather, insureds share the risk that characteristics of those in their risk class that are not taken into account by the classification render the class's expected loss higher than it would be were those characteristics considered in setting premium rates.

The Impact of Separation, Reliability, and Incentive Value on Efficiency

Three of the criteria discussed earlier—separation, reliability, and incentive value—are directly related to the efficiency of a classification system.[28] The greater the potential separation among classes, the more likely the cost of achieving class separation is worth the competitive benefit derived from the additional refinement this separation would produce. The more reliable the variables on which classes are based, the more worthwhile the level of refinement, since it will represent classification on the basis of actual expected loss rather than classification that can be circumvented or confused in practice.

Perhaps the most striking of all the effects of an efficiently structured classification system is its incentive value. Efficient risk classification performs an optimizing function by inducing insureds to compare the cost of coverage with the cost of safety precautions and other forms of loss prevention. As we have seen, if insurance is underpriced, the insured has an incentive to purchase too much coverage and to invest too little in loss prevention. If insurance is priced in accord with expected cost, however, it can help promote optimal investment in insurance and loss prevention.

This optimizing effect can be produced even when the variables on which risk classes are based are not within the insured's control. The insured still has the incentive to optimize his or her overall cost of protecting against risk, through safety expenditures or reductions in activity levels, so long as such expenditures produce greater protection than a similar investment in insurance. Thus, when a noncontrollable variable is used to help set the price of insurance coverage, reducing loss experience will not reduce the price of that coverage, but reducing losses may reduce the amount of coverage needed. For this reason the incentive to optimize loss experience operates even when noncontrollable variables are used. Therefore, although use of noncontrollable variables may sometimes be considered unfair, it is not necessarily inefficient.

Obtaining a related optimizing effect, however, does depend on whether the classification variables used are within an insured's control. Risk classification can perform an informing function by supplying the insured with information about the features of his behavior or operations that are associated with expected loss. This information indicates the types of precautions the insured should take to reduce expected loss. Knowing better how to invest in protection, the insured will need to purchase less insurance to obtain optimal risk protection. The more accurate the classification, the more useful the information may be. But the classification can perform this function only when the variables on which it is based are within the insured's control. If classification sends messages about features outside the insured's control—age or sex, for example—then the messages cannot be converted into action. When such messages are about features within the insured's control, not only may they assist the insured in allocating his protection dollars more efficiently and thereby reduce his need for insurance. They also may help reduce the cost of future coverage, if additional investment in loss prevention serves to reduce the insured's expected loss.

Even experience rating, which points to no particular feature of the insured's activities that might be altered to reduce loss experience, plays a role in the informing function of insurance. Although experience rating does not indicate the kinds of precautions that would reduce the cost of coverage (or mitigate increases in costs), it helps indicate something just as important: the insurance costs that could have been saved this year by avoiding the losses that occurred last year. This figure is a rough estimate of the potential benefit of the expenditures on prevention that would prevent similar losses in the ensuing years.

Unfortunately, each of these possible incentive effects is only the reflection of an ideal. At various points in real classification systems significant slippage occurs. As a consequence, the incentive value of risk classification is sacrificed to satisfy other needs in a variety of ways. First, the cost of obtaining information about expected loss is high enough in many contexts to make accurate classification very difficult. In such cases the proportion of losses that are effectively random, and therefore broadly distributed, is high. The incentive value of the resulting rates falls far short of the efficiency ideal.[29] As Rothschild and Stiglitz have shown in theoretical terms, the problem of distinguishing high- from low-risk insureds may even make it impossible to achieve the competitive equilibrium characteristic of an efficient insurance market.[30] Continual reshuffling of rates and classifications may be the consequence.

Second, in many insured endeavors losses are so infrequent that experience rating can affect rates only modestly. In these endeavors the occurrence of accidents has some predictive value, but the absence of accidents for a period of years proves little. For instance, the average driver has an accident only once every ten years. Therefore, statistical techniques must be used to determine how much the occurrence of one accident increases the probability that the insured will have another.[31] A low-risk driver may, by chance, have more accidents during a three-year period than a driver with a higher expected loss.[32] Because the occurrence of a loss is only a rough indication of the new expected loss that ought to be taken into account in resetting a premium, the incentive value of that premium may be crude.

Third, expense costs (in the language of the trade, "expense loading") may be calculated in simple proportion to expected loss. Yet, if expected expenses in fact are not proportional to expected loss, then the incentive value of the resulting rates will be diluted. For example, a portion of expenses allocable to commissions and administrative costs is incurred regardless of whether the insured makes a claim under the policy in question. Insureds paying high premiums because of high expected losses pay a disproportionate share of such expenses if the latter are assessed in proportion to premiums. Low-risk insureds are correspondingly underassessed. Because the portion of premiums devoted to expenses often is sizable, the distortion that results may have real impact.

Finally, legislative or regulatory intervention may impede accurate classification. Such intervention may be designed to protect against the use of inadmissible variables or for other purposes. Though of course such intervention may be

justified on other grounds, if it encourages inaccurate classification it may hinder
the efficiency of the system. Further, even in the face of intervention, insurers
prevented from classifying in the manner they desire still may use underwriting
decisions to help them continue pricing in accordance with expected cost. For
example, they may refuse to sell coverage to applicants whom they are prohibited
from charging in accord with expected cost, in order to preserve the integrity of
risk classes.[33] As we shall see later, although legal strategies can be designed to
neutralize such moves, they have costs of their own.

Homogeneity and Admissibility

Homogeneity and admissibility are conspicuously absent from the list of criteria relevant to efficient risk classification. Homogeneity is absent because, once
an optimal amount of separation among classes is achieved (where the benefit of
further separation would not outweigh its cost), homogeneity is economically irrelevant.[34] An example will help explain this point.

Suppose that optimal separation already had been achieved by dividing a group
of insureds into two risk classes with a 20 percent overlap between the two: 20 percent of the insureds in each class would have the same expected loss as their coun-
terparts in the other class. By definition, the cost of reducing the overlap any further
would exceed the profit obtainable from that increased accuracy. The profits that
could be captured or the cost savings that could be returned to insureds by charging more nearly in accord with the expected losses of that 20 percent would be
lower than the cost of classification. Therefore, the greater homogeneity of the
classes that would result from further refinement would not be worth the cost of
achieving it.

Thus, separation measures the differences in expected losses among members of different classes. This is the key to achieving accurate classification and
efficient pricing. Homogeneity is irrelevant to this goal because it is merely a residual measure of the differences in the expected losses of members within a given
risk class. Greater homogeneity is often a by-product of greater separation because
separating and charging different risks differently is likely to result in more homogeneous classes. But once there is optimal separation, achieving greater homogeneity will yield no additional economic benefit. This does not mean that homogeneity is never an appropriate concern. This would be true only if efficiency
were the sole consideration of policymakers. The social desirability of treating like
insureds alike by having roughly comparable degrees of homogeneity from class
to class may be worth the sacrifice in separation necessary to achieve it.

Admissibility considerations may also conflict with efficiency. The use of any variable that would improve the reliability of or promote separation among classes would enhance the efficiency of the system because it would assist in charging insureds in accord with their expected losses. If that variable is inadmissible, the efficiency of the system is undermined. To see the significance of homogeneity and admissibility concerns, therefore, we must turn to the set of considerations that may warrant the sacrifice of efficiency in classification.

RISK-DISTRIBUTIONAL FAIRNESS

A series of very different questions may be raised about the ways in which insurance classification and pricing system distribute risk. Because these questions are not always formulated clearly, they need both explication and evaluation. In addition, because the questions are not all of the same order, it is important to consider the different solutions that are available for the different kinds of unfairness these questions highlight. Certain solutions may appropriately be fashioned within the insurance system itself; but for other risk-distributional problems, noninsurance approaches are more suitable. In analyzing such solutions, I first examine the distributional objections to the drive for efficiency in classification and then explore the corresponding problem of the costs of eliminating these distributional objections.

Criticisms of risk classification schemes seem to fall into three general categories. The first cluster of criticisms is composed of what I call "accuracy-equity" concerns: demands that classification and pricing closely reflect expected cost so that low-risk insureds are not forced to subsidize high-risk insureds and so that the burdens of inaccuracy are equitably distributed. Accuracy concerns obviously have much in common with the efficiency notions discussed above. But efficiency is a characteristic of an entire system; risk-distributional fairness is a notion that also pertains to the treatment of individuals and touches upon more than economic considerations alone. The second category of criticisms is composed of "control-causality" concerns. These involve the contention that risk classes should be based on variables that are within the control of or at least caused by the insured. The third set of criticisms questions variables that are suspect even apart from accuracy-equity or control-causality issues. And a fourth kind of argument worth distinguishing is one made in favor of what I call "redistributional policies." This argument does not necessarily raise fairness questions in the same way as the first three; rather, it involves separate objectives of public policy.

Accuracy-Equity

Inaccuracy in General

Criticisms of a classification as being inaccurate or unrefined raise two quite different issues. The first is whether, as a matter of fairness, people should pay for insurance coverage only in proportion to the cost of what they can be expected to consume. If so, then inaccurate classification improperly overcharges some and undercharges others. This notion appears to have libertarian overtones in its expression of a distaste for the supposed subsidies inherent in inaccurate classification. But except in the few instances where insurance coverage is legally mandated, people are at liberty to decline to purchase insurance if it is not priced accurately enough to suit them. The argument against inaccuracy in general seems therefore also to include the idea that there should be a right to purchase accurately priced coverage even when purchasing is not required.

The weakness in this argument is that, because no risk class is completely homogeneous, there always appears to be some subsidy of the slightly higher risks within a class by the slightly lower risks. About half of any class, after all, has expected losses below the class average. Further, inevitably there is some misclassification, and some insureds who are classified properly according to the terms of the system would be classified differently under a more refined one. However, the notion that the risk sharing embodied in a classification scheme constitutes subsidization misunderstands the nature of classification.

In a system of market-supplied insurance, insurers already have an incentive to classify accurately even in the absence of legal intervention. As we saw earlier, they will stop pursuing greater accuracy only when its marginal cost exceeds its marginal benefit. In a competitive market, not only insurers but also insureds benefit when classification is refined up to but not beyond this point because the costs of classification are reflected in the price of coverage. If a decrease in the cost of coverage that would result from greater accuracy would be exceeded by an increase reflecting the extra cost of obtaining that accuracy, then it would not be in anyone's economic interest to have generally more accurate classification.

Critics of inaccuracy in general, then, must be making one of two arguments. First, when the amount of accuracy in the system already is economically optimal, they must be arguing that everyone should be charged more for coverage simply to assure greater accuracy in general. But this is an argument that cuts off its proponent's nose to spite his face. It is hard to see why anyone would favor such a system because no one would benefit from it. Everyone would pay more for coverage unless for some reason the cost of obtaining that extra accuracy were borne disproportionately by different risk classes.

A second and different argument against inaccuracy can be made when the classification system is inefficient—when it is not achieving optimal accuracy. This argument is that because it is wrong to allocate resources inefficiently, inaccurate classification is unfair to everyone concerned. To the extent that the waste entailed in the failure to allocate resources efficiently is morally as well as economically objectionable,[35] this argument has some weight. But it is far from being a claim about individual fairness in risk bearing. Instead the argument is a conflation of efficiency with morality.

In either case, the point to be stressed is that inaccurate classification of any given individual should not itself be objectionable. Any classification system can achieve only a certain level of accuracy; and even if that level has not yet been reached, it is not unfairness but inefficiency that is properly the focus of criticism.

Differential Inaccuracy

An entirely different objection to inaccuracy is based on a claim about the unfairness of uneven distribution of the burdens of inaccuracy. In this view, inaccuracy is not objectionable in itself, if it works to everyone's benefit. But differential burdening of individual insureds may be objectionable. This kind of concern has egalitarian roots; it is based on the notion that the risk of inaccurate classification should be borne by the community of all insureds rather than by a few who suffer the entire disadvantage of inaccuracy.[36]

Differential inaccuracy is likely to be the product of coincidental and contingent differences in the ease of obtaining information about expected loss. It is inexpensive and easy to determine an insured's sex; it is expensive and difficult to determine his or her habits and character. Some variables are made the basis of risk classes, then, not because they are more accurate or preferable to others in any ultimate sense, but because they are available and useful. The two following examples indicate the different ways in which these contingencies can affect distribution of the burdens of inaccuracy.

Example 1. Suppose that drunken driving by young males causes a high percentage of all automobile accidents but that only 10 percent of all young males drive while drunk. Two risk classes are formed: one for young males, one for all other drivers. Young males pay much higher liability insurance premiums than all other drivers.

Figure 4 illustrates the two classes. The class of young males in this example

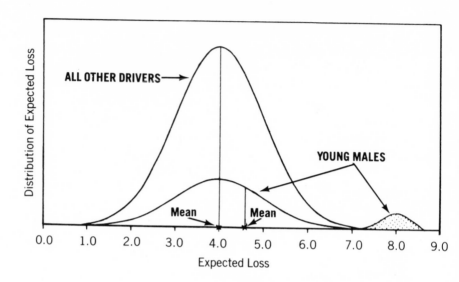

Figure 4

is much less homogeneous than the class of all other drivers. Ten percent of the former class (represented by the shaded area) have very high expected losses, but 90 percent have average expected losses equal to the average of all other drivers. If there is no economically worthwhile method of discovering which young males have high expected losses, then all young males bear the burden of the inaccuracy in this classification scheme. Those young males who have no greater chance of having accidents than other drivers are nevertheless charged considerably higher premiums. In effect, low-risk young males subsidize high-risk young males and all other drivers simply because they happen to be young and male.

Example 2. Suppose that although the causes of automobile accidents are uncertain, young males, older males, young females, and older females have different and separable expected losses. Ten percent of each class have substantially higher expected losses than the other members of the class, but it is not feasible to isolate this group in each class. Four risk classes are formed, each paying a different premium.

Figure 5 illustrates the four classes. The classes have roughly comparable homogeneity (or heterogeneity, depending on one's perspective). Here, one group does not subsidize all the high-risk drivers, while all others avoid this burden entirely. Instead, the comparatively low-risk members of each class subsidize the few high-risk drivers in the class.

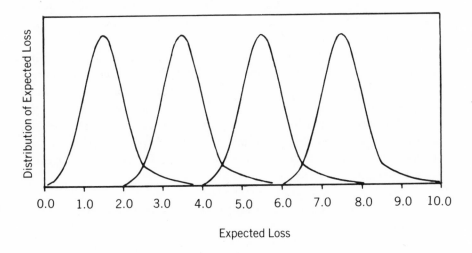

Figure 5

The difference between the two examples is that in the first, a small portion of all insureds bears the burden of inaccurate classification. The young males in the first example have a much greater risk-sharing obligation than all others. By contrast, in the second example all insureds bear a more nearly similar burden of inaccuracy and therefore have similar risk-sharing obligations. In example 1, comparatively few insureds pay a large additional premium, and all other insureds save a smaller amount (except, of course, the high-risk young males, who save much more). In example 2, most insureds pay modest additional premiums, as a result of which a few insureds pay considerably less than they should. Are the large overcharges of low-risk young males in example 1 more objectionable than the sizable undercharges of 10 percent of each class in example 2, or are they equally objectionable?[37]

There is a straightforward differential-inaccuracy argument against permitting the burden of inaccuracy in example 1. Allocating a heavy burden to one group of insureds, merely because a small percentage of those with similar characteristics has high expected losses, fails to treat the members of that group with concern and respect equal to that accorded other groups. This method of classification uses most members of the disadvantaged group as a means to an end: assuring that the few of their number who are truly high-risk are charged higher premiums. Because considerable inaccuracy is unavoidable in this situation, broader and more even distribution of the risk of being overcharged would treat all insureds with more nearly equal concern and respect. If all insureds were unaware of their own characteristics, this argument goes, then enough of them would want protection against the risk of being in the group bearing the burden of inaccuracy that at least some tempering of this burden would be required.[38]

However, the argument holds only weakly if at all when it is levelled against the classification embodied in example 2. In this example differential inaccuracy has been reduced. It is no longer true that a few insureds are overcharged and thereby forced to carry the greatest burden of risk sharing. Instead, because most insureds are overcharged a modest amount, the risk of having to bear the burdens of inaccuracy is tempered. More insureds share the risk that some are being inaccurately classified, although the classes are sex based and therefore are possibly objectionable for other reasons.

Completely even distribution of the burdens of inaccuracy obviously is not feasible without surrendering a great deal of refinement in risk classification. Contingent variations in the ease with which different kinds of information about insureds can be discovered render some tension between equal distribution of the risk of inaccuracy and refined classification inevitable. A crucial question, then, is what amount of uneven distribution is tolerable in return for what amount of refinement? Although an answer may not be specifiable in the abstract, it is possible to specify the two separate factors that are relevant to the issue.

The first is the amount of homogeneity within the burdened class. The more homogeneous the class, the more tolerable the burden. The nine-to-one ratio of low- to high-risk young males in example 1, for instance, meant that the class was not very homogeneous. To establish a class with this much variation in expected loss identifies an entire group with the characteristics of only a few of its members. This kind of classification ignores the fact that 90 percent of the class have an expected loss identical to that of another class charged much less. Nevertheless, standing alone this is nothing more than a statement that, other things being equal, more accuracy in general is preferable to less.

The second relevant factor is comparative homogeneity. If risk classes are relatively heterogeneous, but equally so, as in example 2, then the members of one class do not benefit at the expense of the members of a different class. Instead, low-risk insureds in each class bear a similar burden of inaccuracy. But if one class is more heterogeneous than others, the burden of inaccuracy is spread unevenly. The crux of an accuracy-equity objection to a given classification scheme, then, is the difference in the comparative homogeneity of the risk classes that the scheme has adopted.

It is therefore important to notice that critics of differential risk sharing are not always voicing accuracy-equity objections. Differences in the comparative homogeneity of risk classes do not necessarily underlie such attacks. For example, sex-based life insurance and pension classification often are attacked because about 85 percent of men and women have the same life expectancies. But because the homogeneity of the two classes is roughly similar, an accuracy-equity concern cannot support these attacks. If the only reason for the difference between male and female life expectancies were that 15 percent of all females lived longer than all other females and all males, then sex-based classification would clearly raise accuracy-equity concerns. But this greater female longevity is not the only reason for the difference in life expectancies. The separation between the classes occurs not only at the above-average life expectancy end of the spectrum, but also at the below-average end. That is, the difference between male and female life expectancies is caused not only by a minority of females who have higher-than-average expectancies, but also by a minority of males who have lower-than-average expectancies.[39] The two classes actually have roughly comparable homogeneity.

Both long-expectancy males and long-expectancy females consequently subsidize the other members of their respective classes when they purchase life insurance; and both short-expectancy males and short-expectancy females subsidize the other members of their class when they purchase pensions. Therefore, if sex-based classification is to be soundly criticized for its unfairness, that criticism must be based on the grounds to be explored below.

Control-Causality

The second relevant issue regarding the distribution of risk through insurance classification is whether variables that are neither within the insured's control nor causes of loss should be used to form risk classes. Noncausal variables can be criticized because of their apparent arbitrariness; they appear merely to be statistically correlated with expected loss.[40] Sometimes control and causality are conceptually distinct notions, and the major focus of criticism has to do with controllability. On other occasions, however, the two notions are harder to distinguish, and reference to control-causality objections is more accurate.

Noncontrollable variables can be criticized on the ground that their use makes the exercise of individual responsibility irrelevant to the price one pays for insurance. No amount of care or safety, no period of loss-free behavior can have any effect on the cost of coverage when such variables distinguish risk classes. Thus, use of noncontrollable variables denies individuals the opportunity, through the exercise of individual responsibility, to alter the effect of being grouped.

The choice as to variables that raise these control-causality problems consequently will depend on the critic's conception of individual responsibility and controllability. In common parlance, people are not responsible for their gender, but they are responsible for and can control their smoking and eating habits. In between these extremes lie a variety of actions that are more difficult to characterize. Some people would argue that individuals are responsible for any characteristics that are even theoretically subject to change—only sex, age, race, and birth defects being totally beyond control. In contrast, a more egalitarian conception of responsibility might also consider the results of the natural lottery in skills and talents to be beyond individual control.[41] According to this view, even variables bearing a causal connection to insured losses would be unacceptable if controllability were missing. A driver's congenitally slow reaction time may be a cause of accidents, but it is not within his control. Only the difficulty of distinguishing slow-reaction from quick-but-careless drivers would then justify penalizing the former for errors caused by their slow reactions.

An insured's ability to reduce otherwise uncontrollable risks by varying activity levels is subject to the same kinds of considerations. Though the decision to drive at all is controllable, driving is so often a social necessity that having at least one car is probably not controllable in any practical sense. The element of choice present in most acts of responsibility or irresponsibility is almost entirely absent from this one. But the number of miles driven and the number of cars owned by a family are more clearly determined by free choice.

In short, the notion of control is a normative conclusion about the factors for which individuals can properly be asked to bear insurance responsibility. This notion does not solve risk-distributional issues; rather, it directs attention to them. Do poor people control where they live? Do women control where they work or how much they drive? People with radically different views about these questions will not be able to agree on what constitutes a fair or acceptable classification variable.[42] But conducting the debate about risk-distributional fairness on these terms is likely to be more fruitful than reliance on notions like discrimination or statistical justification. These notions normally are not sharp enough—in this context at least—to help isolate what is at stake in the controversy over classification.

The beginning of a solution of the quandry over how to define the concept of individual responsibility may be to recognize a few ceteris paribus conditions that would be acceptable to many different points of view about this issue. Although these conditions do not completely resolve the tensions among different conceptions of responsibility, they provide a method of ranking alternatives in terms of preferability. The first condition is that the more random the losses in question (in the sense defined earlier), the less reason there is to object to any particular classification variable. When a variable accounts for only a relatively small portion of actual losses, its effect on premium differences will not be great. For instance, the driver's sex accounts for over one-third of the explainable variance of expected loss distribution among drivers—a statistical measure of the efficiency of the variable. However, since all variables in use, including sex, account for only 22 percent of that variance, the vast majority of accidents must be treated as occurring at random.[43] One study showed that if sex were eliminated as a variable, young female drivers' automobile insurance rates would increase 26 percent and young male drivers' rates would decrease 6 percent. (Females are only 24 percent of the youthful driving population.)[44]

Thus, elimination of sex as a classification variable because of its noncontrollability may well satisfy many control-causality objections. It should be noted, however, that a more efficient variable cannot necessarily be substituted whenever a noncontrollable variable such as sex is eliminated. Often an objectionable variable has been used precisely because it is efficient. This point is too often ignored by those who demand that a classification system count past loss experience more heavily in setting premiums. Experience rating cannot safely exceed the credibility of the loss experience on which it is based without risking gross inaccuracy. When the average insured suffers a loss only once every ten or twelve years—as is the case in automobile liability—then the occurrence of a loss only marginally increases his expected loss. The probability is still substantial that the loss was the product of chance. On the other hand, in fields where losses occur more frequently, experience rating becomes more feasible. Because this form of classification leaves the insured with maximum flexibility to affect premium levels through the exercise of individual responsibility, control-causality objections should diminish as reliance on experience rating increases.

A second ceteris paribus condition is that the less efficiency that will be lost by shifting from a noncontrollable to a controllable variable, the more preferable should such a move be. This may seem to be a counterintuitive point since a move to a more controllable variable suggests greater, not less efficiency. It is only superficially a paradox, however, that efficiency could be lost rather than gained by such a move. A noncontrollable variable such as the sex of the insured may be a convenient surrogate for controllable variables such as safety in the workplace or the number of miles an insured is likely to drive. But controllable variables such as the latter two may be expensive to use because of their unreliability and, hence, less efficient than their cruder and otherwise more objectionable surrogates. On the other hand, when the advantage of using noncontrollable variables is only slight, then a shift to controllable variables will sacrifice little efficiency and may increase the perceived fairness and legitimacy of the classification system. Yet it is unlikely that any insurance company would make such a move on its own if the move were even marginally inefficient. Legal compulsion would be required.

It follows that some noncontrollable variables might be prohibited with relatively little loss of efficiency, whereas the elimination of others could be more costly. The amount of the loss would depend on the degree to which the variable in question is a surrogate for one that is controllable and on the cost and reliability of assigning insureds to classes based on a substitute variable. For example, it is often assumed that the prohibition of sex-based life insurance or pension classification will automatically result in the abolition of all classifications other than age. Then males would subsidize female pension rates, and females subsidize male life insurance rates.[45] This will result, however, only if sex stands for no other readily discoverable and easily substituted variable or variables. If instead sex is such a surrogate, for example, for smoking habits or exposure to hazardous substances in the workplace, then following its prohibition as a variable others eventually may replace it. Many insurance companies already take such variables into account in setting rates.

A third condition is derived from the fact that noncontrollable variables do not preclude the exercise of individual responsibility for the control of losses; they merely make the exercise of such control irrelevant to the cost of any given individual's insurance. Insureds whose rates are determined by noncontrollable variables have an incentive to shift their protection dollars away from insurance and into loss prevention. Therefore, the greater the marginal rate of this substitution, the stronger the inference that banning noncontrollable variables would be feasible; the fact of substitution is some evidence that readily controllable variables are at hand. The lower the rate of this substitution, the stronger the inference that the costs of loss prevention are too high to warrant the substitution of prevention for insurance.* In this situation control-causality objections should diminish because, when loss prevention is not easily substituted for insurance, readily controllable variables probably are not available as substitutes for the noncontrollable ones in use.

Suspect Variables

The preceding pages explored two separate reasons why otherwise useful classification variables may be considered inadmissible. Even when these accuracy-equity or control-causality objections are weak or nonexistent, however, certain variables are likely to remain under attack. Symbolic and principled rather than

---

*For evidence of this rate of substitution, one would have to look at the change in coverage levels purchased by individuals after institution of new classification schemes. Because several states have adopted new schemes, such data may eventually be available.

consequentialist concerns often cause criticism of such suspect variables. It is easiest to see the independence of this kind of objection from the two other types by considering an extreme case. For example, even if classification based on race raised neither of the other two risk-distributional concerns, it would be unacceptable to most people on purely symbolic grounds.

Whenever an efficiency-promoting but emotionally or morally suspect variable is rendered inadmissible, a form of redistribution of risk occurs. The risk-assessment goal of insurance is sacrificed to the risk-distribution goal. Subsidies then run from the low-risk members of other groups to the high-risk members of the group identified by an inadmissible variable. Variables that would otherwise be used in classification because of their economic superiority are not used because of their social inferiority. That is simply the cost of avoiding discrimination in insurance on the basis of the suspect variable in question. Indeed, our willingness to ignore variables that would otherwise be useful for classification is largely what defines them as discriminatory in this context. For example, if we were concerned that men and women be treated equally as groups, then sex-based classification would not only be acceptable, but might actually be required.[46] When treatment of men and women as individuals is the predominate goal, however, such classification is likely to appear discriminatory.

Classification variables may be suspect for a variety of reasons. First, a particular characteristic may be used improperly in other fields and, therefore, be objectionable on symbolic grounds. Because women often have been subjected to discriminatory treatment in other social and economic settings, use of sex as an insurance classification variable may be objectionable even if it would be otherwise admissible. Second, the data on which predictions of expected loss are based may not have enough probative power to justify their use in drawing socially questionable distinctions. Life expectancy calculations for men and women may be based on mortality rates formulated before recent improvements in health and safety features of male-populated workplaces. Third, some variables may be suspect because they are used only to disadvantage groups, not to advantage them. Where women have been charged more than men for pensions but the same for life insurance, this objection would hold. Finally, certain variables may help to perpetuate disadvantages that have their origins outside the insurance system. If blacks have lower life expectancies than whites, the reason may be the less healthy living and working conditions under which they have long suffered. If race-based variables were not already inadmissible for other reasons, this factor would render them suspect.

It pays to note here, however, that declaring a variable inadmissible does not necessarily eliminate all the effects that had been associated with the use of the variable. Of course, if the major motivation for prohibiting a given variable is its symbolic effect, then that symbolism is eliminated upon prohibition. But if the concern underlying the inadmissibility of a variable is its actual disadvantaging effect, then the choice of a variable to replace it is critical. For example, when territory of residence functions as a close surrogate for race in automobile insurance, differential treatment on the basis of race has been symbolically eliminated, but such treatment continues in fact through the use of territorial variables. Whether the use of territorial variables is considered an alternative to discriminatory classification or a mere subterfuge depends on whether the purpose of the substitution is symbolic or practical. Further, even when the variables in use are not surrogates for others that are inadmissible, marketing practices can be used to circumvent a mandated classification scheme if suspect variables are easily recognized. Racial or sexual bias in the marketing of coverage is not automatically foreclosed when a classification system is purged of suspect variables.

Because the degree to which a variable is suspect depends on both the nature of the variable itself and the insurance setting in which it is employed, determining whether a variable should be admissible often poses vexing problems. The use of sex as a classification variable is a good example. My view is that the sex of the insured should be an inadmissible variable under almost all circumstances, but my position cannot be ascribed to a single consideration.

In the life insurance and pension fields, as we saw earlier, there are probably no substantial accuracy-equity objections to sex-based classification. However, there are significant control-causality objections to sex-based classification for life expectancy purposes, although the efficiency of alternative variables that are controllable is not entirely clear. As a result, criticism of sex-based classification in these lines of insurance must rest heavily on the intensity of principled objections to this form of classification as suspect in and of itself.

In automobile insurance, to use a contrasting example, there probably are significant accuracy-equity objections to the manner in which young males are sometimes classified.[47] In addition, more controllable variables or greater experience rating could at least temper control-causality objections to sex-based classification. On the other hand, males rather than females are disadvantaged by sex-based automobile classification. To the extent that objections to such classification arise because of past discrimination against women in this and other fields, those objections should be weaker here than in connection with pension classification, where women bear the disadvantage in question.

A separate consideration is that greater inefficiency in automobile insurance seems likely to result in at least marginal increases in personal injuries, whereas the principal effect of any inefficiency in life insurance or pensions will merely be a change in investment patterns. Thus, different considerations might come into play in different insurance contexts. Nevertheless, the symbolic effect of eliminating sex-based classifications only when they disadvantage women would probably be intolerable. On that ground, if some such classifications are eliminated, then all should be abolished.

Notwithstanding this conclusion, the possibility that advantage-giving forms of classification might for some purposes be distinguished from disadvantage-giving forms (though of course each produces both benefits and burdens) is worth recognizing. Whether a variable is suspect is not necessarily independent of the direction in which the benefits and burdens it creates run. This recognition highlights a possibility we have not yet considered directly: the use of classification for the express purpose of creating benefits for certain groups. Notice that sacrificing efficiency in classification for this purpose is not designed simply to assure risk-distributional fairness. Such moves constitute an affirmative redistribution of risk, and occupy our final category.

Risk-Redistributional Policies

Insurance classification can be used to further a variety of risk-redistributional goals. Not only may risk be distributed by ignoring or making inadmissible certain variables that are linked with expected loss: race, sex, age, marital status, and so forth. Classes can be constructed and prices set so that some classes are not self-supporting and others are overcharged. Cross subsidies then run from the overcharged to the undercharged classes. The old can be made to subsidize the young (or vice versa), the healthy the sick, suburbanites city dwellers, or careful insureds the careless. And if one class is largely a surrogate for another recognizable group—when territory of residence substitutes fairly accurately for race, to use an earlier example—then overcharging or undercharging of a territorial group may occur without explicit reliance on a suspect variable. The rich might even be separately classified so that they subsidize the poor (or vice versa), if a good enough surrogate for wealth can be made the basis of risk classes. Moreover, one line of insurance could be used to subsidize another—products liability rates might be set high and auto liability rates low, across-the-board.

Notice that these forms of risk redistribution are not designed to avoid differential treatment of certain risk classes. On the contrary, they are intended to accord special treatment to the classes that benefit in order to increase their welfare. In so doing, such classification may raise accuracy-equity, control-causality, or suspect-variable problems of its own. But it is significant that risk-redistributional classification would create such problems deliberately rather than as a by-product of the search for efficiency. The goal of this approach is to benefit certain people or groups; inevitably burdens must be placed on others if the goal is to be achieved. However, any modification of an economically efficient classification scheme in order to redistribute risk or achieve other goals of public policy is likely to encounter considerable obstacles in its path. We now turn to these obstacles.

THE COSTS OF RISK-DISTRIBUTIONAL FAIRNESS

In any system that relies heavily on the private market to supply insurance, legal regulation designed to assure fair classification or to promote other goals of public policy faces real difficulties. The problem is that the economic interests of insurers and potential insureds do not simply disappear after a reform is adopted. Rather, these interests continue to operate and easily may confound the objectives of the system.

We have already seen such forces at work. The first is that any individual insurer has only a limited incentive to discover new methods of classification. The cost of investing in the discovery of new expected loss data may not warrant the advantages to be gained from discovery, and other insurers may free ride on the innovating insurer's investment in new forms of classification. The solution to this problem of externalized benefit does not always lie in declaring existing classification variables inadmissible in the hope of forcing insurers to develop replacement variables on a now-clean slate. A better solution is collective investment in the discovery of new forms of classification that are more efficient than those now in use. If private collective enterprises such as trade associations have not developed new classifications, then governmental investment in such development might be worthwhile.

A second problem is that any form of limited or partial regulation—such as redistributional classification—is susceptible to circumvention by other forces in the market. Sometimes the form taken by market circumvention of regulatory constraints can be predicted. If the advantages of such market adjustments outweigh their disadvantages, regulation may be designed deliberately to encourage these desirable adjustments. But for a variety of reasons, remedying accuracy-equity, control-causality, or suspect-variable concerns, or implementing wholesale risk-redistribution aims sometimes will require swimming against strong economic currents. Consider the efforts that would be necessary.

First, only a universally adopted scheme could endure. Any insurer voluntarily adopting a classification system that was noticeably counter efficient would quickly find itself afflicted by adverse selection. Low-risk insureds offered less expensive coverage by other insurers would depart, and higher-risk insureds would gravitate in its direction. The greater the cross subsidies, the more likely that a voluntary scheme ultimately would result in insolvency for the insurer adopting it.

Second, even if a counterefficient classification scheme were mandatory, all insurers would be subject to a second and different kind of adverse selection effect. Recall that insurers not only compete among themselves for premium dollars. They also compete with other methods of loss protection for available protection dollars, not all of which need be spent on insurance. A mandatory redistributional scheme will encourage insureds in subsidizing classes to shift their protection dollars away from insurance and into other methods of loss protection. An insured who had previously maintained $10,000 of coverage may now find that his dollars are better spent by purchasing only $8,000 of coverage and investing the money saved on safety precautions that promise more than an additional $2,000 of expected loss protection.

The effects of this option to bail out of the reformed system would depend on the cross elasticity of demand for insurance and loss prevention. The more easily that low-risk insureds can substitute additional investment in loss prevention for insurance coverage, the greater the threat that such substitutions would undermine the system, because substitutions would produce a smaller fund from which to finance subsidies. Correspondingly, insureds in subsidized risk classes would be encouraged to invest less in prevention and more in insurance than they had previously. This would result not only in more losses, but in more losses that are covered by insurance. Even higher rates and possibly greater subsidies then might be required.

This system could eventually fall under its own weight or reach an equilibrium in which a few subsidizers buy small amounts of coverage, and many modestly subsidized insureds buy a little more coverage than they would otherwise. Regardless, there would be a lot less cross subsidization than the system originally envisioned and less insurance purchased by members of burdened risk classes than would otherwise be optimal.

Further, unless there were also some constraints on the discretion of insurers to accept or reject applicants for coverage, underwriting decisions would tend to neutralize the effects of the classification system. Applicants eligible for placement in subsidized classes would be rejected with disproportionate frequency. They would find it difficult in general to purchase the subsidized coverage for which the rules of the system made them eligible.[48] Only strict enforcement of mandatory offer and acceptance rules could restrict the effects of this phenomenon.

In short, the redistributional classification scheme described thus far would have holes through which those supposedly burdened with subsidy obligations could escape. Therefore, yet another device would have to be introduced to stabilize the system. Not only would redistributional classification have to be mandatory for insurers; the purchase of insurance also would have to be required. Such a requirement obviously is realistic in only a few fields.

When the avenues of escape from the system can be closed by making the purchase of coverage mandatory, then a number of different redistributional mechanisms can be adopted.[49] One is an assigned-risk system under which individuals falling into a subsidized category are assigned in rotation to different insurers, which are then required to insure them at the specified subsidy rate. Rates charged other classes are correspondingly higher than they would be in the absence of the subsidy. A different approach uses a governmentally operated fund, which is financed by surcharges against insurers and which itself provides coverage to members of groups to be subsidized. Rates on the private market are again correspondingly higher in reaction to the surcharges that finance these residual-market subsidies. Finally, a hybrid of the first two approaches is a joint underwriting association, financed and operated by all the insurers of the jurisdiction, which writes coverage at subsidized rates for specified classes of insureds. Under any of these schemes, low-risk insureds will tend to purchase less above-minimum coverage than in the absence of the subsidies, and they will tend to spend more on other forms of protection, which now appear comparatively cheaper than before.

This analysis suggests the numerous difficulties entailed in remedying risk-distributional unfairness or in striving for significant amounts of risk redistribution by modifying risk classification practices alone. Voluntary schemes are likely to fall far short of their goal or, even worse, to bankrupt their participants. Programs made mandatory for insurers may have considerable effect, but only at the cost of reducing the amount of insurance coverage that is purchased—something that is generally thought to be an undesirable development. Remedies promising significant risk redistribution must make insurance mandatory not only for insurers but also for insureds—in the end an intuitively obvious point, since risk redistribution is a kind of tax scheme, and when a voluntary activity is taxed, it is likely to draw fewer participants than substitute activities that are not subject to the tax.

This analysis has three related implications. First, remedying accuracy-equity, control-causality, or suspect-variable concerns often will be feasible, but only at a cost. We should recognize this cost rather than assume that the only effect of remedying unfairness is to equalize burdens or benefits. A certain amount of inefficiency in the entire system, a corresponding loss in safety, or an increase in the level of unsafe activities may be part of the price that must be paid to achieve a fairer distribution of risk within the system.

Second, sometimes the risk in question is one that is appropriately redistributed only within the insurance system. On other occasions, however, the risk is the kind that society as a whole should more appropriately bear. Accuracy-equity concerns normally fall into the former category because they arise mainly from the difficulty of determining expected loss. Some control-causality and suspect-variable concerns, on the other hand, arise from notions of equality whose costs should be distributed broadly. If the form of insurance involved is nearly universal—mandatory automobile coverage, for example—perhaps the risk-sharing population is already broad enough to warrant using the insurance system as a partial remedy for the inequality in question. Because so many people already participate in that kind of coverage, society as a whole effectively bears the cost of the redistribution. But if the insurance involved is specialized—professional liability or private disability coverage, for instance—then it is not at all clear that the cost of risk redistribution within the system should be borne only by those participating.

An example may help illustrate this point. Suppose we decided that hemophiliacs and nonhemophiliacs should be charged the same rates for disability insurance. In such a case there would be no particular reason why disability insureds alone should be forced to bear the risk we have decided hemophiliacs alone should not have to bear. The decision to protect hemophiliacs is not designed to remedy a risk-distributional unfairness inherent in disability insurance but to remedy an unfortunate outcome of the natural lottery for physical health. Unless there already has been an across-the-board effort to subsidize hemophiliacs, of which the change in disability insurance classification is but a part, it seems inappropriate to ask disability insureds to bear the full cost of subsidies to hemophiliacs. However, where more generalized efforts at redistribution of a particular risk have occurred—by eliminating sexual or racial discrimination at large, for instance—asking the holders of specialized forms of insurance coverage to bear their proportionate share of the cost of this effort is much less problematic.

This insight leads to a final point. There are much simpler ways of redistributing risk wholesale, if that is desired, then by regulation of insurance risk classification. Members of risk classes deserving subsidies can simply be given money out of selectively assessed taxes and allowed to use it as they wish. If some forms of insurance are considered merit goods—those that society as a whole believes people should have regardless of whether they would choose to purchase them—then insurance can be bought for the classes whom we wish to subsidize. For example, certain groups might be issued insurance stamps that would purchase insurance only. Or a governmentally financed insurance system could be maintained to cover those whom it considers desirable to subsidize. And if certain forms of insurance are not merit goods, but subsidies to some groups nevertheless are considered desirable—perhaps because the market improperly overcharges them—governmentally provided reinsurance may be a workable solution.

These more straightforward methods of redistributing risk are likely to be much more effective at wholesale redistribution than is a method that relies on risk classification to do the same job. More direct forms of redistribution that do not rely on insurance at all, such as flood control, may be even more effective in particular situations. But these methods are not always politically feasible. So the legal system has developed other devices for achieving small scale or local redistribution. Making regulatory adjustments in the risk classification system is only one such method. These ad hoc methods of risk distribution may be inefficient, subject to circumvention by the market, and only partially effective. But they have the virtue, at least for proponents of risk redistribution, of being possible to implement. More than anything else, this may explain their attractiveness.

Assessing the efficiency and fairness of insurance classification systems is a complex undertaking. Different notions of fairness are likely to lead to obviously different assessments; and the claims of each notion of risk-distributional fairness must make their peace with the inherent demands of any classification system and with countervailing considerations of economic efficiency. Although efficiency may be a more monolithic concept in this context than risk-distributional fairness, the safety incentives produced even by efficient classification may be less powerful than desired. Limitations on available information and the diminishing returns of increasingly refined classification make pricing in accordance with expected cost an ideal, but never a wholly attainable one.

Because a classification system is unavoidably influenced by the effects of market incentives, attempts to make it fairer or to redistribute risk by regulation of risk classification and pricing require significant legal interventions to be successful. Mandatory insurance and government operation of substitute or residual insurance markets may even be necessary to maintain an effective redistributional scheme. In the end, therefore, it is likely that the compromise between efficiency and the broad distribution of risk that is inevitable in any insurance system will never fully satisfy the proponents of either value.

5   Judge-Made Law and Judge-Made Insurance

We now make a transition from topics of obvious significance for public policy to several that at first glance may seem to be of more specialized interest. But in fact many issues that would traditionally be considered the exclusive domain of the insurance specialist have just as much significance for public policy as toxic tort problems or sexual and statistical discrimination in risk classification. One of those problems is the judicial creation of legal doctrines governing insurance. Since judge-made law is the vehicle through which the courts exercise legal supervision over the relations between insurers and insureds, this is a matter of the utmost importance.

Traditional and unsurprising as this activity appears to be, in the field of insurance it produces very interesting consequences. Judges in insurance cases not only make insurance law; sometimes they also make insurance. This practice is part of a widely recognized but only dimly understood fact of legal life: courts seem consistently to favor policyholders in disputes with insurance companies. To be sure, insurers often win in litigation. But the sense remains, from reading judicial opinions and from more subtle clues, that the balance is tilted in the policyholder's favor. The casual observer often can find little doctrinal support for this attitude other than the maxim *contra preferentem*, which directs that the ambiguities in a legal instrument be construed against the drafter. Sometimes the courts even seem to search for ambiguities in an insurance policy where none exists so that they can then invoke this maxim. The consequence is that judicial techniques of interpretation frequently create insurance coverage when policies do not provide for it. It is too easy, however, to conclude that this practice simply reflects an unprinci-

101

pled judicial preference for the policyholder at the expense of insurers with deep pockets. The practice turns out to be considerably more complicated than that.

In this chapter I want to examine the nature of what I call "judge-made insurance" and to uncover the principles that might justify it. My main focus will be a single important development in insurance law doctrine: in many states a principle authorizing the courts to honor the reasonable expectations of the insured is emerging.[1] This expectations principle is used to justify a wide range of decisions granting policyholders coverage in spite of policy language that seems to deny it. In some ways the expectations principle parallels such traditional contract law doctrines as the principle of unconscionability and the duty to bargain in good faith, through which courts commonly alter otherwise enforceable agreements between contracting parties. But the expectations principle is not simply a combination of basic contract law doctrines under another name. Many expectations decisions are unique because they turn on the nature of insurance marketing or the purposes particular kinds of insurance are designed to serve. Still others must be explained primarily as judicial efforts to fill the vacuum created by weak administrative regulation of the insurance industry.

The courts, unfortunately, have not been very articulate in explaining their decisions or isolating the justifications underlying them. Nor have they been effective in stating the scope of the expectations principle and the points at which its strength runs out. Nevertheless, in my view, there can be little doubt that the expectations principle is more than an unprincipled judicial preference for the insured. It is a discrete legal principle that can be analyzed, shaped to serve a variety of ends, and appropriately limited.

To accomplish this task, we will first take a close and careful look at the cases that have employed the expectations principle. The details of these cases are important, for they demonstrate that the expectations principle has a basis in principle: in most instances when the principle is invoked, the insurer has been responsible for creating the policyholder's expectations of coverage. I contend that this link between the insurer's behavior and the insured's expectations is the primary justification for the long-standing judicial preference for policyholders now reflected in the expectations principle.

There are, however, secondary justifications that also need to be explored. When the insurer is not responsible for the policyholder's expectations, separate justifications for disregarding the policy language in question are required. The search for such justifications leads naturally to the second feature of my analysis: an examination of the manner in which the expectations principle can promote the economic, equitable, and risk-distributional purposes of insurance law discussed throughout this book. Finally, with the cases analyzed and the purposes of the expectations principle outlined, we can pinpoint the limitations of the principle and suggest guidelines for its appropriate application by the courts.

THE EXPECTATIONS DECISIONS

Although there were rumblings earlier, it was not until the 1960s that courts in several different states began routinely to accept the argument that they should honor the reasonable expectations of the insured, despite policy provisions denying the coverage claimed by the insured. The argument first succeeded in connection with accident,[2] life,[3] and liability[4] insurance but was soon successfully invoked in other situations as well. By 1970, there were enough decisions in enough jurisdictions for Professor (now Judge) Robert Keeton to express the principle in formal terms: "The objectively reasonable expectations of applicants and intended beneficiaries regarding the terms of insurance contracts will be honored even though painstaking study of the policy provisions would have negated those expectations."[5]

In the next decade the principle was invoked frequently.[6] It is now clear that the expectations principle is being employed in varying situations and with varying justifications. The courts have employed the expectations principle in cases where the insured's expectation of coverage was probably real and reasonable.[7] They also have employed it when an expectation of coverage was less probable, but the policy's denial of coverage seemed unfair.[8] Finally, they have relied on the principle even when an expectation of coverage was improbable and the denial of coverage did not appear unfair.[9] In short, the judicial concept of an expectation of coverage is not a monolithic one.

Several themes common to these opinions are worth noting in advance. First, almost all the cases involve ordinary consumers without a sophisticated understanding of insurance. The expectations principle is not primarily a device for ordering commercial relations; it is a tool for protecting consumers. Second, the likelihood that an insured actually expected coverage is relevant to, but not decisive of the decision to honor any such expectation. Although literal application of the principle seems to require that the insured actually expected coverage, courts have generally focused instead on whether any reasonable insured might have expected it. Third, other factors, such as the substantive unfairness of a policy provision or the desirability of making a certain form of coverage available, are often relevant to a court's decision. Sometimes these factors merely support the court's determination that the alleged expectation should be honored; in a few cases they appear to be central to the decision. Finally, the courts have tended to avoid explaining why an insured's expectation, even though reasonable, should override the language of an insurance policy. An effort to understand why courts have honored expectations, therefore, must focus not only on the language of judicial opinions, but also on the underlying facts of each case and on the patterns that emerge from application of the principle in a variety of disputes.

In the discussion that follows I have divided the judicial decisions into a series of categories. Any such classification risks oversimplifying the interplay of factors affecting each decision. But identifying patterns organizes the analysis and enhances its value. It is impossible, of course, to discuss all the cases that have employed the expectations principle. My analysis attempts instead to deal with a sizable number that are representative of the patterns displayed in this body of law. The cases fall into two major categories: those in which the insurer misleads the insured about the scope of coverage or influences his expectations in some other way (what I call the "misleading impression" cases),[10] and those in which the insurer does not act misleadingly but the courts nevertheless hold the insurer liable (the "mandated coverage" cases).

The distinctive fact about the misleading impression cases is that the insured could reasonably have expected coverage largely because the insurer's words, conduct, or a situation for which the insurer is responsible have created that expectation. In contrast, although the courts speak of the insured's "reasonable expectations" in the mandated coverage cases, it is much less likely that ordinary insureds would have expected coverage in the situations in question. In those cases, the courts have gone beyond honoring actual or reasonable expectations. They have relied on the expectations principle when in truth they are mandating coverage where it seems desirable. The courts have engaged most frequently in this kind of activity when the omitted coverage is otherwise unavailable from other sources. When such coverage is available elsewhere, the courts generally have refrained from indulging in the fiction that the insured expected coverage, and they have not mandated its extension. In short, the mandated coverage cases seem more concerned with encouraging broader risk spreading than with equitable or economic goals.

The Misleading Impression Theme

Automated Marketing

Many forms of insurance are sold impersonally, either through vending machines or printed solicitations. Two leading pairs of cases in which the expectations principle has been invoked to control this form of marketing are worth exploring. The first pair involved flight insurance sold through airport vending machines; the second two involved accident insurance offered and sold through the mail. In all four cases, each court's principal concern was that impersonal marketing methods prevented the insured from determining whether the policy in question actually provided the expected coverage—a fact that underscored the insurers' responsibility for the mistaken expectations of coverage held by their insureds.

In *Lacks v. Fidelity & Casualty Co.*[11] the insured died on a charter flight, the kind of trip the insurer claimed the policy excluded from coverage. The insurer, however, had placed its vending machine directly in front of the charter airline's counter. Although the policy specifically excluded coverage on nonscheduled airlines, and a large sign near the charter airline counter listed it as nonscheduled, the court found the policy exclusion ambiguous. The court reasoned that the placement of the machine could constitute an invitation to purchase insurance for flights on the nearby airline. It also assumed that the decedent expected coverage and would not have purchased the insurance had she been informed that it would not cover her trip.

In a subsequent case, *Steven v. Fidelity & Casualty Co.*,[12] a leg of the deceased's scheduled flight was cancelled because of poor weather conditions; he died on a substitute charter flight that the insurer also argued was not covered by the policy. The court again found for the decedent's estate, reasoning that because the purpose of "taking out the insurance was to obtain insurance protection for the trip," and because "his contract covered the trip," the insured would reasonably expect coverage for any reasonable substitute emergency transportation on that trip.

In contrast to the situation in *Lacks*, there was no evidence in *Steven* that the insurer's marketing techniques actually created a misleading impression. The court noted instead that had the insured in fact mistakenly expected coverage (something it could not know since the insured died in the crash), the marketing techniques of the insurer would have precluded the insured from correcting or clarifying those expectations in deciding whether to embark on the substitute flight. Because the policy was sold by a machine there was no agent to warn him of the gap in coverage; the insured probably could not examine a specimen policy before deciding to purchase coverage; and he could not examine the relevant provision when the need to substitute flights arose since the machine had instructed him to mail the policy to his beneficiary before beginning his trip. Notwithstanding the insurer's responsibility for these effects of its marketing technique, the court also felt compelled to stress that the challenged policy provision "tended toward the harsh and unconscionable." Use of this extra ground to justify the decision is an addition whose significance we will note again and again in later cases.

The two leading solicitation-by-mail cases also reflect judicial concern that insurance marketing techniques may inhibit clarification of coverage expectations. In *Klos v. Mobil Oil Co.*[13] the insured received his policy but died before its specified effective date. The court nevertheless held that there was coverage at the time of death. It found that the guaranteed acceptance of the insured's application, coupled with the language of the insurer's advertising brochure, would lead an average layman to expect coverage upon receipt of his policy.[14]

In a similar case, *Fritz v. Old American Insurance Co.*,[15] the insured had actually signed an application stating "I understand that the policy becomes effective when issued," and died before that policy was issued. Nevertheless, the court held that the insurer's use of the mails, the language of the solicitation, and the absence of an agent all encouraged the expectation that there was immediate coverage upon mailing the application. As in the other cases, the court emphasized that the insurer's choice of impersonal marketing conditions made it responsible for any reasonable but misguided expectations that persisted because of that choice.

Accident Insurance: Coverage Bearing a Misleading Name

Insurers have also created misleading impressions about coverage by selling insurance bearing a commonly understood name—accident or disability—but providing coverage far narrower than the common name would lead the ordinary person to expect. In such cases the issue is whether the court should read the terms of the policy literally and deny the expected coverage or enforce the transaction to comply with the insured's expectations.

Like life insurance, accident insurance provides coverage in the event of the insured's death. Often it also provides coverage if the insured suffers bodily injury. Unlike life insurance, however, accident insurance is limited to death and bodily injury caused by *accident*, a term that is variously defined. One of the earliest cases to employ the expectations principle involved accident insurance.[16] In *Kievet v. Loyal Protective Life Insurance Co.*,[17] the insured's policy covered certain specified injuries and "loss resulting directly and independently of all other causes from accidental bodily injuries." On its next page, the policy excluded coverage of "disability or other loss resulting from or contributed to by any disease or ailment." The insured received an accidental blow on the head that activated his preexisting but unknown Parkinson's disease. Despite the company's reassuring name, it denied coverage, pointing to the policy provisions that gave meaning (and took it away) from the term *accident*.

The court, nevertheless, found that Kievet was covered. It reasoned that an average member of the public would expect accident insurance to cover "accidental injury which results (in the commonly accepted sense) in his disability." The court reasoned that its interpretation was justified because, if the policy were read literally, it would be of little value to the plaintiff. The policy that Kievet purchased at age forty-eight was renewable to age sixty-five. By that time, "disability or death resulting from accidental injury would in all probability be in some sense contributed to by the infirmities of age."[18]

Thus, the result in *Kievet* turned on both an objectively reasonable interpretation of the language of the policy and the fact that the insurer's interpretation would have emasculated expected coverage.[19] By implication, the insurer was held responsible for coverage because it did not dispel an expectation that was so common and so central to the value of the policy that the insurer must have been aware of that expectation.

The accident insurance cases are similar in several respects to the automated marketing decisions. As in the latter, the insurer is responsible for creating a misleading impression that is independent of anything gleaned from the policy other than its title; and in both, the insurer can escape liability by dispelling the insured's inaccurate expectation of coverage. This is unlikely to occur, however, because adequate disclaimers would interfere with persuasive marketing. Furthermore, the clear implication of the accident insurance decisions is that the courts disapprove of provisions emasculating coverage and that they will scrutinize the substance of such provisions regardless of the insured's actual expectations. Yet the court's disapproval of restrictive coverage is not the sole nor necessarily even the major explanation for these decisions. A substantive attack on a restrictive policy is triggered only after the insurer has created or encouraged a misleading impression about the scope of the policy. This influence of substantive concerns on judicial calculations about the expectations an insured would reasonably hold becomes even more evident in the decisions analyzed below.

Temporary Life Insurance

Life insurance often is sold by agents who accept an application and a first premium and then forward them to the home office for processing and a decision whether to insure. Disputes arise when the prospective insured dies after submitting an application and first premium but before a policy is issued. The insured's beneficiary then claims that although the application had not been accepted at the date of death, there was temporary coverage in effect at that time. In a sizable body of cases, the courts have vindicated such claims.

For instance, in *Smith v. Westland Life Insurance Co.*[20] the insured applied for life insurance, paid the first month's premium, and received a conditional receipt providing that: "[I]f the Company . . . after investigation shall be satisfied that on the date hereof . . . each person proposed for insurance was insurable and entitled under the Company's rules and standards to insurance . . . , the insurance protection applied for shall . . . take effect from the date hereof." The insured was later informed that he had not met the Company's conditions for insurability, but he died the next day, before his premium could be refunded.

Despite the language in the receipt and the rejection of the insured's application, the California Supreme Court held that he was covered at the time of death. The court first applied California's rule (and that of a number of other states) that temporary life insurance comes into being upon payment of a first premium, subject to later termination if the insured does not meet the insurer's conditions for permanent coverage. This rule is based on the premise that an insured who signs an application and pays a first premium can reasonably expect that he is immediately covered.[21] Yet the court held further that the temporary coverage created by accepting a first premium with the application could not be terminated merely by providing clear notice of rejection, but only by returning the first premium as well. The court apparently concluded that the insured can reasonably expect that he still is temporarily covered even after being notified of the rejection of his application, so long as his premium has not yet been returned.[22]

Standing alone, this conclusion is so preposterous that another of the court's determinations has to be considered if the decision in *Smith* is to make any sense. That second determination was this: "it is unconscionable for an insurance company to hold premiums without providing coverage." The connection between this presumed unfairness and the reasonableness of an insured's expectation of coverage is a key to understanding the decision.

In cases like *Smith*, although insurers' conditional receipts purport to provide retroactive coverage if the application is accepted, such retroactive coverage is likely to be illusory. Suppose the application contains a provision like the following: "If the first premium is paid with this application, and if the applicant is insurable on the date of issue for the type and amount of coverage applied for at the rate applied for, then coverage shall be effective from the date of application."

Call the date of application date 1 and the date of issue date 2. If the terms of the application are binding, then no applicant ever will benefit from the supposedly retroactive coverage described in the application. Any applicant who dies before date 2 will be uninsured, because he will not have been insurable on date 2; any applicant who survives until date 2, and thereby becomes insured retroactive to date 1, will have had no need for that coverage because he will still be alive. The class of persons who will die between date 1 and date 2 and be covered is nonexistent. In short, the promise to provide retroactive coverage is almost meaningless.[23]

This kind of unfairness arises independently of and is distinct from frustrating an insured's reasonable expectations. An empty promise made in return for value is unfair regardless of the promisee's expectations about it. Still, the unfairness is certainly exacerbated if the promisee expects that the promise has value when it does not. This notion links the expectations principle, the *Smith* court's remarks about the unconscionability of accepting a first premium without providing immediate coverage, and the court's holding that temporary coverage obtains until the premium deposit is returned. An insured would expect something in return for his premium, since the application promises it, in the form of retroactive coverage. If this promise of retroactive coverage is largely illusory, the insured's expectations have not been honored.

In these life insurance cases, then, a substantive unfairness in the policy or application and the insured's expectations influence each other and thereby play an important part in the court's decisions. The insured expects coverage because it would be unfair to deny it, and he does not expect unfairness. In the following cases, the substance of the coverage provided, rather than the insured's expectations, becomes even more important. Nevertheless, the courts continue to rely on the expectations principle as a ground of decision. Without actually saying so, in these mandated coverage cases the courts go even further in modifying their conception of an expectation of coverage.

The Mandated Coverage Theme

In the misleading impression cases we have just analyzed, the policy's language, the potential expectations of a reasonable insured, and the substantive unfairness of restrictions on coverage all play a role. These elements vary from case to case, and the strength of one may compensate for the weakness of another in explaining the decision. In the mandated coverage cases to be analyzed next, however, each of those elements is weak or nonexistent. The policy language denying coverage is relatively clear; it is also unrealistic to suppose that the insured would actually or reasonably expect the coverage in question; and the policy's denial of coverage does not appear to be unfair. The courts nevertheless pay lip service to the idea that the insured's reasonable expectations justify their decisions in his favor. The opinions speak of expectations without satisfactorily pointing to their source.

A better and more realistic explanation of the mandated coverage cases does not depend on expectations as such. Instead this explanation concerns the desirability of somehow providing coverage that is currently unavailable to most insureds. Reference in the opinions to the insured's expectations or to the unfairness of denying the insured coverage makes much more sense if it is viewed not as a description of any individual insured's expectations or any individual insurer's conduct, but as criticism of the insurance market as a whole. The mandated coverage decisions involve forms of coverage that generally are not marketed. The courts make such coverage available by tacking it onto conventional liability policies. In doing so, they step into a vacuum that neither the market nor administrative regulation has filled. But by mandating coverage only when it is otherwise unavailable, even this activist approach observes an implicit limit.

The Duty to Defend

Liability insurance policies typically impose two major duties on the insurer: (1) the duty to indemnify—to pay damages for which the insured is legally liable, and (2) the duty to defend—to provide or to pay for the insured's defense against suits alleging liability for damages that are payable under the policy, regardless of whether the insured ultimately is found liable. The duty to defend normally extends even to a claim that is groundless, false, or fraudulent, so long as damages would be payable under the policy if the claim were successful. But to guard against moral hazard, policies generally exclude coverage of liability for intentionally inflicted injuries.[24] Disputes over the insurer's duty to defend arise when it is unclear whether the damages claimed from the insured would be payable under the policy if the suit against the insured proved successful. Courts traditionally have resolved such disputes by examining the complaint in the suit against the insured to determine whether it pleads a liability for which the insurer would be bound to indemnify the insured if the suit were successful.[25]

In several leading cases on the subject, the courts rejected this pleadings test and instead based their decisions on the reasonable expectations of the insured. For instance, in *Gray v. Zurich Insurance Co.*[26] Gray was insured by the defendant against liability for bodily injury and property damage. The policy contained a standard insuring clause[27] and a separate clause excluding coverage of "bodily injury or property damage caused intentionally by or at the direction of the insured." Gray was sued for "wilfully, maliciously, brutally and intentionally" assaulting the plaintiff. Gray's insurer refused to defend him, arguing that because the suit did not seek damages payable under the policy, it had no duty to defend.

The court disagreed for several reasons. It found that the insured's alleged expectation that the policy required a defense was reasonable because the policy contained a broad and apparently unqualified duty to defend. The scope of that duty and its relationship to the separate exclusionary clause (excluding coverage of intentional injuries) were unclear in the policy itself. The insured therefore could reasonably expect a defense in this situation. The opinion reached beyond concern with the policy's language, however, and addressed the substantive fairness of the policy itself. The court noted that the limitations imposed by the company would "defeat the basic reason for the purchase of the insurance." Consequently, it indicated that an ordinary insured would expect a defense under the circumstances in *Gray*, apparently apart from any expectations the policy language alone might create.[28]

There are several flaws in the court's reasoning. First, the court's claim about the ambiguity of the policy provisions is unpersuasive. Most insureds would not derive any expectations from the policy language because they would never read it. If they did, few would understand the paragraph embodying the duty of defense well enough to be misled by it. Those who did read the provision carefully enough to understand it would probably also understand the exclusionary clause modifying the scope of the duty.

Second, there is little reason to believe that an insured would develop expectations of coverage independently of the policy language. A reasonable insured will not commonly expect defense coverage to include defense against claims of assault and battery since coverage of intentional torts is not reasonably expected. Moreover, in contrast to cases where an exclusionary clause would have emasculated coverage,[29] the exclusionary clause in *Gray* did not strike at the basic coverage purchased, as the court claimed; the policy limited that coverage only tangentially. The main coverage provided by a liability policy is against liability for negligence or carelessness, and this coverage was unaffected by the exclusion.

Finally, unlike the misleading impression cases, there is little evidence in cases such as *Gray* to support the court's assertion that the insured would not have purchased the policy had he properly understood the scope of the defense coverage. The policy still provided extensive coverage, even given this limited exclusion. Consequently, it is difficult to conclude that the exclusion of defense of allegedly intentional tort claims is unconscionable or unfair.

This analysis suggests that in the duty-to-defend cases the courts are concerned much more with the substance of coverage than with the expectations of the insured. When they find that it would be desirable to have the excluded coverage in policies, they mandate this coverage into existence, regardless of the insured's expectations or their reasonableness. Under these circumstances, the judicial creation of coverage is not a remedy for an individual contractual malfunction, but a substitute for the insurance market's failure to provide this specific form of defense insurance: insurance against the costs of defending groundless intentional tort suits is not independently available. Yet the cost to the insured of defending even groundless claims could be so significant that in spite of victory in the underlying law suit, the insured will have suffered a substantial loss. *Gray* and the cases that follow it remedy that situation by tacking such coverage onto the duty of defense contained in the typical liability policy.[30] The rationale for such judicial action seems to be that regardless of whether anyone actually expects such coverage, people have a right to expect it from some source, and that it is most appropriately provided by primary liability insurers.

Extending the Duration of Coverage

The last major setting in which the expectations principle appears is in disputes over the duration of coverage. In the simplest of situations, the effect of the policy period on coverage is clear. The policy provides coverage for the period between time 1 and time 2. If an insured loss occurs during that period, there is coverage; if the loss occurs before time 1 or after time 2, there is no coverage. Obviously, disputes do not arise when events and policy provisions are this simple.

For the plaintiffs in *Gyler v. Mission Insurance Co.*,[31] the problem was far more complicated. The plaintiffs were attorneys covered by a malpractice policy issued by the defendant for the period 1964 to 1967. A former client filed suit against them in 1969, alleging malpractice in 1966. The policy insured "against any claim or claims for breach of professional duty as Lawyers which may be made against them during the period set forth in the Certificate." Mission denied coverage, arguing that this provision covered only those claims actually made during the policy period. Plaintiffs argued that there was coverage of any claim that "may" have been made during the policy period, whether or not the claim actually was made during the period. The court sided with the plaintiffs, concluding that the phrase "may be made" was ambiguous in this respect and should be interpreted against the insurer.

The court's conclusion that the phrase "may be made" was ambiguous is questionable and suggests once again how significant a factor the expectations principle is even in cases that turn in part on the ambiguity of policy language. The court understood the word *may*, in the phrase "any claims . . . which may be made against them during the period," to mean *could*. But another provision in the policy extended coverage to occurrences "which may subsequently give rise to a claim" if the insured gave written notice to the company of such a potentiality during the policy period. If *may* means *could* in the first provision, then this second provision appears to be redundant, apart from the addition of a reporting requirement. So the court interpreted the second provision to apply not to all claims that could be made during the policy period, but only to legal services provided during the policy period that did not cause injury or loss until after the period. Such claims would not fall within the first coverage provision because they *could not* be made until after the period.

This is a tortured interpretation indeed. The combined effect of the court's interpretation of these two provisions is that the policy contains a variable policy period covering some claims that could have been brought before the period began but were not, some claims made during the policy period, some that could have been made during the period but were not made until after its expiration, and some that could not have been made during the policy period at all.

A reasonable insured, especially an attorney, could be expected to adopt a much simpler and more plausible interpretation of the policy. The first coverage provision—claims "which may be made against them during the period"—covers claims actually made during the period; the second—occurrences "which may subsequently give rise to a claim"—extends coverage to errors the insured thinks he may have made, but which have not yet been reduced to claims. On this reading, the plaintiffs had purchased a simple claims-made policy, with the additional right to coverage of claims that have not yet been made, so long as the act exposing the insured to potential liability has already occurred and is reported.

Perhaps recognizing the fragility of its interpretation, as in *Gray* the court also insisted that plaintiffs were covered by the policy because they could reasonably expect coverage under the circumstances. Without coverage, the court argued, attorneys would have no insurance for claims brought against them after retirement.[32] Only claims actually made during previous policy periods or at least reported by the insured during such periods would be covered under the more straightforward interpretation of the policy. Retired attorneys therefore would have to continue purchasing policies in order to remain covered against future claims arising out of preretirement services. The court thought that the need to continue purchasing such coverage after retirement was contrary to reasonable expectation. But it gave no reason why attorneys who had not yet retired would expect such coverage, or why they would need it, although they too would be covered against post-policy period claims under the court's holding.

In short, in light of the seemingly straightforward language of the policy, the fact that the insureds were attorneys capable of understanding it, and the fairly clear difference between claims-made and occurrence coverage, it appears that the decision was based as much on the supposed desirability of including postretirement coverage in preretirement policies as on any actual expectation by the attorneys that it already was included in standard coverage.

WHY HONOR AN INSURED'S EXPECTATIONS?

The preceding analysis of the expectations decisions now provides a basis for exploring the purposes underlying the expectations principle. Why should a court honor an insured's expectations, especially when they are contradicted by the terms of the insured's own insurance policy? Several themes that recurred throughout the analysis can lead to answers to this question. First, we saw that the insurer generally can avoid liability by clearly informing the insured that the expected coverage is not included in the policy being purchased. This will dispel the insured's expectations and make the expectations principle inapplicable. Second, in the vast majority of cases, the insurer's misleading conduct significantly influences both the finding that the insured's expectation of coverage is reasonable and the decision to honor it. Finally, as the two preceding considerations wane in importance, the courts' preference for desirable but currently unavailable coverage plays an increasingly important role.

These themes correspond to the three major purposes of insurance law we have been examining throughout this book. First, proper use of the expectations principle may promote the disclosure of more information about the scope of coverage offered prospective applicants. This will help promote economic efficiency. Second, the expectations principle may serve equitable interests by encouraging a more fully informed choice by the insured and by permitting the courts to look beyond the formal transaction between the parties to their actual expectations. The appropriate issues then will be whether the insured truly understood the terms of what he agreed to and whether the insurer should be held responsible for expectations that it may have created. Finally, the expectations principle may serve a variety of risk-distributional aims by spreading the cost of otherwise uninsured losses and by encouraging a diversity of coverage options that will help promote risk spreading. Of course, to say that the expectations principle may serve these purposes is not to say that it will always serve them well or consistently. The following pages explore the manner in which the expectations principle may serve such purposes and begin to assess its limitations in doing so.

Economic Efficiency

Assuring accurate information about insurance coverage is a central concern of the expectations principle. As I argued above, the insurer is held liable in an expectations case primarily because it is in some way responsible for the insured's inaccurate understanding of the scope of the coverage provided by the policy in dispute. Without such information, it will be difficult for consumers to make decisions that effectively serve their interests and resources will be allocated inefficiently. Thus, part of the theory behind the expectations principle is that imposing liability on the insurer when the insured possesses inaccurate coverage information should encourage the production of more accurate information and thereby help create a more efficient market. In effect the principle strives to reduce transactions costs by placing responsibility for producing coverage information on the party who can most cheaply do so. With such information, the insured may better assess the value of coverage offered him and may shop for coverage more completely meeting his expectations. If a particular form of coverage is unavailable but desired, promoting disclosure of its absence from standard coverage may encourage insurers to offer it.

Although generating increased information is a valid goal, there are limits on both the extent to which increased information will promote efficiency and on the capacity of the expectations principle to generate more coverage information. First, it is unclear whether requiring the generation of increased information would, in fact, promote efficiency. Such a requirement is efficient only if its economic benefits outweigh the costs it imposes. At some point the cost of producing more information would outweigh its benefits. The difficulty of evaluating these costs and benefits has resulted in sharp disagreement among economists over which approach is actually more efficient—government intervention or a hands-off attitude toward an imperfect market.[33]

Second, even if requiring increased information were guaranteed to promote efficiency, it is questionable whether reliance on the expectations principle would produce a great deal more coverage information than would be produced without it. The principle does not mandate disclosure; it merely imposes liability for failure to comply with judicial guidelines. Therefore, insurers will disseminate additional information only when the risk of increased liability outweighs the costs of dissemination. In deciding whether to provide additional information, an insurer will consider both the cost of anticipating the insured's expectation of coverage and the cost of dispelling it. It is important to recognize these cost restraints in analyzing the probable effectiveness of the expectations principle in generating increased information.

Finally, because estimates of these costs are likely to be very imprecise, the expectations principle may encourage the production of information generally, but it cannot dictate whether the production of that information will be efficient in a particular case. In theory a competitive market should produce optimal amounts of information and a desirable variety of coverage alternatives without legal intervention. If for various reasons, however, a particular insurance submarket is not fully competitive—because of a history of price regulation or the high capital requirements for entry, for example—encouraging the production of more information through an expectations principle may help make the market more competitive.

In light of these limits, several generalizations can be made about use of the expectations principle to promote the disclosure of coverage information. First, there is an important connection between the insurer's responsibility for a misleading impression about coverage and the feasibility of dispelling inaccurate expectations. The greater the insurer's responsibility for creating the insured's expectations, the better the position it will be in to anticipate them. Even if the insurer is not directly responsible for the expectations, they may be so common that an insurer could easily anticipate them. The accident and life insurance cases are good illustrations of this point. On the other hand, in the duty-to-defend cases not only did the insurer do nothing to create a misleading impression, but the disputed coverage probably was not commonly expected. The expectations principle is less likely to produce increased information under the latter circumstances.

Second, the fact that the insurer is responsible for the insured's expectation provides strong evidence that the conduct creating the expectation is within the insurer's control and that it has the capacity to dispel it. This does not mean, however, that such conduct can be altered inexpensively or that accurate information can be distributed inexpensively. It may be relatively easy to change the location of a vending machine or the wording of a printed solicitation, but if expectations are created or furthered by the entire marketing situation, the insurer may be able to dispel them only at the cost of a complete revision of its marketing practices. And even if coverage is sold through an agent, disclaimers may be only partially effective in dispelling false expectations. In the life insurance cases, for example, payment of a first premium was largely responsible for the expectation of immediate coverage. In order to dispel that expectation effectively insurers will have to dispense with the requirement that an insured submit a first premium with the application[34] or assume the additional costs of issuing oral and written disclaimers. Insurers will weigh these costs carefully before assuming them simply to avoid liability at the hand of the expectations principle.

Finally, other transactions costs may hinder attempts to use the expectations principle to promote information disclosure. Expectations may be difficult and costly to dispel when they involve minor or highly technical components of coverage. And the difficulties of case-by-case application may render the expectations principle less effective in practice than in theory.[35] In sum, the expectations decisions promise only limited success in promoting the dissemination of coverage information. Although the expectations principle may encourage alterations in insurer conduct that can be achieved easily and inexpensively, it is unlikely to influence more fundamental features of behavior whose change would be contrary to the economic interests of insurers and, in the aggregate, the community of insureds as well.

Equity

The expectations principle plays an important role in promoting equity in two respects. First, the principle is a means emphasizing the importance of what I call "informed assent"—the making of contractual decisions with a complete understanding of the scope of the undertaking. Second, the expectations principle recognizes the influence of the insurer's conduct on the insured's expectations about the insurance coverage he purchases.

A striking feature of both these equitable themes is their focus on present parties and present fairness. Equity is largely concerned with correcting unfairness that has already occurred and only to a much lesser extent with ordering future relations. And equity deals with relations between insurer and insured rather than among insureds. Yet any legal intervention to achieve equity in the present is likely to affect future relations of both sorts. Consequently, the equitable interventions we examine below also have risk-distributional implications that must be examined afterward.

Informed Assent

Encouraging fully informed choice about coverage alternatives is not only a means to an economic end; in a sense informed assent is also an end in itself. Decisions made in comparative ignorance are more like guesses than choices. The disclosure of coverage information facilitates genuine choice and thereby serves the interests of autonomy and freedom of contract as well as economic efficiency. Legal doctrines such as the duty to obtain informed consent to medical treatment and to warn consumers about the hazards of dangerous products encourage the dissemination of information to protect these interests. The expectations principle is analogous to these doctrines and serves similar interests.

The sole justification for honoring expectations, therefore, does not lie in the efficiency of doing so. The expectations principle has a principled justification even when its success in promoting the disclosure of coverage information is likely to be limited. Regardless of whether a decision to honor an insured's reasonable expectations affects the future behavior of a particular insurer or the industry at large, honoring expectations acknowledges the value of informed assent. By treating the absence of informed assent as a circumstance of special legal concern, the expectations principle recognizes an ideal. It signifies the connection between informed assent and the value of individual autonomy that is at the heart of freedom of contract as a matter of equity, quite apart from economic efficiency.

The Insurer's Responsibility for Coverage Expectations

Many courts have pointed to the insurer's role in creating or failing to dispel expectations as a justification for imposing liability under the expectations principle. In such cases, the courts have relied implicitly on equitable principles of fairness to override even clear policy provisions. They have not, however, attempted to link their decisions with more conventional legal doctrine. Yet such links exist.

A very important source of current law is furnished by the doctrines developed in the Courts of Equity that were created hundreds of years ago. Courts of Equity provided flexible justice when the rigid rules of the law courts failed to do so. Today the functions of both law and equity are performed by one set of courts. But talk of "rules of equity" persists, as a way of referring to doctrines with origins in the equitable concerns of the original Courts of Equity.

Equity developed a number of doctrines regulating the rights of parties who suffer losses due to misinformation, especially when remedies at law for such losses were limited. Courts applying strict legal doctrine were and are hesitant to impose liability for losses caused by misinformation in the absence of fraud[36] or proof that there was a special relationship between the parties that would oblige the defendant to exercise reasonable care in transmitting the information in question.[37] In most of the expectations cases—even those involving misleading impressions—the insurer's conduct generally would not meet the legal requirements of either fraud or negligent misrepresentation. Equity, however, often grants relief based on the relative blameworthiness of the party from whom misinformation flows. To this end, contract reformation has long been available in a variety of contexts, and the courts often have invoked the doctrine of equitable estoppel to prevent one party from benefiting from the mistaken impression it has conveyed to another. Both reformation and equitable estoppel operate in a fashion that is analogous to the expectations principle.

Reformation. Courts may invoke the equitable remedy of reformation when, due to the mistake of one or both parties, a written instrument fails to express the real agreement of the parties.[38] This remedy has its origin in a body of contract law that holds that the parties must come to a meeting of the minds before a contract is formed.[39] Reformation was first invoked when the mistake in the instrument was mutual and the court's only task was to reform the written instrument to conform to the actual agreement of the parties. As the remedy developed, it was extended to include relief when only one party was mistaken about the contents of the contract, but the other party was aware of that mistake.[40]

Though by its terms this extension still turns on the parties' contractual intent, when the mistake is not wholly mutual, whether reformation is granted also seems to turn on the relative faults of the parties.[41] In either case, whether one party actually induced the other's misinterpretation or only knew of it, he is the more blameworthy for having allowed his counterpart to labor under delusions about the contract's contents. Of course, when actual inducement is not involved, it may be difficult to show that the first party knew of the other's mistake. Thus, the more likely it is that the first party caused the misinterpretation, the stronger the inference that he knew or should have known of it.

Equitable Estoppel. The doctrine of estoppel also provides some insight into the equitable foundations of holding the insurer responsible for the insured's expectations. The doctrine applies when one party's representation or failure to speak induces another to believe the truth of certain facts and to rely on that belief. A person may be estopped from asserting as a defense the truth of a matter that he has misrepresented to another, if the latter has relied on the misrepresentation.[42] For instance, the misrepresenting party might be estopped from relying on a contract provision if he had induced the other party to believe the contract provided otherwise.

Estoppel focuses directly on the injuring party's conduct, but it does not require an intent to deceive. If the misrepresentation is active—involving words or conduct made with reason to believe another would rely—then the misrepresentation alone may be sufficiently blameworthy to hold the other responsible.[43] If the misrepresentation is passive—failure to disabuse another of his misconceptions—estoppel requires that this silence at least be negligent. In the latter instance, unless the offending party had reason to know of the other party's misconceptions and of his intention to act on them, the representation probably would not be considered negligent.

The Expectations Principle as a Doctrine of Equity

An analysis of the expectations cases as an equitable balancing of relative faults requires consideration of three interrelated factors derived in part from the principles underlying reformation and estoppel. First, if the insurer knew or should have known of the insured's expectations, the equities weigh heavily in favor of holding it responsible for fulfilling them. The principles underlying reformation would then apply. The policy would be reformed to conform to the insured's expectations. Second, if the insurer also created or helped create those expectations, equity would suggest even more strongly that those expectations be fulfilled. The insurer would be estopped to deny the truth of the expectations it had induced. Finally, the insured's expectations must be reasonable before equity should demand that they be honored. In most cases, this criterion will be met if one of the other two is. If the insurer knew of or created an insured's expectation concerning the scope of coverage, it is probably reasonable for the insured to have that expectation. In short, the principles of equity at work here seem to turn on an information imbalance whose consequences are considered the insurer's responsibility.

A brief second look at the expectations decisions will help reveal to what extent they can be explained as a balancing of equities of this sort. For two reasons the factor that distinguishes the decisions in this respect is the directness of the insurer's responsibility for the insured's expectations. First, when the insurer actually creates an expectation of coverage, it bears more blame than when it merely fails to dispel them. Second, equity might well hold the insurer responsible simply for knowing of but not dispelling the insured's false expectations. In most situations, however, knowledge alone would be difficult to prove. But if the insurer actually created the expectations, it is also more likely to have known of them.

Conversely, the less direct the link between the insurer's words or conduct and the insured's expectations, the less blameworthy the insurer and the less justifiable the inference of knowledge from causal responsibility. It is not surprising, then, that in the expectations cases where the insurer's causal responsibility is least direct, the courts have reached for collateral support to justify honoring the insured's expectations. Because these cases are more difficult to explain by reference to traditional equitable principles, courts have sought additional justification in considerations of substantive fairness. The following examples illustrate how the equitable component of the expectations principle varies with the directness of the insurer's responsibility for the insured's expectations.

When the Policy Itself Creates the Expectation. The venerable maxim that ambiguities in an insurance policy should be construed against the drafter is itself a reflection of the comparative responsibilities of insurer and insured. Because the insurer could have drafted to avoid ambiguous policy language, it is fair that of the two parties, the insurer should be the party whose expectations are disappointed when ambiguous policy language is interpreted against its interests.[44] This balancing of responsibilities is also manifested by the courts' tendency to limit the construction of ambiguities to meanings that could reasonably have been expected by the nondrafting party.[45]

The fairness of construing ambiguities against the insurer is underscored by several factors. First, insurance policies, even the new plain language policies, often are difficult to understand. It is easy for insureds to derive inaccurate expectations from them or to be unable on their own to correct preexisting expectations by reading a policy. Second, policies customarily are not issued and made available to the insured until after sale. Package policies of automobile and homeowner's insurance, for example, are often ordered by telephone. Insureds cannot easily check their expectations against policy language. Finally, the typical personal insurance consumer has little opportunity to bargain with an insurance company over the terms of a policy. Standard forms are not altered for individual purchasers, and there is little incentive to compare the terms offered by competing companies since terms (though not necessarily prices) tend to be identical. The consumer therefore has no incentive to try to have his expectations incorporated in the policy.

These factors not only help explain the maxim *contra proferentem* (construe ambiguities against the drafter); they also support the extension of the expectations principle beyond the construction of ambiguities against the insurer to situations where the insurer has caused an expectation of coverage despite clear and contrary policy language.

When the Insurer Is Directly Responsible for the Insured's Expectations. Although many expectations cases purport to be based in part on the ambiguity of policy language, the expectations in these cases are often derived independently of the policy. In such cases, the equities clearly favor the insured if the insurer is directly responsible for the expectations. Thus, in the solicitation-by-mail cases, the insurer was responsible because its solicitation had a tone of urgency creating the expectation of immediate coverage. And in the temporary life insurance cases, insurers created the expectation of immediate coverage by accepting a first premium with the application. In both sets of cases, the inference that the insurer was aware of the expectations it had created seems legitimate. This combination of causal responsibility with presumptive knowledge of the insured's expectations explains balancing the equities in the insured's favor.

When the Insurer Is Only Indirectly Responsible for the Insured's Expectations. In this situation the relative responsibilities of the parties are more difficult to assess. In such cases, the courts have tended to reach beyond expectations and the equities related to them to justify finding for the insured. In each of the flight insurance cases, for example, the insurer was indirectly responsible for the insured's expectations in that it chose an automated marketing technique. In *Lacks*, the insurer went further and created an expectation of coverage a bit more directly, by placing its vending machine in front of the charter counter. The insurer in *Steven*, however, did nothing directly to create an expectation of coverage. The court therefore supported its decision to hold the insurer responsible by finding that the exclusion of coverage was not only unexpected, but "harsh and unconscionable."[46] Similarly, in the accident insurance cases, there was no evidence that the insurer actively encouraged the insured's expectations. The insurer could be charged with knowledge of the insured's expectations only because of the common understanding of the word *accident* in the title of the policy. As in the other indirect responsibility cases, however, the decisions were reinforced by the find-

ing that the coverage the insurer offered was not only unexpected, but was disproportionately narrow considering the substantial premium the insured had paid.

*When Expectations Are Created by Forces for Which the Insurer Is Not
Responsible.* In most cases the less responsibility the insurer has for the insured's
expectations, the less notice it will have of the probable existence of those expectations. If there is neither causal responsibility nor presumptive knowledge of the
insured's expectations by the insurer, the balance of equities between insurer and
insured is nearly equal. In these cases, the insured simply has an independent expectation—sometimes reasonable, sometimes not—that happens to conflict with
the equally reasonable expectation of the insurer that the policy provisions are
binding. Because the equities are balanced, from an exclusively equitable standpoint there is no reason to displace the contract terms. Although a scattering of
cases refusing to invoke the expectations principle may be explained on this basis,[47] certainly the mandated coverage cases ignore the point.

When disputes of this sort are resolved in the insured's favor, therefore, it
must be for reasons that transcend equity. As we saw above, although it might be
conducive to economic efficiency and informed assent if the insureds in the mandated coverage cases were informed of various omitted coverages, it is unlikely that
the expectations principle would often have this effect. Only risk-distributional
justifications, therefore, seem available to support the decision to honor expectations in these cases. These distributional implications are examined below.

Risk Distribution

Even after the economic and equitable justifications for the expectations principles have been exhausted, risk-distributional reasons for honoring an insured's expectations may remain. Of course, there are also risk-distributional reasons for
criticizing the expectations principle and its application in particular settings. The
ultimate effect of any particular decision depends on the kind of expectations being
honored and the kind of coverage involved. The results of the cases may therefore
be evaluated by tracing these distributional effects and by assessing their impact
on the forms of insurance coverage that are modified by the expectation principle.

The expectations decisions have both general risk-spreading effects and more
focused risk-redistributional consequences. The immediate effect of a decision
honoring an insured's expectations is to spread a loss broadly rather than to focus
it on the insured. In the short run, in this respect, there is little basis for distinguishing between the misleading impression and the mandated coverage cases.
Whether the absence of coverage is unexpected, both unexpected and unfair, or

merely undesirable has little relevance to the advisability of mitigating the effects of an otherwise uninsured loss.

In the long run, however, increased risk spreading may or may not occur. If the expectations decisions induce insurers to add expected coverage to their policies expressly, there will be increased risk spreading among those who continue to purchase policies, presumably at an increased cost. But insurers may not add expected coverage as a result of the expectations principle. They may continue to behave as before, risking occasional judgments rendered in accordance with the expectations principle; they may offer the expected coverage only as an option, in which case some but not all the increased risk spreading the courts envision probably will occur; or, finally, they may simply disclose the absence of expected coverage and thereby avoid liability .

The availability of a risk-distributional justification for invoking the principle, then, depends in part on what consequences one expects it to produce. If one is concerned mainly with short-run risk spreading, the principle obviously can be successful since it provides a litigant with coverage. But that is largely an equitable rather than a distributional concern. If the principle is designed to promote long-run spreading, a court must be confident that insurers will add expected coverage as a result, and that most insureds will continue to purchase the policies that contain such coverage. Yet this will not necessarily occur.

If actual expectations of coverage are involved, moreover, then most of the justifications for legally promoting increased risk spreading that we surveyed in chapter 2 will be absent anyway. First, people will not have underestimated the risks they face since they will actually believe that they have purchased coverage to guard against these risks. Second, they will not have refused to share risk for any of the other reasons that might justify mandatory spreading—faulty statistical reasoning, the desire to free ride on others' efforts at philanthropy, or the dynamic character of preferences. Their very expectation that they have purchased the coverage in question suggests just the opposite. Finally, if in fact there were enough demand for the expected coverage, then in the absence of some special imperfection in the market that might justify legal intervention for nondistributional reasons, the coverage would already have been made available by the market. These observations underscore the insight that emerged in analyzing the mandated coverage cases: these cases seem mainly concerned not with honoring expectations, but with making desirable coverage available even apart from any actual expectations about it.

A second and separate set of effects of the expectations decisions are risk redistributional. The increased possibility of adverse selection is the first such effect that should be noted. For example, the flight insurance cases may increase the number of charter flyers who purchase coverage, the temporary life insurance cases may increase the number of applicants for insurance who have a better-than-average chance of dying during the application period, and so forth. If this pressures insurers to raise premiums, then other insureds will have to pay higher premiums than their expected loss would otherwise require because of this adverse selection. The adverse risks then will be subsidized by the good risks. Even when such adverse selection is minimized, at least some of the cross-subsidization that is characteristic of risk redistribution will be produced by the expectations decisions.

The justification for these subsidies—whether they encourage adverse selection or they do not—depends on the theory of distributive justice one holds. From a libertarian point of view no such redistribution is justified; and from a utilitarian standpoint the justification for these redistributions is speculative, although there is no apparent reason to suppose that they would increase social utility. The egalitarian approach examined in chapter 2, however, probably would favor some, but not all the expectations decisions.

Recall that the critical factor for the egalitarian evaluating a risk-redistributional scheme is the extent of the insured's control over risk-increasing characteristics. The notion of control is by no means unproblematic since it expresses a conclusion about the scope of individual moral responsibility. But the notion can help the analyst refine his intuitions about the proper allocation between individual responsibility for, and collective sharing of, different risks. For example, some people prefer not to fly on unscheduled or charter airlines because of their safety records; others willingly take the increased risk of flying on such carriers. These are voluntary choices very much within the control of the insureds who make them. Decisions like *Lacks* and *Steven* tend to force these two groups, somewhat arbitrarily, to share the risk of mishaps on such flights. Similarly, the duty-to-defend cases pool two distinct groups: those who are sued for committing intentional torts and those who are not. To the extent that the former group has some control over the activities that give rise to this litigation, it seems inappropriate to ask the latter group to help subsidize these activities.

In contrast, many of the other expectations decisions have distributional effects that seem intuitively acceptable because they promote the sharing of largely uncontrollable risks. For instance, in the accident insurance cases, the extension of coverage to all losses commonly understood as accidental spreads the risk of having an unknown natural handicap or physical infirmity to all those in the insurance pool. This does not appear to produce an inappropriate subsidy because the odds are good that everyone has infirmities that could combine quite fortuitously with external forces to cause accidental injury. This conclusion, of course, depends very much on the acceptance of both generally egalitarian values and a particular interpretation of the notion of controllability of losses.

Furthermore, for anyone holding what I have called a "pragmatist" approach to risk-distributive justice, the problem is complicated by the infringement of liberty entailed by decisions taken for redistributional reasons. The risk spreading and redistribution achieved by the expectations decisions limit the insured's freedom of choice by involuntarily increasing the scope of the coverage he purchases. Any increase in a policy's package of insurance protection also often increases its price. Those who would prefer the narrower but cheaper coverage then are forced to accept more insurance than they want in order to obtain the coverage they need. When having insurance coverage is optional, some people then will choose not to buy it at all—the increase in cost caused by the expectations principle will have priced them out of the market. And when the coverage is effectively mandatory—automobile liability or fire insurance on mortgaged real estate—insureds will have to give up other noninsurance goods in order to buy the mandated but overly broad coverage.

In short, the importance of tracing risk-distributional effects when they are a significant factor in a decision should not be underestimated. It is deceptively easy for a court to invoke equitable principles in order to find an insured's expectations reasonable and then to require that they be honored in order to mitigate the consequences of the insured's unfortunate loss. It is more difficult, but equally important, to realize that the short-run risk spreading in such cases may have more profound effects than a simple reduction of the insurer's profits. Saving one insured from catastrophe may not simply spread a neutral risk to all insureds; it may spread it in ways that a court sensitive to the consequences of its actions would find both disturbing and counterproductive.

GUIDELINES FOR ADJUDICATION

This analysis of the expectations decisions and the purposes the expectations principle serves has shown that the capacities of the principle are not unlimited. In an effort to formulate guidelines for use of the principle, I will now examine three kinds of limits on the usefulness of the principle: (1) the constraints that courts should observe in regulating insurance coverage, especially in light of the concurrent authority of other legal institutions; (2) the legitimacy of the courts' use of the principle to pursue economic, equitable, and distributional goals, considering both their complexity and interdependence; and (3) the probable effectiveness of judicial regulation in view of the limits of adjudication and of the form of the expectations principle itself.

Institutional Constraints

Legislation in every state has established an administrative agency—usually a state insurance commission or commissioner and his staff—with authority to regulate the prices and terms of insurance coverage. The scope of that agency's authority and the means that may be used to exercise it vary, but in every state the agency has the authority to affect, directly or indirectly, the terms of most policies of personal insurance. It is therefore sensible to ask whether, in light of this administrative authority, the courts have a legitimate role to play in this field.

There are several strong arguments in support of the role the courts have played in creating the expectations principle. First, the enactment of regulatory legislation indicates that the insurance industry's activities sufficiently affect the public interest to justify legal control over those activities. Although the exercise of this regulatory authority may on occasion preempt judicial involvement in this field, most regulation should not be viewed as preemptive. General administrative authority to approve of or to acquiesce in premium levels and policy terms should not foreclose inquiry into their acceptability in exceptional cases. Moreover, approval of the substance of policy terms does not necessarily indicate approval of the procedures used to market the policies containing them. In both respects, the tradition of judicial intervention to guard against the more egregious examples of insurer misconduct is strong enough to counter any inference that a judicial role has been foreclosed, except when the intent to preempt has been specifically expressed by a regulatory agency or a legislature.

A second argument in favor of the principle is that insurance regulation often has been unsystematic and ineffective. In many states, the flexibility necessary for effective regulation has not been available, resources provided regulatory agencies have been insufficient, and the industry has sometimes dominated the regulators. These deficiencies tend to justify judicial intervention.[48] Finally, judicial intervention is subject to an administrative check against radical or otherwise unacceptable innovation: although judicial decisions are final, the rules they establish are not. Just as the courts and legislatures sometimes engage in a colloquy over the meaning and validity of legislation, so regulatory action subsequent to a judicial decision may send a message to the courts that such intervention contravenes considered regulatory policy. In such instances, the courts generally should refrain from further intervention.

In sum, the courts should be respectful of administrative authority when regulation already has addressed the specific question at hand, but the mere existence of unexercised paramount regulatory authority does not preclude judicial action in the field. That judicial action may be legitimate, however, does not necessarily mean that it will be effective in pursuing its goals. The limits on judicial effectiveness are both substantive and formal.

Substantive Limits

The economic, equitable, and distributional justifications for the expectations principle considered earlier all offer support for judicial use of the expectations principle. Each also suggests clear limits on the extent to which courts can and should pursue those goals.

Efficiency

Promoting efficiency through the expectations principle is likely to be an elusive judicial goal. Determining optimal amounts of coverage information inevitably will be an uncertain process; and encouraging the production of that information may be little more than an exercise in exhortation. In contrast to legislative or regulatory disclosure requirements, the expectations principle is likely to be most effective when the cost to the insurer of anticipating and dispelling inaccurate expectations is not high. Thus, although this is not a perfect test, the more likely it is that the insurer actually created the insured's expectations, the more likely that the benefits of anticipating and dispelling those expectations will outweigh the costs of doing so. The vagueness of this test and the difficulty of implementing it with confidence suggest that economic efficiency should be viewed as a subsidiary goal of the expectations principle. The potential for achieving it may add support to decisions made for other reasons but normally should not suffice as the sole justification for judicial action.

Equity

Allocating equitable responsibility between the parties to an insurance contract is an acceptable judicial function. That function, however, cannot be pursued liberally without sacrificing the certainty and predictability afforded by written policies of insurance. Therefore, the courts should exercise prudence in their equitable supervision of insurance transactions. Limiting the application of the expectations principle to cases where the insured's expectations of coverage are reasonable is one way to reconcile the need for equitable flexibility with the particular demand of the insurance industry that its obligations be predictable. But the reasonableness test will not effectively regulate the application of the principle until the courts clarify its content. Otherwise, insurance companies may be subject to endless claims of coverage at variance with policy provisions.

The likelihood that the insurer actually created a misleading impression about coverage provides a reliable index of the equities in most of the insurance disputes analyzed here. The misleading impression standard not only serves as a test for blameworthy conduct by insurers; it also grounds the expectations principle in fundamental principles of contract law by establishing the relevance of the insurer's knowledge of the insured's interpretation of the contract. If this way of understanding what counts as a reasonable expectation is adopted, the situations in which the principle may be invoked will become more predictable and the competing concerns of equity and certainty may be reconciled.

Risk Distribution

Courts are understandably uncomfortable with legal doctrines designed to achieve distributional aims. Doctrines that promote risk spreading in general, however, may be somewhat less controversial than those that redistribute risk, because society increasingly favors spreading of the risks against which personal insurance typically protects. Nevertheless, mandatory risk spreading itself is a controversial judicial aim even in the insurance context. Judicial decisions promoting greater distribution may appear inconsistent with democratic values;[49] the courts also seem institutionally ill-suited to make decisions, such as these, that require weighing a series of incommensurable factors in determining the best course of action.[50] Further, in the insurance context, decisions made for risk-distributional reasons alone threaten the statistical basis of the insurer's decision making. They may therefore render some forms of coverage actuarially unsound or unmarketable. They will certainly make some forms of coverage more expensive. Perhaps these factors help explain the courts' tendency in the mandated coverage cases to base their decisions on fictional expectations instead of revealing more forthrightly the latent risk-distributional reasons for their actions.

Although the courts are probably not the proper branch through which to achieve significant risk redistribution, there are justifications for taking distributional consequences into account in resolving insurance disputes. First, common law courts historically have considered distributional effects relevant to their decisions, and the practice has gained some legitimacy simply through precedent. Second, the courts have long been thought capable of determining what kind of conduct falls below minimum standards of justice, even though they may not be as capable of structuring optimally just arrangements in the first instance.

Consequently, although the expectations principle might not be invoked for distributional reasons alone, distributional factors are certainly relevant because expectations decisions have distributional consequences.[51] Awareness of those consequences may assist decision making in cases where other considerations are closely balanced. For example, the flight insurance decisions may be suspect because they work a redistribution of risk between passengers of charter and regularly scheduled flights. On the other hand, the apparently undesirable short-run distributional consequences of such decisions might be acceptable if they encourage a variety of coverage options in the long run. The threat of liability for the deaths of an entire charter party can eventually encourage insurers to offer charter coverage at appropriately higher premiums. At many airports now, both chartered and regularly scheduled airline coverage are available at different rates.

Finally, proper analysis of the expectations decisions requires a clearer understanding of the relationship between risk-distributional concerns and substantive unfairness. In the insurance context, a decision that a particular policy provision or gap in coverage is substantively unfair has special significance: it represents a judicial determination that the risk the policy fails to cover is one that insureds as a group should have an opportunity to share, even if this means increased premiums in the future or curtailment of coverage in other ways. Such a decision need not constitute a finding that the coverage it mandates is the fairest or best that could be fashioned. That is, invoking the expectations principle need not constitute a dictation by the court of its own ultimate coverage preferences. It is merely a judicial determination that whatever the acceptable possibilities, the one embodied in the policy does not meet minimum standards of fairness in risk sharing. But this recognition cannot be the end of the matter.

The courts then need to articulate their standards of risk-sharing fairness, and indicate why the future risk-distributional effects of applying these standards are desirable or at least tolerable. Earlier I showed that these standards might be based on the right to be informed of the scope of coverage one purchases, on a rough equivalence between price and coverage, on a combination of these two factors, or on the bare desirability of coverage even when these other factors are absent. And I noted when the risk-distributional impacts of these standards did and did not seem acceptable, given the moral theory through which the issue is viewed. At the very least, courts relying even partly on substantive dissatisfaction with particular coverage provisions or omissions should explain the basis of their dissatisfaction. Insurers then can determine with some measure of predictability whether their policies meet judicial standards.[52]

The Practical Consequences of Form

The effectiveness of judicial involvement in regulating insurance contracts depends not only on the goals the courts pursue, but also on the form and procedure under which they pursue them. The first formal consideration here is the comparative strength of administrative and judicial rulemaking; the second concerns the advantages and disadvantages of general standards, as opposed to discrete sets of rules, as methods of judicial regulation.

Administrative or Judicial Rulemaking

The major advantage of adjudication is its flexibility. Courts have a special ability to accommodate and respond to individual claims and needs as they arise in particular fact situations. For example, administrative regulation could require that insurers provide temporary life insurance unless they disclaim coverage in a designated color and size of type. Judicial rules need not be so rigid; they can allow inquiry into the effectiveness of the disclaimer rather than into its form alone.

Adjudication also allows the insurer to choose between compliance and the threat of liability. Yet this element of choice is also the greatest limitation of the expectations principle: the principle's capacity to alter standard practices is limited by the strength of the economic incentives it can create. Thus, the principle is likely to be more effective as a remedial measure in cases where there have been losses sufficiently severe to justify a lawsuit than as a force for industrywide reform.

In contrast, administrative regulation could circumvent this limitation by requiring insurers to provide generally expected coverage or by prescribing disclosure procedures. A state insurance commissioner desiring to address the problems highlighted by the temporary life insurance cases, for example, could do so with relative dispatch. He would not have to wait for the parties to a dispute to present it to him; his factfinding authority and capacity would almost certainly be greater than that of the courts, and he could take broader and more systematic remedial action than the courts. Consider also an administrative directive that liability policies contain the duty to defend mandated in *Gray*, for example, or a refusal to approve a proposed premium increase until such coverage is offered. Each and every policy issued thereafter would be affected by such action. Decisions such as *Gray* cannot hope to have such a systematic effect.

Despite the limitations of adjudication, the expectations principle may mesh with administrative regulation in a valuable way. By making the courts available to resolve individual coverage disputes, the principle may help regulators with limited resources determine which problems are sufficiently widespread and severe to justify regulatory intervention. The issues that are most commonly litigated are probably those most in need of the attention of a regulatory agency equipped to resolve them through its rulemaking authority.

General Standards or Specific Rules

The expectations principle still functions more like a general standard than as a discrete set of rules. The courts have not arrived at a systematic understanding of the purposes the principle should serve, and there is no common standard against which to measure the reasonableness of an expectation. This is not unusual early in the development of a legal principle. Discrete purposes are not determined all at once because adjudication occurs in piecemeal fashion. A broadly formulated standard prevents premature specification. Nevertheless, powerful reasons suggest that it is time for the expectations principle to mature into a body of doctrine composed of a discrete set of rules.[53]

First, the move from general toward specific explanations of the principle may focus judicial inquiry on exactly what makes an expectation reasonable and why such an expectation should be honored. This chapter has indicated the ways in which the three interests served by insurance law affect the expectations principle. It also has formulated two considerations of great importance from the equitable point of view—the insurer's causal responsibility for and knowledge of the expectation—that often appear to be decisive. Others may emerge, but in all cases, courts should make an effort to explain their decisions in ways that will establish some uniformity in this field.

Another reason for greater specification is that concrete rules will provide better guidance for the parties whose conduct the principle governs. If insurers can determine from established rules what conduct on their part renders the expectations of an insured reasonable, they can alter that conduct and correct false expectations more easily. Without the predictability provided by rules, insurers can only guess at the kind of conduct governed by the expectations principle. Where uncertainty exists, they may well disregard the principle, especially if the consequences of altering behavior to avoid liability in all the situations conceivably regulated by the principle would be too costly.

Third, casting the principle into a set of more specific rules will tend to legitimize it. Broad standards are intrinsically and deliberately vague; they suggest a desire by appellate courts to avoid explanation of the specific grounds for decision. Such standards allow judicial retreat or inconsistency without acknowledgment. Judicial wavering of this sort appears to have occurred in the mandated coverage cases. Rules, on the other hand, call much more clearly for close factual analysis, explicit recognition of concern for decisions in analogous cases, and reconciliation with traditional legal doctrine. Shaping the expectations principle into a set of rules will compel this more focused inquiry.

Finally, the expectations principle will operate much more effectively if it is applied pursuant to a discrete set of rules. Appellate courts sometimes make law, but they cannot always enforce it. Specific rules will provide lower courts with the guidance necessary for them to apply accurately and effectively the law determined by the courts above. Moreover, in reality appellate courts must justify their decisions to the lower courts before the appellate courts can expect those decisions to be enforced with complete fidelity and enthusiasm. The formulation and explanation of rules helps to provide the justification necessary to gain this support from the lower courts.

No legal rule is ever immune to change. As legal and economic needs evolve, rules are modified to meet these needs. When courts make new law governing insurance, often they also create new insurance coverage in the process. The expectations principle is the most prominent example of this phenomenon. The principle serves a variety of objectives, some of which are not entirely consistent. The principle must therefore be assessed holistically, keeping in mind the purposes it serves. Although the courts have generally applied the principle correctly, the strong temptation to use it to achieve risk-distributional purposes alone has not always been resisted. This should come as no surprise, for the principle provides not only a stage on which private parties and insurance companies can trace responsibility for their respective misfortunes, but a vehicle for implementing these allocations of responsibility.

6 Toward a Theory of Coordinated Coverage

Over the past few decades the growth in the amount and kinds of insurance that are now commonplace has been enormous. More individuals, businesses, and institutions have more insurance, against more risks, than ever before. Well over two hundred billion dollars is spent on private insurance each year.[1] Vast sums are paid for publicly provided social insurance as well. The problem that we examine next is the product of this heavy reliance on so many different forms of insurance and of the relatively disorganized way in which all this coverage has come into being. Different policies and sources of protection continually overlap or conflict; and different sources of legal authority are called upon to resolve these issues of insurance jurisdiction. Because insurance has become so important an instrument for achieving social policy, there is a critical need for more effective ways of allocating coverage responsibility when more than one insurance policy or source of protection potentially covers a loss. I call this process of allocating coverage responsibility "coordination."

Complex problems of coordination are extremely common. Consider a simple automobile accident. Suppose that Harriet is directed by her employer to drive the company car across town. On the way, Harriet's vehicle and one driven negligently by Susan collide. Harriet is hurt and the company car is damaged. This simple problem of tort liability is likely to be overwhelmed by the array of insurance coverage available to the parties. Harriet probably has her own health insurance and her own automobile personal injury protection (PIP) insurance[2] covering both medical expenses and lost wages, even though the accident occurred in someone else's vehicle. In addition, she may be eligible for workers' compensa-

133

tion that will pay her medical expenses and lost wages, and she may be entitled to claim disability or Social Security coverage if she is out of work for more than a few months or is permanently disabled. Her employer's automobile PIP insurance also will cover Harriet's medical expenses and probably her lost wages as well. Susan—the other driver—will almost certainly be covered by liability insurance that will compensate Harriet for her medical expenses, lost wages, and pain and suffering if Susan is found liable to Harriet. The same policy probably covers Susan against liability for damage to Harriet's employer's vehicle. And if Susan is not covered by liability insurance, then Harriet will be covered both by her own and her employer's uninsured motorist insurance for medical, wage loss, and pain and suffering damages.[3] In addition, Harriet's employer probably has automobile collision insurance. There may be other coverage as well.

The problems of coordinating all this coverage not only reflect the proliferation of different kinds of insurance that provide overlapping forms of protection. They also suggest that a simple contractual model of the standard insurance relation is no longer adequate to the task of conceptual organization that the problems of coordination pose. Insurance today is not merely a transaction between a single insurer and an insured. The typical insurance arrangement increasingly involves several insurers, each providing somewhat different coverage, and each not only bearing overlapping responsibilities to the insured, but also having separate legal claims against each other. For the law to make sense out of such arrangements, they must be seen as something more than a series of independent, two-party contracts. A theory that accounts not only for the independence of each insurance relation, but also for their interrelation is required.

This chapter begins to build such a theory by demonstrating how the process of coordination can serve the economic and distributional purposes of insurance law. The need for coordination arises precisely because in practice insurance arrangements are not merely bilateral, but multilateral. Yet because such arrangements have their roots in bilateral contracts, legal devices that help to mediate between the bilateral building blocks and the multilateral purposes of insurance have been developed. When coordination is understood as serving these purposes, then a different picture of the insurance relation starts to emerge.

At present, unfortunately, there is no well-articulated way of thinking about the problems of coordination or of comparing the different ways in which different coordination questions can be resolved. Rarely is there any sustained discussion in judicial decisions or commentary of the purposes that may be served by a system of coordination.[4] Nor has there been more than a glimmer of recognition that a whole series of apparently independent legal devices governing multiple sources of coverage actually is concerned with the same problem: coordination. There has therefore been no attempt to view these legal devices as part of one system directed at the same set of ends.[5]

I will demonstrate that, in fact, there is a developing system of coordination and that it makes use of two very different mechanisms to pursue its objectives. On the one hand, the private market has developed a number of distinct contractual devices for coordinating coverage. These mainly serve to promote economic efficiency; yet they are subject to the inevitable limits of any imperfect market. The legal system has therefore developed a second set of coordination devices, sometimes to remedy the imperfections of the market and sometimes to substitute more collective risk-distributional objectives for those pursued in unregulated private transactions. For example, a number of legally prescribed coordination devices promote broader loss spreading than the private market would achieve on its own. These devices are not necessarily efficient; they supersede rather than simply assist the market.

The first step in building a theory of coordination is to analyze the strengths and weaknesses of this developing system of coordinating insurance coverage. I shall evaluate both market and legal methods of coordination, showing where and why market methods fail, and how the legal system could do a better job of helping to remedy these market failures. I shall argue in particular that the courts need to promulgate much clearer standards for resolving coordination disputes so that the insurance market can anticipate judicial action through pricing and sales practices. In addition, I shall try to show how legislatures and regulators could play a more assertive and helpful role in setting such standards when the courts face difficulty in assisting the market in this way. Policymakers need to be much more conscious of their place in the system of coordination so that they can aid the market when it is in need of assistance and regulate it effectively when collective, risk-distributional goals rather than private incentives should predominate. Any approach to coordination should take the loss prevention, cost reduction, and loss distribution capacities of different insurance policies into account in setting coverage priorities and allocating rights among the insurers and insureds who are parties to them.

Such an approach would recognize that coordination problems not only raise straightforward questions about bilateral contract rights; they involve the rights and obligations of the parties to complex, multilateral risk-sharing arrangements. This conception of insurance relations and a theory of coordination should go hand in hand. My examination of this new conception of insurance relations is very much exploratory, and I want to be careful not to push the notion too far. It is intended as a complement, not as an alternative to the dominant understanding of insurance arrangements. Both ways of looking at insurance capture something important about it. But a more expansive understanding of insurance as part of a larger system of risk sharing and allocation will reveal how much potential the coordination of coverage has to serve economic and distributional goals and how that potential can be tapped.

To address these questions, I first discuss the ways in which coordinating coverage can serve the purposes of insurance law. With these purposes and their impact on coordination isolated, I then survey and analyze the market and legal devices that are used for coordination. In the course of this analysis I try to show how these devices have begun to reflect the multilateral aspects of insurance relations. This requires a good deal of immersion in somewhat technical insurance and legal devices for coordination. Finally, I make suggestions that would help the courts, regulators, and legislatures play a more effective role in coordinating coverage and that would enable them to contribute to the development of a theory of coordination.

THE PURPOSES OF COORDINATION

Businesses and individuals may find themselves with duplicative or overlapping coverage for a variety of reasons. I may have purchased two different kinds of insurance that happen to cover some of the same losses—health insurance and automobile PIP coverage commonly overlap. Or I may have purchased two policies of roughly the same kind from different insurers in the hope of obtaining double recovery or to guard against possible gaps in the coverage provided by both policies. For example, people sometimes have two or more health insurance policies covering many of the same risks. On the other hand, duplication may occur even when I have purchased only one policy. I may be covered by my own policy and as an additional insured or beneficiary by a policy purchased by someone else. This is often the case under various forms of automobile and homeowner's insurance. Finally, I may be covered by my own private insurance but also be eligible for benefits under a public or social insurance program such as Social Security or Medicare.

The coordination of insurance coverage in such cases performs both economic and risk-distributional functions. Coordination can promote economic efficiency in several ways. First, it can protect against the moral hazard of overinsurance by implementing the principle of indemnity—the idea that insurance is designed to guard against net loss, not to produce net gain. It can achieve this aim through rules that prohibit or limit stacking: that is, duplicating or combining coverage provided by two or more policies. Second, coordination can encourage optimal loss prevention by setting coverage priorities and channeling coverage responsibility through the policies most likely to create incentives for insureds to engage in prevention. Third, coordination can help reduce the cost of insurance by providing clear directives that preclude the need for litigation and thereby minimize administrative and legal costs. Finally, certain kinds of rules regarding coordination also may promote deliberation by insureds about available coverage options.

Coordination not only may promote economic efficiency; it may also be used to help achieve desired distributions of risk. It can do this in two ways: first, coordination can help to spread risk broadly by permitting the stacking of duplicative coverage; second, coordination can redistribute risk by setting priorities that channel responsibility away from policies covering certain groups of insureds and allocating that responsibility to other policies whose insureds will bear more of the redistributed risk. The latter then will subsidize the former. Because these risk-distributional aims often conflict with the operation of private incentives that produce economic efficiency, risk-distributional directives normally must originate in the legal system rather than in the private market. In order to understand how the system of coordination operates, we need first to have a more detailed idea of these purposes and the ways it can serve them.

Economic Goals

Protection against Overrecovery

The first purpose of coordination is to serve the principle of indemnity by preventing overrecovery by the insured. The principle holds that the purpose of insurance is reimbursement of loss, not the production of gain.[6] It is served whenever two or more sources of coverage are coordinated so that the insured receives, from all sources, no more than the amount of his loss.

There are two often-given justifications for the principle. The oldest is that it expresses a policy against wagering.[7] It is difficult to credit this justification with much current force since wagering of various sorts is now authorized by law and in some places is actually administered by government for profit. Probably this idea has been confused with the second justification for the principle, to which it is related. This is the need to guard against the moral hazard arising out of over-insurance. In this sense the principle of indemnity is one means of helping to optimize loss prevention, a purpose discussed below at length. If overinsurance were permitted, insureds would have an incentive to destroy insured property in order to collect insurance in excess of the property's value. This rationale does not rest on the evil of wagering, but on the opportunity and incentive to tamper with odds after a bet has been made. Thus, although moral hazard also affects life and liability insurance, the principle of indemnity rarely applies to these forms of coverage since the insured cannot capture any net gain by overinsuring.

Very little is required of a system of coordination for it to serve the principle of indemnity. Any of a variety of rules governing stacking, priorities, or contribution among policies will be satisfactory so long as the limit of the insured's total recovery is the amount of his loss. Any approach limiting recovery to an amount less than the insured's loss exceeds the demands of the principle of indemnity. At this point the approach must be understood to be serving other ends.

Optimal Loss Prevention

Coordination can promote optimal loss prevention by reducing the sum of the costs of loss prevention and insurance. As we have seen time and again, the key to promoting loss prevention through insurance is the nature of the risk classification and pricing system used. Setting premiums to reflect expected loss provides the insured with the incentive to compare the cost of coverage with the cost of taking safety measures that will reduce that cost. Promoting loss prevention through coordination, therefore, requires allocating coverage responsibility in a way that will maximize the loss prevention incentives produced by premium rates.

Risk-controlling capacity is by far the most important factor to be considered in fashioning a strategy of coordination that aims at loss prevention. Coverage responsiblity should be allocated to the insurance policy whose insureds have the most control over the risk in question. For example, suppose that the owner of a power boat is sued for injuries caused by its operation and that he is covered by two policies. One policy (call it policy A) is a homeowner's policy with standard coverage protecting the insured against liability of various sorts. A second policy (call it policy B) covers only liability arising out of the use of recreational water vehicles. Normally a homeowner's policy excludes coverage of some but not all uses of water vehicles. Let us assume here that the use in question is covered by both policies.

Loss prevention concerns would dictate that policy B bear primary coverage responsibility in this situation because a much higher percentage of holders of policy B will own power boats. As a result, premiums for policy B should be much more responsive to changes in power boating safety than premiums for policy A, because liability for power boating accidents is only one of many risks covered by the latter. An increase in claims and payments made under policy B would therefore have a more substantial impact on premiums and a concomitantly greater impact on loss prevention incentives. Policy A should therefore bear secondary responsibility only.

This hypothetical discussion, of course, raises issues more clearly than many duplicate coverage problems. Implementing a loss prevention coordination strategy may be more difficult in certain situations for a number of reasons. First, the differences between the loss controlling capacities of the insureds holding each type of policy may not be as straightforward as those in the above example. Suppose that one group of policyholders has little ability to exercise control over the safety of individual acts (power boating may involve certain unavoidable dangers) but can control the amount of an activity that it engages in. Loss prevention effects will be felt by allocating coverage responsibility to that group only if premium increases cause a shift to a relatively safer activity—for instance, from power boating to sailing or swimming. On the other hand, when one group of policyholders has activity level control and another group has act safety level control, the problem will be even more difficult. Allocating coverage responsibility to the former group may have more immediate but perhaps ultimately less efficient effects.

Second, the appropriate loss prevention strategy may depend not only on the degree of control exercised by those in the insurance pools in question, but on the amount of refinement in the risk classifications of each type of policy. In a related context, Guido Calabresi has called this the problem of "externalization due to insufficient subcategorization."[8] If a form of coverage uses little classification or is not sensitive to changes in claims experience through experience rating, the degree of control that might in the abstract be exercised by those who have that coverage is not very relevant. A given strategy of coordination will not affect their exercise of that control because premiums will not be responsive to variations in their claims experience. At best such a loss prevention strategy will affect the level of the activity engaged in, but not the safety of the activity itself.

Finally, in some cases it may be clear that, in the aggregate, each of two (or more) insurance pools will be equally good risk controllers. Each pool may tend to have equal control when different characteristics of the pools have differential effects on loss prevention. A common example of this phenomenon is the non-owned automobile problem. Omnibus liability coverage in standard automobile policies extends liability insurance to anyone driving the insured vehicle with the permission of an insured. Drive-other-cars coverage in the standard policy extends protection to the named insured and members of his family while driving a nonowned vehicle with its owner's permission. When suit is brought against the driver of a borrowed car, which liability policy should provide primary coverage, the owner's or the driver's?

Loss prevention concerns suggest that the owner's policy should be primary to the extent that proper maintenance, supervision, and careful lending decisions are the most important influences on safety; but the driver's policy should be primary to the extent that care and skill in operation are most significant. By making the owner's policy primary, the standard policy suggests that the owner is in the best overall position to exercise risk control. But this will not always be the case.

These considerations suggest that the choice of a coordination strategy properly emphasizing loss prevention will not always be easy. Ideally the market itself should arrive at strategies of coordination that create efficient loss prevention incentives and an optimal allocation of resources between safety and insurance. As we shall see later, however, when the market fails to coordinate efficiently or fails under some circumstances to coordinate at all, then legal decision makers must be called upon to confront the problems of fashioning a strategy of coordination that is effective at loss prevention.

Reducing the Cost of Insurance

Any system of insurance should be concerned with the costs of achieving its goals. Coordination of coverage can reduce costs in several ways. In any instance where coordination limits the amount of insurance actually available to the insured, it will help reduce the cost of coverage. The less coverage a policy provides in fact, the less it will cost. Further, when a system of coordination clearly and completely specifies coverage responsibilities and priorities, duplicate investigation and claims processing by each insurer involved are more easily avoidable. Finally, by providing clear guidelines about coverage responsibility, coordination can reduce the costs of uncertainty and the litigation that is necessary to clarify coverage responsibility. In fact, settling coordination questions in advance may be more important than the particular rule that does the settling. Once an approach to coordination is set, in the long run prices can be adjusted in accordance with it. An approach that leaves questions unsettled, often by slowly accumulating a body of judicial decisions governing coordination, will not be a satisfactory means of reducing costs until it has matured.

It is important, however, to note that while coordination obviously will help reduce the cost of coverage if its effect is to limit the amount afforded in any given case, the reductions are likely to benefit policyholders as a whole rather than the individuals whose coverage is coordinated. This is because an individual normally gets no discount on a second policy simply because he or she already has a first. Suppose that Susan decides to buy a policy from the Old Reliable Insurance Company. Susan then decides she wants a second policy, from Safety and Security Mutual, that overlaps the first. She may buy the Safety and Security policy because it covers other risks not covered by Old Reliable, because she believes (probably incorrectly) that she will be entitled to double recovery if she suffers a loss, or because the second policy is heavily subsidized.

The price of Susan's second policy is likely not to vary depending on whether she has the first, even though she may be unable to stack the two policies together in the event of a loss. Only when a potential coverage overlap is extremely common and the savings that coordination will produce for the insurer are highly predictable (in the case of exclusively excess coverage or insurance for a second family car, for instance) does the policyholder whose coverage is coordinated pay a reduced premium. This is even more obviously the case if Susan has purchased only one policy, but she is covered by another as an additional insured. The company from whom she buys her policy has no way of knowing the extent to which Susan is incidentally covered for the same risks under policies she has not purchased herself. It therefore has no way of lowering the price of her own policy.

In short, coordination helps to reduce the cost of insurance generally and to eliminate some unnecessary duplication of administrative and legal expenses. But it does not automatically help individual insureds to maximize the value of their insurance dollars.

Encouraging Deliberation about Coverage Options

As we have seen, encouraging informed choice about coverage options is a goal that runs through much of insurance law. It would be surprising if this concern were not at all reflected in the body of law governing coordination of coverage. Still, I note this possible goal here not because it should play an important part in a system of coordination, but because the principal justifications of some of the devices for coordination surveyed below seem to rest on the need to encourage deliberation.

In fact, however, if insurance is regarded by many purchasers as a highly technical and complex subject, then coordination questions are doubly so. Until coordination issues arise in concrete form, most people will be uninterested in anticipating and deliberating about them. This problem plagues many efforts to encourage informed choice about coverage options, whether concerning coordination or other issues. The perceived obscurity of the problems presented makes it very difficult to hold the applicant's attention long enough to allow deliberation. A few choices may reasonably be demanded of him; a long series of choices will only produce shots in the dark.

Realistically, we cannot expect deliberation by ordinary insureds to produce coordination, and we cannot expect policy provisions or legal rules regarding coordination to produce very much deliberation. The insured will engage in much the same thought process regardless of what the relevant policy or statute says about coordination. He will think mainly about how much coverage of a given type he wishes to purchase. Whether and how that coverage may be combined or otherwise linked with other coverage will not often influence the decision whether to purchase or the combination of coverage to purchase. In large measure an overall strategy of coordination must come ready-made to the insured—he will not construct a strategy to suit his needs except by choosing the major forms of coverage to purchase. Further, the strategy or strategies of coordination that are adopted can be formulated largely without regard for their effect on individual choices that might fine-tune an insured's package of insurance protection. Such choices will be made without being significantly influenced by these strategies.

Risk Distribution

The demand that a system of coordinated coverage promote appropriate levels of risk distribution poses a problem similar to the dilemma that confronts insurance law as a whole. On the one hand, loss prevention is constantly a concern of those fashioning an insurance system. Risk classification and the many other devices that deal with the moral hazard of insurance are directed at this goal. On the other hand, the essence of insurance is risk distribution. Without the distribution of risk, and the distribution of losses that naturally follows it, the system would be pointless. Yet the problems of how much distribution to have and how to arrive at that determination are consistently troubling.

Individual transactions in the private insurance market provide in rough measure the amount of risk distribution that people individually desire. But legal promotion of greater spreading or a different distribution of risk may be justified for one or more of the reasons discussed in chapter 2: the nonrational character of people's risk-taking decisions, collective preferences for other people's security that cannot be satisfied through free market transactions, and the dynamic character of people's desires, among other reasons. These are largely utilitarian concerns, for they turn mainly on people's failure to purchase levels of coverage that would increase their own welfare.

Of course, these justifications for nonvoluntary forms of distribution do not always apply. Some would charge that it is undemocratic to promote risk distribution through legal devices. Moreover, often people are so risk-averse that there is no need to encourage them to obtain additional protection against risk. But in other settings—depending on the salience of the risk, the information they have about it, or the way risk-safety issues are posed—people may act as risk preferrers. In such cases promoting more extensive risk distribution may well be justified. That purpose can be pursued in this field through rules of coordination that permit stacking together the coverage of two or more policies so long as total recovery does not exceed loss. In this way the amount of the loss covered by the second policy is spread among all its policyholders instead of being shouldered by the insured alone.

Legal regulation of coordination also may be designed not simply to promote greater risk spreading in general, but to achieve risk redistribution. Coordination can serve as a redistributional tool in two ways. First, if recognizable groups tend to have duplicative or overlapping coverage, then rules of law permitting stacking, regardless of policy terms prohibiting it, are redistributional at least in the short run. Premiums charged the subsidized group eventually may increase; but only if that group can separately be charged extra will the redistributional effect be entirely neutralized. Thus, greater risk spreading itself can be redistributional if the market cannot efficiently charge those who derive special benefit from that spreading.

Consider the power boat example discussed earlier. If coverage under the recreational water vehicle policy and the homeowner's policy can be stacked despite policy provisions providing otherwise, then risk is partially distributed away from power boat owners and shifted to homeowners not owning power boats. The former are subsidized by the latter. Eventually the power boat owners may be charged additional premiums for their homeowner's coverage, but only if the cost of separately classifying them is worth the economic gain it produces. Second, similar effects can occur even if stacking is prohibited. Allocation of coverage responsiblity to one of two duplicative policies will have redistributional effects if a distinct subgroup of its policyholders tends to suffer the loss in question. For instance, if exclusive coverage responsiblity were allocated to the homeowner's policy (notwithstanding loss prevention concerns), risk would be redistributed away from power boat owners and shifted to homeowners not owning power boats.

Redistributional effects may be the result of a coordination strategy deliberately designed to achieve them or may be the by-product of a strategy designed to accomplish other ends. For instance, Social Security, workers' compensation, and Medicare sometimes have coverage responsibility that is primary to no-fault automobile PIP and uninsured motorist coverage in order to minimize the cost of these auto coverages. But the effect of this allocation is that wage earners subsidize the risk taking of drivers and their passengers. To the extent that these groups do not coincide, a redistribution of risk occurs.

Although risk spreading and redistributional issues such as this run through all insurance law, they arise in a special way here. Their resolution depends not only on the role of distributional values in the overall system of insurance, but also on the special character of coordination problems. Two factors seem especially relevant to any determination of the proper role of a system of coordination in promoting risk spreading or redistribution: (1) the relation between loss prevention and the different kinds of distributional effects that can be produced by coordination; and (2) whether a given strategy of coordination contradicts deliberate choices already made by insureds. As is often the case, neither of these factors yields a precise test for the use of risk-distributional aims in fashioning legal rules that overturn market decisions about coordination. Rather, these considerations incline a decision in one direction or the other by directing attention to the presence or absence of potentially significant influences on decisions.

The Relation between Loss Prevention and the Distributional Effects of Coordination

Because of the tension between these two goals, as loss prevention concerns decline, risk-distribution aims become more legitimate. This notion is a corollary of the ever-present concern of insurance with the problem of moral hazard: insurance reduces loss prevention incentives. However, sometimes noninsurance mechanisms create especially effective safety incentives; then risk distribution may be a more legitimate concern. The extreme case is life insurance. The incentive to preserve life is so strong that, once the requirement of an insurable interest is satisfied, there is heavy emphasis on distribution: there are no real legal limits on the amount of life insurance coverage or number of policies permitted, and the practical limits are also high. In effect, risk spreading is permitted to take priority.

At a lesser extreme are forms of insurance like uninsured motorist (UM) coverage. UM coverage protects the insured in the event that he is injured by a judgment-proof (insolvent and uninsured) driver. The insured may recover from his own insurer upon showing that the uninsured driver is legally liable for the insured's losses but cannot pay them. It is unlikely that such coverage decreases very much whatever incentives already exist for the insured to operate his vehicle safely. Concern for his own safety and for his liability premium rates ought to be a great enough safety incentive to render loss prevention an insubstantial issue in connection with this form of coverage. In short, there is little moral hazard associated with uninsured motorist coverage. Concern with broad distribution of losses caused by uninsured motorists can therefore be correspondingly greater. In this respect, allowing the stacking of coverage available under two or more UM policies in order to promote risk spreading makes considerable sense.

On the other hand, sometimes noninsurance mechanisms do not provide especially strong loss prevention incentives. Then the legitimacy of distributional aims should depend on the strength of the incentives produced by insurance mechanisms. As we saw earlier, channeling coverage responsiblity through a form of insurance that uses unrefined risk classification instead of a form with relatively refined classification is likely to reduce loss prevention incentives. This was the point of the power boat example used above.

But a decision to shift the focus of responsibility from one unrefined classification system to another will have less effect on incentives. Suppose that coverage responsibility could be allocated either to privately financed but crudely classified private insurance or to a social-security-type system of financing. The choice will have little effect on the level of safety at which the insured activity is conducted. Rather, it will affect only the amount of the activity that is engaged in. If through social insurance the public as a whole bears the risk posed by the activity in question, the level of that activity will be greater than under a private insurance scheme. If privately financed insurance bears primary coverage responsibility, the risks posed by the activity will be borne largely by those engaging in it, and some optimizing of the costs and benefits of engaging in the activity at all will occur. But the safety of the activity itself will not be noticeably affected since premiums for insurance covering the activity will not be sensitive to changes in the loss experience of those who engage in it.

All this pertains to the setting of coverage priorities among two or more sources of coverage. But refinement in the risk classifications of two sources of coverage is also relevant to the permissibility of stacking the sources together. If classification in both forms of coverage is refined, then in the long run allowing them to be stacked will not dilute loss prevention incentives. Higher levels of coverage may be encouraged, but because premium rates will reflect stackability, the loss prevention incentives embodied in each source of coverage will be preserved.

If one form of coverage is only crudely rated, however, permitting it to be stacked onto the other may reduce loss prevention incentives since rates in the former will not closely reflect expected loss. Thus, if health insurance and automobile personal injury protection benefits can be stacked, any additional moral hazard that is created derives largely from the absence of careful (and periodically revised) rating of these forms of coverage rather than from the permissibility of stacking itself. In sum, depending on the kind of coverage involved, sometimes risk-distributional aims can be pursued without very much sacrifice of loss prevention incentives. On other occasions, however, the two goals may conflict, and a choice between them will have to be made.

Whether a Strategy of Coordination Contradicts Deliberate Choices Already Made by Insureds

Promoting risk spreading through coordination threatens the autonomy of policyholders: it may produce more insurance coverage than they have chosen to purchase. Whether they actually pay for this extra coverage depends on the state of the market, though in fact they are almost certain to bear some if not most of the additional cost. It would seem, then, that the legitimacy of promoting spreading through coordination also should depend in part on how deliberately insureds have chosen to limit the extent of their coverage. The less clear the message sent by that choice, the greater the legitimate scope of distributional considerations.

The least deliberately chosen forms of coverage are those that are mandatory or effectively so: automobile liability and (often) uninsured motorist coverage, as well as fire insurance on mortgaged real estate. There can be no deliberation about the minimum amount of such coverage, and, at least as regards the automobile insurance, popular consent to the requirement almost certainly exists. Adjustments at the margin to enable coordination to serve distributional aims—for example, by permitting stacking these forms of coverage—seem least objectionable in cases like this. It does not follow, however, that such adjustments are the best way to promote risk distribution. Requiring higher minimum coverage certainly would be a more straightforward approach. But sometimes it is not politically feasible.

Next on the continuum fall those forms of coverage that are not mandatory, but whose purchase is not the product of careful deliberation either. Some of these are ordinarily included in package policies or suggested as endorsements at the time a basic type of coverage is purchased. The coverage may be sold quickly over the phone or in a hurried interview. As a consequence, sometimes the insured makes a split-second decision or is given no real choice, and he is covered. But the amount of coverage purchased is not considered in detail, and its scope may not be well understood at all. Students in courses in insurance law require five or ten minutes of discussion before they begin to understand the way that automobile liability, uninsured motorist, and personal injury protection coverage mesh, even in broad outline. The ordinary insurance consumer certainly will not be quicker to grasp the purposes of these forms of coverage, and often insurance agents' explanations are perfunctory or confused. The idea that the community of policyholders with only minimum coverage somehow has its intentions ignored when an insured is allowed to stack together two such policies presupposes an intention on the part of purchasers that never really exists. Some are informed and have truly assented to purchasing only minimal coverage; others have only an incomplete understanding of the scope of the coverage they have purchased.

A rationale, however, that reaches beyond the notion that there is implied assent to stacking is necessary to support the importation of risk distribution concerns into areas where careful deliberation is more likely. Paternalistic rationales generally come to the fore here. For example, there is growing evidence that ordinary statistical intuitions are quite faulty.[9] If people tend to undervalue very low probability risks, then a coordination principle that neutralizes this error may be in order. The risk of a judgment in excess of a basic policy limit is just such a low probability risk. This low probability is the reason that the first $20,000 of liability or other coverage, for example, costs so much more than an additional $20,000. If less of this additional coverage is purchased than would be statistically warranted in light of aggregate individual risk aversion, principles of coordination favoring additional distribution through stacking could be an obvious antidote. A complementary approach would encourage greater use of deductibles or coinsurance provisions in policies that normally do not carry them. The result would be less extensive spreading of small losses, and more extensive spreading of large ones.

These then are the outlines of the major purposes of coordination. At this stage it will be useful to underscore a point that will help make the transition to the next subject—the devices actually used for coordination. The purposes of coordination outlined above not only describe what a system of coordination can achieve; they also reflect a conception of insurance that is more than a simple relation between individual insurers and insureds. The notion that economic efficiency can and should be served by coordination implies that insurers may have claims, vis-à-vis each other, to particular rules of coverage priority, since pursuing efficiency requires setting such priorities. And the idea that coordination can and should further risk-distributional aims suggests that risk-sharing relations among insureds should be given consideration in coordinating coverage. Indeed, the assertion that coordination can promote economic efficiency and appropriate forms of risk distribution is a way of saying that there are rights (or claims or entitlements—call them what one will) between insurers and among insureds, even when there are no formal contracts between insurers or among insureds.

That noncontracting parties might have legal rights or obligations to each other should not be particularly surprising, although this way of thinking about insurance relations is unusual. Such legal obligations are imposed all the time through the law of torts and through other noncontractual forms of civil liability. Taken together, however, the combination of contractual and noncontractual relations that is emerging in this field hints at an understanding of insurance that may be a bit surprising until it becomes familiar: the notion that insurance is a set of multilateral risk-shifting arrangements that make use of both contractual and noncontractual sources of obligation.

THE DEVICES OF COORDINATION

We now turn to the devices by which the purposes of coordination can be achieved. Because not every device is capable of achieving all the purposes of coordination, we need to look carefully at the kinds of objectives each is best at pursuing. There are two very different ways to coordinate coverage. First, coordination can be directed through contractual devices produced by the private market. These include: (1) differentiation between the interests and risks covered by different kinds of policies, (2) policy provisions that govern coordination when policies duplicate or overlap, and (3) agreements among insurers specifying coverage priorities and responsibilities in the event of duplication. Second, coordination can be regulated through mechanisms supplied by the legal system: (1) judicial rules governing coordination when market devices fail, and (2) statutory or administrative mandates superseding market mechanisms and substituting mandatory directives regarding coordination.

The market devices often do not achieve perfect coordination, and sometimes the coordination they do achieve is objectionable for other reasons. As a consequence, we must look not only at how the market devices operate, but also at how they fail. And we must look not only at how the legal methods achieve the goals of coordination when the market does not do so on its own, but how the legal system might better achieve these goals.

Market Devices

The most important characteristic of contractual devices for coordination to be surveyed below is that their potential is limited by the costs of reaching and defining agreements that embody them. For example, it would cost money for ordinary, individual policyholders to search for coverage that is coordinated. They would have to scrutinize policy provisions in several policies to see how they mesh or hire experts to fashion an appropriate package of protections for them. Commercial enterprises that use insurance brokers may find it worthwhile to customize a package of carefully coordinated coverage. Individual insureds are likely to find it too costly to do this.

The alternative is for insurers to provide ready-made coordination. This approach, however, also is costly. It would require including detailed coordination provisions in all policies. But this strategy cuts against the trend toward simplified policy language, and it can be only haphazardly successful because the coordination provisions in two or more policies will not always be consistent. A different

approach circumvents this problem by providing for coordination through cooperative agreements among insurers about the coverage each type of policy should
provide and about methods of coordination when policies nevertheless overlap.
But reaching and defining such agreements also may be costly.

In short, the insurance market provides for only imperfect coordination. Since
coordination is not likely in any direct way to increase the attractiveness of coverage to most potential customers, its main benefit lies in the avoidance of litigation
that results when coordination fails. But risking occasional litigation is worthwhile because the cost of fashioning an airtight system of coordination in the private market would exceed its benefits. In economic terms, efforts are made to
coordinate in advance until the costs of doing so exceed the benefits of coordinating. Once that point is reached, no further private coordination occurs, and the
legal system must coordinate when coverages conflict or coordination has failed
in some other fashion. This inevitable limit is reflected in the coordination devices that the market has generated.

Coverage Differentiation

By far the most straightforward method of coordinating coverage is for insurers to draft coverage language so that different policies cover different interests and
risks and therefore cannot overlap. Earlier in the history of insurance, such coverage differentiation was easily accomplished. Marine insurance did not (and still
does not) overlap fire insurance; fire and life insurance have never overlapped. As
the forms of insurance have proliferated, however, the possibility of overlapping
has increased. Business interruption coverage and fire insurance must be deliberately drafted to cover different interests, or they may overlap. Umbrella, or excess,
coverage must be designed to take effect only if the insured has purchased other
primary coverage. Homeowner's liability and automobile liability coverage may
be structured to overlap or simply to dovetail, and so forth.

Although this approach is a sensible way to achieve some coordination, it
has unavoidable limitations. First, it obviously cannot help coordinate coverage available under concurrent policies providing the same kind of insurance—two health or automobile policies, for example. Second, unanticipated
issues may confound the effort to coordinate when claims actually are made.
The most noteworthy recent example involves the liability insurance of asbestos manufacturers. Over the years most manufacturers purchased a series of
policies from a series of insurers, each covering bodily injury occurring during
the policy period. The policy periods in the policies appeared to be coordinated
in that there was neither duplication nor omission of coverage—the day one
policy terminated, the next one began.

But when suits against the insured manufacturers (and business users) of asbestos began to be brought, which policy or policies provided coverage was unclear. The meaning of the term *bodily injury* had not been satisfactorily defined. Asbestosis, for example, has a latency period of about twenty years. Each inhalation causes bodily injury, though the disease does not mature and manifest itself for years thereafter. The provisions of the liability insurance policies involved provided little guidance because liability for diseases with very long latency periods was not anticipated when the policies were drafted.[10]

The second shortcoming of industrywide policy differentiation results from competition among insurers and from the nature of consumer demand. Auto and homeowner's policies, for example, are now packaged combinations of different forms of insurance including liability, property damage, medical payments or personal injury protection, and uninsured motorist coverage. As the types of insurance increase and the scope of coverage included within particular policies expands, the probability of overlapping among policies increases. Yet the desirability of providing coverage within one policy rather than two favors expanding coverage. The tendency of insurers to seek a competitive advantage by providing expanded coverage is thus at war with any method of coordination that relies on sharp distinctions among different forms of coverage to avoid duplication. As coverage expands, differentiation between policies can be maintained only by devising separate policy provisions prescribing methods of coordination in the event of overlapping with other coverage. At this point the simple guideline that different kinds of policies cover entirely different risks and interests is no longer adequate. Coordination through coverage differentiation has reached its limit.

It is interesting, however, that when coordination by differentiation among coverages is successful, a bilateral model of insurance relations accurately describes what occurs. The insured has a series of separate contractual relations with different insurers, the sum of which exactly equals the scope of coverage protecting him. Each relation is entirely separate and independent of the others; a dispute related to one policy can be resolved without reference to any other policy. The bilateral model can account for the resolution of such disputes without recourse to any notions concerning rights and obligations between insurers or among insureds. Neither economic nor distributional goals need be considered in resolving coverage disputes. The only question is the meaning of the policy under scrutiny. When insurance begins to proliferate and overlap, however, the coverage available under separate policies cannot simply be aggregated. Other methods of coordination must be called into service, and a more expansive conception of insurance relations is required.

Policy Provisions Governing Coordination

The next type of coordination also is provided for by contract between insurer and insured. Policy provisions can govern coordination by indicating coverage priorities when two or more policies in which they are contained both supply potential coverage. A variety of standard provisions perform this function. Although these other-insurance, subrogation, and limits-of-liability provisions all play roles in coordinating coverage, often they are discussed as though they do not arise out of this same need. They do, of course, foster coordination in different ways. Yet each involves not only the basic insurer-insured relation, but also the multilateral risk-sharing arrangement of which that relation is a part.

Other-Insurance Clauses. The most notable policy provision governing duplicate coverage is the standard other-insurance clause found in policies of almost all kinds except life insurance. There are three ways in which an other-insurance clause may provide for coordination. The clause may indicate that the policy shall escape entirely if other coverage is available, that it shall provide only excess coverage after the other policy limits are exhasuted, or that it shall contribute on a pro rata basis with other policies.[11]

It is rarely noticed that at least in theory the market can select the type of provision that will mesh best with different loss prevention and distribution goals. An escape provision can be used when loss prevention concerns are great and premiums for the policy containing the clause are not carefully risk classified. Then other policies, presumably accompanied by more carefully classified premiums, will bear coverage responsibility. The insured will bear any excess above policy limits. An excess clause can be used when one policy has superior loss prevention capacity than others it may meet, but distributional concerns are strong enough to warant stacking the coverage of both. A pro rata clause can be used when both insurance pools are equally good risk controllers and distributional goals warrant stacking.

Often such clauses work well. For example, because they rarely contain escape clauses, most automobile liability insurance policies are stackable. One policy is primary and the other excess, or they provide for prorated responsibility. In a simpler world such provisions alone would be fairly effective at coordinating coverage. But in the more complicated settings in which the clauses actually operate, they have limitations. First, using such clauses to promote loss prevention is not as simple as it may appear. Whether the insureds who have purchased a particular policy are better risk controllers than the holders of overlapping policies is obviously a relative, not an absolute notion. Insureds under one policy may be better risk controllers relative to insureds under some other policies, but they may be worse relative to others. To solve this problem, it would take not just one other-

TABLE 1

First Clause	Second Clause	Clauses Consistent?
Escape	Escape	No
Escape	Excess	Sometimes*
Escape	Pro rata	Yes
Excess	Excess	No
Excess	Pro rata	Sometimes*
Pro rata	Pro rata	Yes

*When an escape clause is paired with an excess or pro rata clause, the policy containing the former normally escapes because the latter provides that there must be other valid and collectible insurance before it applies. Another way to understand this is to see that the escape clause exhibits a general intent to avoid liability in the event of duplication, while the other two reflect a general intent to share it. The most difficult cases involve the pairing of pro rata and excess in different ways. The courts are split on the question whether such a pair is consistent. When they are found to be consistent, the policy with the pro rata clause usually first pays up to its limits, perhaps because it is the only one of the three types reflecting an intent to bear at least some primary liability even when it meets other coverage.

insurance clause in each policy, but a whole series, each indicating whether the policy is to escape, bear excess, or pro rata liability when it meets a series of specified types of other insurance. Few policies attempt to construct the complicated matrix of alternatives that would be required to make this approach work.

The second limitation is that other-insurance clauses function best when only one of the policies applicable to the loss contains such a clause. If only one of every two overlapping policies contained an other-insurance clause, the policy containing the clause would pay only a pro rata or excess share, or escape liability altogether, depending on the clause involved. It takes no great imagination, however, to see that in most cases all the policies involved will contain other-insurance clauses. These clauses normally must be read together in order to determine coverage responsibility. Several pairs of the three types of clauses are perfectly consistent and yield clear priotiries. Others pairs are not consistent, and combinations of more than two also may be difficult to reconcile. Table 1 shows the combinations of other-insurance clauses that are and are not consistent.

The problem is that other-insurance clauses normally do not condition coverage responsibility on the kind of clause found in the other policy because they could not always be successful at doing this. Each clause could still provide that it was secondary when it met other clauses. As a result, each other-insurance clause often ends up playing Alphonse to the other's Gaston. Competing escape clauses, for example, are obviously irreconcilable, as are competing excess clauses.

When the other-insurance clauses in two policies are consistent, the process of coordination is not complicated. Though a relation among three parties is being untangled, the untangling takes place without reference to any relation between the two insurers. There are simply two bilateral relations at work. Each other-insurance clause speaks only to the insured, by way of reference to the insured's second insurance interest. The insurers have no direct rights or responsibilities to each other. Each other-insurance clause is merely a statement of the insurer's obligations to the insured in the event of a specified condition—the existence of other insurance against the loss in question.

When the other-insurance clauses in two policies conflict, however, focusing on the two separate insurer-insured relations leads nowhere. Each insurer has attempted to place itself in a position of secondary responsibility only or none at all. The individual contracts in question do not solve the problem, they cause it. Yet on the face of it there is nothing oppressive or objectionable about the clause in either insurance policy when considered separately. Either would be valid and enforceable were it not for the coincidence of its conflict with the other. Nor is there any fully satisfactory way to solve the problem merely by adjusting each insurer-insured relation separately. Drafting clauses to anticipate the provisions of corresponding clauses would require extremely detailed elaboration of the policy's coverage responsibility in the face of each possible corresponding clause. But conflicts between one policy's treatment of each possible combination and another's could still occur since each could provide that it would be secondary even if the other did the same. At this point the capacity of other-insurance provisions to coordinate coverage is exhausted, and the legal system must provide a solution to the conflict between clauses. [12]

Subrogation. Subrogation is the process by which an insurer recovers from a third party the amount the insurer has paid its insured. [13] The insurer is subrogated to the insured by succeeding to the insured's rights against the third party, who usually has injured the insured and is or could be sued by him. For example, if Stanley is injured by Michael, Stanley's hospital and medical expenses may be paid by Blue Cross–Blue Shield. Stanley's Blue Cross–Blue Shield policy then will provide that it is subrogated to Stanley's rights against Michael to the extent of its prior payment to Stanley.

Subrogation coordinates coverage by making the third party—Michael in our example—or his liability insurer primarily responsible for the insured's loss and providing the insurer with reimbursement for its expenditures when such reimbursement is available.[14] Rights of subrogation thus transform the insurer's role as an insurer into something like that of guarantor of third-party obligations to the insured. If the third party can pay, then ultimately the insurer avoids its own obligation to do so.

Subrogation may further a number of economic goals. It prevents the insured from obtaining a net gain by transferring to the insurer part of the insured's right to recover from the tortfeasor. In this sense subrogation advances the principle of indemnity. But subrogation goes further since it is directed at assuring that the third party who is liable to the insured bears ultimate responsibility for the insured's loss. In this sense it is also concerned with loss prevention. And by affording the insurer a right to reimbursement from the tortfeasor for payments made to the insured, subrogation also may help to reduce the cost of insurance in the long run.

Like other-insurance clauses, rights of subrogation recognize that individual insurance policies are working parts in a larger system of risk sharing and allocation. But while subrogation is obviously a powerful tool, its single-minded use can result in a very monolithic and clumsy approach to coordination. A standard subrogation provision automatically affords the insurer a set of rights against the insured and third parties liable to him. For several reasons, the exercise of these rights may not always be consistent with some of the purposes of coordination. First, although subrogation may help to reduce the cost of the subrogated insurer's coverage, it increases the cost of insurance covering parties held liable to subrogated insurers. The price of making this transfer from one sizable insurance pool to another is the cost of litigating subrogation suits. Some insurers have agreed to arbitrate subrogation claims in order to reduce these costs; but even arbitration is not without cost.

Second, subrogation provisions in insurance policies normally do not distinguish between those situations in which subrogation can realistically hope to influence loss prevention and those in which it cannot. Allowing subrogation against insured defendants will have more effect when the form of the defendant's coverage is very different from that of the original insured and the defendant is in fact a relatively good risk controller. Otherwise subrogation will merely shift a loss from one good or bad risk controller to another in a similar class. Subrogating auto medical payments or collision insurers to the rights of their insureds against other drivers is a notable example of the problem. Whether the cost of such subrogation actions is worthwhile depends very much on how sensitive automobile liability premiums are to such claims. No-fault systems, with one goal the reduction of administrative and legal costs, often foreclose subrogation rights and thereby sacrifice the ability to fine-tune loss prevention incentives in order to avoid just such costs.

Third, indiscriminate use of subrogation obviously ignores the distributional differences between subrogating against insured and uninsured defendants.[15] Subrogating against insured defendants incurs litigation costs in order to shift responsibility from one sizable risk-sharing pool to another. Whether incurring this cost is worthwhile depends on the strength of the loss prevention effects of the subrogation arrangement in question. But subrogating against uninsured defendants, whatever its loss prevention effects, shifts loss out of broad channels of distribution and focuses it on a single party. In such cases the benefits of loss spreading are entirely ignored.

Finally, subrogation may impair full indemnity if the insurer's right to reimbursement is exercised by making a claim against the insured's recovery from the third party who injured him. In such cases, if the insurer is entitled to reimbursement off the top of this recovery, the insured's net recovery may not fully compensate him for his losses.

Limits-of-Liability Provisions. We have already seen that other-insurance provisions typically govern what is known as "inter-policy" stacking, by permitting or limiting the stacking of coverage under two separate policies. On occasion, however, the opportunity for "intra-policy" stacking also arises. For example, package automobile policies often cover more than one vehicle. In the event of a loss that is payable under the liability, personal injury protection, or uninsured motorist coverage contained in the policy, the insured might claim that the policy limits applicable to each vehicle should be stacked in order to determine the total available coverage. Under this view a policy providing $20,000 in uninsured motorist coverage, and applicable to two owned vehicles, actually would afford $40,000 of coverage.

On the face of it this is a plausible claim, but the terms of the typical limits-of-liability provision appear to preclude this result.[16] Such clauses provide that the limit of liability stated in the policy to be applicable to each person is the limit of the company's liability for injury sustained by one person as the result of any one accident.[17] When the limit for each person is stated to be $20,000, then no more than that coverage is available. The insurance industry's argument in favor of such limitations is straightforward: if the insured desires $40,000 of coverage, he should buy it directly instead of trying to obtain it indirectly by stacking coverage that is not intended to be stacked.

However, as we shall see when we explore judicially created devices for coordination, arguments attacking the validity of limits-of-liability clauses frequently succeed. The main appeal of such arguments, obviously, is distributional. Limits-of-liability clauses inhibit risk spreading, in order to encourage more careful deliberation about coverage and to make pricing actuarially sound. When clear drafting has not made the latter two purposes secure—and sometimes even when it has—the judicial preference for broad spreading often supersedes them.

Inter-Insurer Agreements

As the forms of coverage have proliferated and the number of insured individuals and institutions has increased, the devices for coordination described above have proved unwieldy. Industry coordination through differentiation among policy types has achieved only very rough coordination; the use of policy provisions to coordinate has provided additional assistance, but this approach has encountered limits of its own. In order to circumvent some of these problems, several sets of guiding principles have been promulgated by groups of insurers to promote cooperation and coordination in cases of duplicative or overlapping coverage.

Of the several sets of guiding principles, by far the most significant for our purposes are those governing first-party property losses.[18] Subscribed to by six trade associations in 1963, these principles specify coverage responsibilities in the event of the overlapping of coverage provided by subscribing companies. The principles are designed not to "operate to reduce recovery to the insured below that which would have been obtained under any policy or policies covering the risk" in question.[19]

In disputes between insurers, the principles supersede any other-insurance clauses contained in the policies involved. In structure, however, the principles resemble other-insurance clauses in prescribing priorities among policies. But the principles are much more detailed than other-insurance clauses; they leave less room for uncertainty as to the proper allocation of coverage responsibility. And because they are the product of agreement among insurers, there can be no conflict between different principles, as there can be between other-insurance clauses. Each insurer has subscribed to exactly the same principles of coordination: when prescribed priorities are equal, the policies contribute on a pro rata basis.

The fundamental notion that appears to underlie the coverage priorities prescribed by the guiding principles is what might be called the "specificity-of-purpose" principle. Insurance covering a specifically described individual article or object at a designated location is primary to any other insurance. Insurance covering a specifically described individual article or object without designation of location is excess as to the above-described coverage but primary to any other. Insurance covering a specifically described group of articles or objects has a lower priority, and so forth. Detailed conditions assisting interpretation of the principles are included, along with twenty-eight pages of numerical examples illustrating their application.

By adopting this specificity-of-purpose principle, the guiding principles recognize an approach to coordination that has a relatively consistent aim. A policy specifically describing a risk, other things being equal, is more likely than a less specific policy to afford special rather than general purpose coverage. Premiums for the more specific policy will therefore be more responsive to changes in loss rates and, as a result, will have greater capacity to influence loss prevention behavior by insureds.

The very isolation of a single principle suggests, however, that the guiding principles have a limited view of the purposes of coordination. They naturally are concerned primarily with loss prevention, channeling liability through that group of policyholders most dominantly concerned with the risk in question. They are secondarily concerned with providing a clear directive about allocating responsibility in the case of potential conflicts between policies. Other factors do not appear to be very influential in shaping the guidelines. This seems the almost inevitable result of an agreement among insurance companies, which are, after all, likely to be more eager to refine their actuarial calculations and to avoid costly litigation than to reconcile these needs with distributional concerns. Finally, the use of inter-insurer agreements to coordinate coverage is hampered by the obvious difficulty of assuring that insurers subscribe to the agreement and that insurers subscribing actually follow it in practice. The guiding principles, for example, are applicable only to certain kinds of first-party losses and have not been universally adopted. Further, a number of insurance professionals suspect that while the claims departments of home offices adhere to them, personnel in the field pay less attention to the principles than might be expected. Their effectiveness in promoting coordination is thereby reduced.

Legal Devices

The strength and weaknesses of the devices we have just surveyed help to demonstrate that the private insurance market provides for coordination only when the benefits of coordination exceed its costs. At some point almost every device exhausts its power, and the legal system must be called upon to supply the necessary coordination. Because market devices mainly make use of bilateral contracts to achieve coordination, their capacity to reflect the multilateral character of the insurance arrangements they create is limited. The potential of legal devices in this regard is much greater, but this potential has been only partially realized.

Two reasons for legal as opposed to market coordination should be distinguished. First, the legal system can coordinate coverage when the cost of providing coordination through contractual devices is prohibitively high. Legal intervention in such cases should be designed to substitute for the market by promoting economic efficiency after the market's capacity to do so has run out. Second, in order to further distributional aims, legal devices can be used to supersede the arrangements that are or would be made by the private market in the absence of legal intervention. In such cases efficiency is sacrificed in order to achieve a fairer or more desirable distribution of risk.

The courts, legislatures, and insurance commissioners all participate in this process. The courts are called upon to resolve problems of coordination when the private market has authority to coordinate but has not succeeded in doing so. Judicially supplied coordination, therefore, almost always is displaceable by private agreement. Although the solution arrived at is mandatory in the dispute before the court, the parties to policies providing identical kinds of coverage are free to provide by contract in the future for alternative forms of coordination. Legislative and regulatory directives governing coordination, on the other hand, usually are not displaceable. They tend to be mandatory for all the forms of coverage to which they apply.

In my opinion the most satisfactory explanation for this division of labor is traceable to the difference between the purposes the two forms of coordination are designed to achieve. Because generally the courts accept whatever coordination the market actually achieves, they are logically committed to acting mainly as a substitute for the market when it fails. Sometimes distributional calculations enter their decisions, but only when market devices result in conflict that requires judicial resolution. The courts rarely intervene when the market approach to coordination works. The displaceable directives upon which the courts rely reflect this priority of the market. On the other hand, legislative and regulatory devices often are more concerned with distributional goals. They are sometimes imposed even when the market seems to be functioning smoothly. Because transactions in the private market can circumvent distributional directives that are only optional, legislative and regulatory standards tend to be mandatory and nondisplaceable.

Although this general arrangement makes sense, the entire process could be improved in several ways. The courts should recognize their place in the overall scheme and strive to generate precise rules that will facilitate the functioning of the market. Legislatures should consider more extensive use of displaceable standards that supplant judicial efforts which are not effective. And insurance commissioners should play a more active role on both fronts. The system's potential for improvement is revealed in the following analysis.

Judicial Coordination

When private coordination fails, the insured and his insurers must resort to the courts, which have developed their own methods of coordinating the coverage involved in multiparty disputes. The need for judicial action arises in several contexts. By examining each, we can evaluate the success of judicial action in this field and determine the sense in which the legal system has begun to recognize an expansive, multilateral conception of insurance relations.

The Failure of Coverage Differentiation. The courts sometimes are called upon to determine the scope of policies that overlap or conflict because attempts at coverage differentiation have failed. For instance, in the asbestos coverage cases mentioned earlier, the courts have had to determine which of several liability policies issued to asbestos manufacturers over the years provide coverage. Most courts have adopted an exposure theory, by reading policies so that those in effect at the time of the claimant's exposure to asbestos provide coverage, regardless of the time when asbestos-related disease actually is manifested. In *Keene Corp. v. INA,* the U.S. Court of Appeals for the District of Columbia decided that there was a triple trigger of coverage, holding that insurers whose policies were in effect at exposure, during the period of latency, or at the time of manifestation are jointly and severally liable.[20]

Over the long term, the exposure and triple-trigger theories would have similar economic effects, so long as the insured has purchased a series of uninterrupted policies that are never terminated. If a manifestation theory were adopted, however, then very different and undesirable effects might result. Insurers could thereafter refuse to offer coverage against future liability, thereby avoiding liability for exposures that have already occurred but have not yet been reduced to claims. Defendants then would be left without coverage and without any way to obtain it. As Judge Bazelon put it in *Keene,* "If we were to hold that only the manifestation of disease can trigger coverage, the insurance companies would have to bear only a fraction of Keene's total liability for asbestos-related disease."[21] Since the scope of potential liability for asbestos-related disease is so great, this approach could threaten every manufacturer with actual bankruptcy.[22] The result could be a serious threat to the distribution of asbestos-related losses. The exposure and triple-trigger theories neutralize this threat. It should be recognized, however, that because of the potential liability of several insurers under these theories (because of exposure spanning several policy periods), the cost of allocating coverage responsibility among insurers may be high.[23]

Coordination decisions that take prevention and distributional effects into account in this way reflect the multilateral conception of insurance relations that is necessary to effective operation in this field. Admittedly, the different insurers involved in each asbestos case have no formal contractual rights or responsibilities in relation to each other. Similarly, the pools of insureds to which different policies have been sold have no formal responsibilities to each other. The only formal rights and responsibilities in these disputes exist between each insurer and each individual insured: they are reflected in the insurance policies in question. Yet through the resolution of coordination questions, factors independent of these individual contracts can play a role—sometimes a central one—in fixing the scope of the rights embodied in the contracts. When the loss prevention or distributional effects of allocating coverage responsibility are made relevant to such decisions, then insurers have begun to have something like rights among themselves. They become entitled to have these effects considered in allocating coverage responsibility. The establishment of such entitlements is the beginning of a recognition that insurance relations are not only bilateral, but involve more complex risk-sharing arrangements than a bilateral model can comfortably describe.

Other-Insurance Conflicts. A second situation in which judicial methods of coordination must be called upon occurs when the other-insurance clauses in two or more policies conflict. The courts have adopted a series of different approaches in resolving conflicts between other-insurance clauses. The earliest method was to adopt a rule of thumb to break the tie between clauses: allocate liability to the first policy issued[24] or to the policy that more specifically covers the risk in question.[25] A more recent approach is termed the Lamb-Weston doctrine, after the first case to employ it.[26] Lamb-Weston requires that conflicting other-insurance clauses be disregarded. Coverage responsibility is then prorated in proportion to the coverage limits of each policy, and stacking is permitted up to the amount of their aggregate limits. Thus, neither other-insurance provision governs under Lamb-Weston; a judicial solution is entirely substituted for the clauses that generate the problem. A third approach (originating in Minnesota) disregards conflicting clauses but does not automatically prorate. Instead, primary coverage responsibility is allocated according to a multifactored test directed at determining the policy most closely related to the risk in question.[27]

These approaches all have begun to recognize that a system of coordination can serve more than merely technical or tiebreaking purposes. They are concerned with substantive ends. Although the rules of thumb sometimes appear to be merely arbitrary, even they implicitly recognize this function. One policy is chosen as primary for reasons that compare the policies rather than focus on each insurance relation separately. For instance, the rule of thumb that makes the more specific policy primary certainly suggests loss prevention as a goal since premiums for that policy are likely to be more responsive than general purpose policies to claims involving the specific risk covered. The Lamb-Weston and Minnesota doctrines use the occasion of a conflict between other-insurance clauses to reorder a faltering risk sharing arrangement in accordance with a view of the underlying function of that arrangement. Lamb-Weston is blunt about that function, mandating that responsibility always be shared roughly in proportion to the maximum exposure undertaken by each insurer. This assures loss distribution by making both policies available for coverage, and it reduces litigation costs by declaring in advance a standard allocation in the event of conflict. But Lamb-Weston achieves these aims only by sacrificing an ability to fine-tune loss prevention aims. The Minnesota approach allows for fine-tuning, though only in the vague sense of attempting to discover which policy seems most appropriately the primary risk bearer in light of the coverage regime that has been adopted. It searches for an underlying intent that may or may not be discoverable.

None of these approaches goes very far in articulating the factors to be taken into account in coordinating the coverage available under typical insurance arrangements. Each first leaves the parties to whatever coordination they are able to achieve through the combination of independent policy provisions governing coordination. When this semiplanned, semicoincidential form of market coordination fails, the courts are called upon to solve the problem. They have seized upon very simple criteria to guide the process—a tiebreaking rule of thumb, a proportional sharing principle, or an imprecise notion of the total insuring intent of both policies.

If the application of these criteria could be predicted with certainty, their simplicity would not be a drawback. The parties to an other-insurance dispute could determine in advance how it would be resolved in court and settle among themselves. But the comparative specificity of different other-insurance clauses and the underlying intent of an insurance arrangement are not self-applying concepts. Even the outcome of the Lamb-Weston test is not entirely predictable since its application depends on the court's conclusion that the language in two other-insurance clauses is irreconcilable. The result is that none of the judicial devices provides the market with the kind of rule certainty that would minimize resort to litigation.

Limits-of-Liability Issues. The last important setting in which courts make coordination decisions arises when they are called upon to interpret limits-of-liability provisions. Recall that these provisions purport to restrict intra-policy stacking of coverage but that insureds often have attempted to circumvent their effect. Insureds have argued, for instance, that restrictions on stacking are ambiguous or that accepting a double premium without providing double coverage is unconscionable.

Judicial reactions to these arguments, whether or not favorable, have not been as helpful or enlightening as they could be.[28] The reason is that the opinions seem to limit themselves to the narrow issues raised, without placing their treatment of the stacking question within a larger framework. The overriding issue here seems to be a distributional one, especially in regard to personal injury protection or uninsured motorist coverage. Yet few courts have seen fit to analyze the issues forthrightly in these terms. If the insured, or someone acting on his behalf, has paid for two sets of coverage, why should both sets not be accessible?

One argument is that a no-stacking rule will encourage deliberation about coverage options. If the insured wants $40,000 of uninsured motorist coverage, then he should purchase it directly and not be entitled to it merely because he has insured two vehicles for $20,000 each. The weakness of this argument is that anything resembling real deliberation on this issue is very unlikely. When ordinary consumers buy coverage, they have to make half-a-dozen choices about coverage limits. By the time they must decide how much uninsured motorist coverage to purchase, serious deliberation probably will not take place, even assuming that the nature of the coverage offered is clear to them.

The strong distributional argument for intra-policy stacking, however, is undercut by two other considerations. First, a distinction should be drawn between stacking by named insureds or family members, on the one hand, and by passengers or employees, on the other.[29] Insureds and family members have a plausible claim to a right to stack, but others do not. It is pure coincidence that a passenger or employee happens to be injured in a vehicle that is only one of several owned by his host or employer. These guests have no connection with the other vehicles. But the insured and his or her family have a kind of interest in all the vehicles. As a matter of equity they have a more legitimate expectation that the coverage they have purchased is part of an overall package of protection that can be drawn upon in the event of loss. In addition, passengers and employees are likely to have separate insurance associated with their own vehicles. Any stacking to which they are entitled should involve these policies rather than the coverage on vehicles with which they have no connection whatever.

A second consideration is that allowing stacking has implications for what might be called "claim prevention" to distinguish it from loss prevention. Uninsured motorist insurance is highly vulnerable to fraudulent claims because the uninsured driver need not be located. A hit-and-run driver usually is considered uninsured if there is proof of physical contact with another vehicle and a report of the accident is filed within twenty-four hours. In some states even the physical contact requirement is invalid.[30] Placing restrictions on stacking UM coverage is a way of limiting exposure to fraudulent claims in the cases where the temptation to commit fraud is greatest—those involving very serious personal injuries. This limit is especially important in the jurisdictions without a physical contact requirement.

Yet none of these considerations has played much of a part in the courts' treatment of stacking questions. The courts therefore have some distance to cover before their approach to these matters can be effective. They have not located the reasons for their decisions about stacking within a systematic framework of analysis—the decisions are not explicitly linked with considerations relevant to analogous coordination questions. Nor do the decisions provide sufficiently clear guidance to the market. Rationales for judicial decision that rest on the ambiguity of policy language or substantive unconscionability call for subjective judgments that can only be applied in case-by-case adjudication. Decisions that permit stacking by insureds holding a given status (a named insured or family member) without indicating whether this right extends to those with a different status yield similar uncertainty. As a consequence, litigation over these issues is frequent and continuing.

Legislative and Regulatory Devices

Legislative and regulatory directives governing coordination have the potential to be much more effective than judicial resolution of coordination questions. In contrast to judicial methods of coordination, legislative and regulatory approaches to coordination tend to be mandatory. They are not displaceable by contract provisions fashioned by insurers and insureds. Rather than providing a starting point away from which the parties may contract, they are meant to fix a strategy of coordination that the parties may not alter.

Mandatory directives governing coordination express a certainty about the correct way to coordinate that is missing from displaceable directives. Although judicial decisions do not always reflect the agreement that all the parties would reach if the costs of doing so were not prohibitive, in allowing private agreements to govern when they are consistent, the logic of judicial action subordinates collective standards about the goals of coordination to the economic incentives of the market. Only if concerned parties fail to coordinate successfully are courts called into play.

Framers of mandatory rules of coordination, however, are not skeptical of their ability to dictate proper methods of coordination. Sometimes this posture reflects their certainty about how to move the market toward more efficient coordination. But the exercise of this kind of confidence would be puzzling, if in fact assisting the market's search for efficiency were its aim. Legislators or regulators desiring to promote efficient coordination have everything to lose and nothing to gain by promulgating mandatory rules. Displaceable rules leave the parties free to construct more efficient alternatives when they exist, whereas mandatory rules do not.

This is strong evidence that legislative and regulatory approaches to coordination, precisely because they are mandatory, are not designed, at least directly, to achieve economic goals. Rather, they are intended to foreclose or countermand judicial approaches that are inefficient, or they are themselves designed to promote noneconomic aims. The distributional effects of these approaches, then, are prime candidates for analysis. Unfortunately, regulatory actions governing coordination are rare. I shall therefore have some recommendations later about the course that regulators should pursue. The following discussion examines the contribution of two different kinds of legislative directives to the coordination process. These are: (1) statutes prohibiting or authorizing the stacking of coverage; and (2) statutes mandating set-offs in the amount due under one form of coverage by amounts payable under others.

Stacking. Many state statutes require the purchase of motor vehicle liability, personal injury protection, and uninsured motorist coverage. When more than one such policy is potentially available to the insured, but policy provisions in each purport to limit stacking, the insured must turn to the statutory mandate for support of his claim to coverage under both. The interpretation in favor of stacking is that by mandating the purchase of minimum amounts of coverage, the legislature intended that each and every policy issued to satisfy the mandate provide at least that amount. A policy limitation on the right to stacking would render the policy defective within the meaning of the statute because it would not provide the required coverage.[31] Behind this interpretation there is unstated but obvious emphasis not only on achieving the explicit statutory purpose, but also on assuring, insofar as possible, full indemnity to the insured. This concern with broad distribution is an important feature of the prostacking interpretation.

The antistacking interpretation presupposes a narrower statutory purpose. The legislature's concern, according to this view, was merely to assure that a minimum amount of coverage be available for any loss. Policy provisions precluding stacking are entirely consistent with this purpose, as long as one of the applicable policies supplies the statutory minimum.[32] Once that minimum is provided, concern with indemnity ceases. Coverage beyond the minimum is then available only if the insured has made a deliberate decision to purchase it. That is, the amount of coverage the insured has chosen may not be fortuitously supplemented by a second source of coverage with policy limits no higher than the first.

In both cases, although the issue is joined on the question of how to interpret the statute, the answer does not depend on a close reading of its language, Rather, the debate is conducted by referring to the purposes of coordination in order to pour content into the statutory language. Logically, the purposes of coordination come first; the meaning of the statute follows from them. Under both interpretations, the two policies are not independent, free standing sources of coverage; they are pieces in an overall coverage scheme that the statute brings into being.

The statutes subject to these two interpretations usually do not refer explicitly to the stacking question. Other statutes often regulate stacking more explicitly, however, by prohibiting[33] or authorizing[34] it or by setting coverage priorities in specified circumstances. Such statutes exhibit the same themes that appear in interpretations of the purposes of mandatory coverage legislation: promoting broad loss spreading by allowing the combination of coverage through stacking versus assuring only minimum protection by leaving responsibility for deliberately purchasing coverage with higher limits to the insured. Both kinds of statutes and both interpretations of underlying legislative purpose reflect mainly distributional concerns. The prostacking approach favors broad loss spreading. Yet even the no-stacking approach has a conscious distributional (or antidistributional) purpose. It is intended to preclude broad loss spreading when insureds have not deliberately purchased it.

Of course, the most direct and obvious way to achieve greater spreading of losses covered by uninsured motorist or personal injury protection insurance is to raise the mandated minimum amounts of such insurance. But that may be politically difficult for two reasons. First, increasing the minimum required coverage will increase its price. This is a highly visible move that may draw objections from the electorate at large. Second, when there is strong rate regulation, the insurance industry also may object. Raising minimums means that high-risk drivers must be provided high-limits coverage; yet regulatory approval to charge these drivers accurately is not always automatic. Explicitly permitting stacking or leaving the courts to interpret mandatory coverage legislation as permitting it, however, is likely to be less objectionable.

This more covert approach to encouraging loss spreading has two political advantages. First, it is less visible, and therefore less likely to engender public opposition. Second, it meets some of the insurance industry's objections to the overt approach. Intra-policy stacking can occur only when the insured owns two vehicles—a situation more characteristic of the middle class suburban driver than the urban driver who resides and drives in congested, high-risk territories. So this form of increase in mandatory coverage sweeps within its scope fewer drivers whom insurers are apprehensive about covering. Moreover, permitting intra-policy stacking affords greater protection to some insureds who have low-limits coverage not because of their clear preference for it, but because they do not fully understand the nature of the protection provided by uninsured motorist or personal injury protection insurance.

There is, nevertheless, much to recommend the antistacking view. PIP coverage is not risk classified sufficiently to create strong loss prevention or claims limitation incentives, and uninsured motorist coverage is susceptible to fraud and exaggerated claims of pain and suffering damages. Allowing stacking exacerbates both problems. Further, higher limits of both forms of coverage can be purchased by the deliberate insurance consumer; and both PIP and UM provide medical care insurance that largely duplicates what is elsewhere available in the form of health insurance, but the latter has premiums producing somewhat superior incentive effects.

If this were all that were involved, the antistacking view would clearly be preferable. However, one factor remains to be considered. Minimum amounts of uninsured motorist and personal injury protection are not always sufficient to compensate the insured for all wage loss resulting from his injuries. Yet unlike health care insurance, the majority of the population is not covered by other wage loss insurance with high limits. Workers' compensation and Social Security provide only subsistence levels of coverage; and private disability insurance is not widespread. Allowing stacking of uninsured motorist and personal injury protection can help to supplement this incomplete coverage against wage loss. Until private wage loss insurance is more widely purchased, therefore, there are plausible arguments for permitting stacking automobile coverages that provide wage loss protection. Whichever choice is made, however, it should be made clearly. If stacking is clearly permitted by law, insurers will adjust their rates to take account of that exposure. But if legislation is unclear on the question, then judicial interpretation will be required, and the uncertainty characteristic of the delays and incrementalism of adjudication will reconfuse the process.

Set-off Statutes. The last legislative device we will examine is the set-off statute. Many state insurance statutes contain language directed not at stacking in general, but at the combination of specified types of coverage. Often such statutes direct that PIP coverage be set-off, or reduced, by amounts paid or payable by collateral sources such as workers' compensation, Social Security, disability insurance, and Medicare. Similar legislation governing uninsured motorist insurance and basic no-fault automobile insurance (usually a form of PIP coverage) is also common.[35] These relatively obscure pieces of legislation establish the relation between basic sources of social welfare protection and the most widespread form of private coverage, automobile insurance. Yet, perhaps because of their technicality, their importance as a reflection of social policy has gone largely unnoticed.

Under these statutory provisions, the amounts payable from the collateral sources are counted as set-offs against automobile coverages. Thus, stacking these automobile coverages with others is not simply disallowed: the insured is entitled to the difference, if any, between the limits of each automobile coverage and the other source. If the insured has received $10,000 in Social Security disability payments and his PIP limits are also $10,000, then the statute directs that he receive nothing from the latter—the auto insurer escapes responsibility, notwithstanding that the insured's losses exceed $10,000. If the insured's Social Security payments are only $7,000, however, then he receives $3,000 from his auto insurer—the excess over payments from the collateral sources up to the limits of the secondary automobile coverage. Thus, insurance subject to set-offs is only a primary source of protection in the absence of other sources. The insured is guaranteed the amount of his coverage. But he never recovers more than that coverage, even if he has other sources of protection, unless those sources provide it.

Set-off provisions are a powerful tool for coordinating coverage because they can be selective about the forms of coverage they govern. They work like subrogation provisions by reducing one insurer's liability, but without litigation and without the overbroad effects sometimes produced by subrogation. Unlike some subrogation, however, these statutes not only set coverage priorities; they may also impair full compensation of loss. The justification for this impairment depends on the other objectives they can achieve.

Several objectives appear to underlie set-off statutes. First, they reflect the obvious legislative concern with minimizing the cost of auto insurance. Many set-off provisions are part of comprehensive no-fault automobile insurance statutes;[36] others are part of statutes creating add-on no-fault coverage.[37] Political opposition to legislation proposing such mandatory coverage is often said to be based on the potentially high cost of the coverage. By reducing auto coverage to the extent that coverage is available from collateral sources, the cost of the former can be minimized; primary coverage responsibility remains on collateral sources that are federally financed or on workers' compensation, the cost of neither being affected by the additional auto coverage.

A second objective of set-off statutes reflects the nature of the coverage they coordinate. The sources such statutes designate as primary tend to provide social welfare maintenance only—minimal Social Security and disability insurance, Medicare, and workers' compensation. The natural inference to be drawn is that mandatory PIP and UM coverage are intended mainly to fill gaps in the fabric of these sources of social welfare maintenance. When these social insurance sources provide protection equal to the amount of mandatory auto insurance, the latter is not to be available because the social welfare need has been met. Only by deliberately purchasing more than the mandated minimum can the insured obtain protection exceeding the safety net provided by the social welfare sources. In this sense a conscious limitation on distributional aims is the motivation behind set-off statutes.

The form of the distribution effected by these statutes, however, is also revealing. Set-off statutes produce very broad but very shallow spreading. Allocating primary coverage responsibility to public sources such as Social Security and Medicare spreads loss among a most extensive pool of loss sharers. But setting-off auto coverage by the amounts paid from these public sources results in shallow spreading since the effect is to preclude any stacking of the auto coverage onto these sources. The distributional message of set-off statutes is that the basic costs of automobile accidents are a cost of living in our society, not just a cost of driving. These costs therefore should be borne first by the insurance pools that spread loss as nearly as possible to society as a whole. The way to achieve this aim is to assure that public sources of protection are primary. Only after their protection is exhausted do private sources come into play.

This breakdown of responsibility, however, underscores the limited scope of wage loss coverage noted earlier. Social insurance tends to provide only subsistence level wage loss protection. Yet because of set-off statutes, the wage loss protection provided by auto coverage is of no value unless its limits exceed that provided by social insurance sources collateral to it. In short, unless the insured deliberately purchases high-limits coverage in order to have it available as a supplement, it will not be available at all. And of course any consumer deliberate enough to make this choice would be better advised instead to purchase broad-based disability coverage to supplement his or her public sources of protection.

IMPLICATIONS AND RECOMMENDATIONS

The preceding analysis isolated and examined a set of purposes, both economic and distributional, that are served by different methods of coordination of different kinds of coverage. And it explored the connections between a series of ambiguously related contractual and legal devices by arguing that each is concerned with coordination—the allocation of coverage responsibility when more than one policy or source of coverage is potentially available. Together, these two efforts constitute a descriptive theory of coordination, if by that term one means a generalized, formal, and detailed account of how and why that legal activity proceeds.

The analysis has also advanced toward a normative theory of coordination. It has shown that insurance relations cannot be accurately described only as a set of bilateral contract rights, nor even as a set of contract rights plus a body of rights at variance with policy provisions.[38] The methods of coordination in use and the purposes they appear to serve belie the adequacy of a bilateral, contractual model of coordination. Legal intervention often is necessary just to make contractual coordination work, and it is sometimes necessary also to supersede the purposes of contractual coordination. In short, insurance is a complex, multilateral risk-sharing arrangement that requires a combination of contractual and legal devices in order to operate effectively. These insights have important implications for the way that the courts, legislatures, and administrative regulators play their roles in the system of coordination.

First, the courts should recognize that for the most part their role is to act as a surrogate for the market when private devices have failed to achieve coordination. This role is implied by the fact that market solutions take precedence over judicial ones—the latter apply only when multilateral private arrangements are not entirely consistent.

This is not to say that distributional considerations should be irrelevant to the courts. Coordination decisions have distributional effects that may be taken into account, and the courts traditionally have engaged in a certain amount of interstitial risk redistribution at common law. But since the courts are acting here as substitute markets, even though perhaps with more social conscience than private ones, providing clear solutions that give real guidance about future judicial action should have a high priority. The market may not always be able to circumvent a given form of judicial coordination, but insurers may anticipate judicial action by varying prices if they can predict the action with confidence. The legal priority of the market over the courts in this context entitles the market to that kind of guidance.

Second, legislative and regulatory participation in the process of coordination also could be more effective. Both institutions are better equipped than the courts to balance the demands of loss prevention, cost reduction, distributional effects, and other goals. Yet insurance commissioners have hardly entered the field at all, and legislatures have entered it only selectively. The legislative approaches examined did seem to recognize the complexity of the insurance relations involved in arriving at directives to govern coordination. Certainly the complexity of the problems and the attention to detail necessary to solve them are part of the explanation for the limited scope of coordination legislation to date.

Another explanation may be legislative reluctance to interfere with market-based strategies of coordination. But legislators should recognize that statutory solutions need not be mandatory. Instead, they could be invested with the same effect as judicial coordination, by making statutory standards available in the event of a conflict between coverages but displaceable by contract. For example, legislative standards for resolving conflicts between other-insurance clauses would have distinct advantages over judicial solutions to the same problem.[39] They could be general, resolving a series of different issues in one statute; they could provide statutory clarity of the sort more difficult to extract from a judicial decision; and they could deal systematically with the many combinations of other insurance clauses that give rise to the problem. In this way legislatures could offer the industry a set of solutions that the costs of transactions and difficulty of reaching agreement on cooperative solutions appear to have precluded. Yet this approach could be circumvented by contractual readjustment whenever it turned out not to be the efficient solution.

In addition, legislatures might save costs for the entire system by scrutinizing more carefully the situations in which policy provisions permit subrogation. The cost of subrogation actions is high, and as we saw earlier, their benefits are not always great. In any given case an insurer may profit by subrogation; but on the whole, subrogation actions and the collateral source rule that serves them could wisely be limited. Insurers themselves often arbitrate subrogation claims in order to save costs; and some state statutes have placed limits on selected rights of subrogation.[40] But more limits are necessary. The governing principle should be that subrogation generally is not permitted unless it promises significant loss prevention or cost reduction benefits. It certainly should not be permitted to impair full compensation. Legislatures are the legal institutions best equipped to put these principles into effect through a series of specific prohibitions.

Because their weapons are not the same as those in the legislature's arsenal, insurance commissioners cannot play quite the same role. They cannot simply fashion regulations dictating how coordination conflicts should be resolved because these directives will not necessarily be binding on the courts to whom the parties turn for assistance when private coordination has failed. In order to achieve the same end, however, commissioners could promulgate separate schemes of coordination applicable field by field (e.g., one to auto liability insurance, another to private health care coverage, and so forth) to which insurers would have to subscribe in order to do business in the jurisdiction. These administratively prescribed schemes of coordination could be superseded by market action, but not through the action of any individual insurer. Each scheme should be displaceable only by agreement between two or more insurers on an alternative method of coordination that would minimize the need for costly litigation to resolve coverage problems.

This strategy could have several advantages. It would require insurance commissioners to determine, field by field, the extent to which the market is successfully achieving coordination on its own. This knowledge would be a prerequisite to decisions about what fields to focus upon. Where a uniform system of coordination is economically desirable but the costs of reaching agreement on one have been prohibitive, this approach would provide a uniform system. Yet the approach also would permit insurers cooperating together to opt out of the uniform scheme in situations where the scheme was inefficient. The scheme's only drawback would be the cost to insurers of opting out through separate agreements. In deciding whether to adopt a scheme, the insurance commissioner should compare the costs of reaching private agreements governing coordination with the costs of contractually opting out of administratively provided coordination schemes. Whenever the former costs are greater, an administratively prescribed approach should be more effective.

Insurance commissioners might also address the intra-policy stacking issue through rulemaking procedures. As we noted earlier, the stackability of coverage is a subject about which the typical insurance consumer is not likely to deliberate. As a consequence, it is difficult for competition among insurers to produce a range of alternatives regarding the stacking of policies. Pricing of identical coverage often may be competitive without there being much competition over the scope of coverage provided. To remedy this competitive imperfection, insurers could be required to offer insureds the option of purchasing stackable or nonstackable coverage at different prices.

Ideally this is a sensible approach, but it should be recognized that it could have weaknesses in practice. Consumer attention spans and lack of interest place practical limits on the effectiveness of disclosing coverage alternatives. Disclosure of obscure or intricate coverage provisions is a good way to encourage informed assent, but only a limited amount of disclosure is feasible. If emphasis is placed on options regarding stacking, disclosure of other important features of coverage is likely to diminish. If some disclosure is to be mandated in order to encourage greater risk spreading, disclosure of the modest additional cost of purchasing coverage with higher limits probably would be a preferable route to this end.

On the other hand, if insurance commissioners were to conclude that the typical consumer, if informed, would prefer to pay slightly more to obtain stackable coverage, then such a requirement might be imposed. Policies would then have to provide for stacking in order to meet administrative standards. Such action would constitute a recognition that the costs of informing insureds about the possibility of stacking had been preventing the market from reaching an otherwise more efficient allocation of resources.

The courts, legislatures, and insurance commissioners should recognize the place of legal approaches in the overall system of coordination. These legal institutions will be only partially effective in regulating coordination unless they make use of an expansive conception of the functions of coordination. Greater clarity about the purposes of coordination and about the role that can be played by such institutions in assisting or countermanding the market's objectives should help aid the process.

This chapter has focused on two themes. The first was clearing the conceptual ground on which issues regarding coordination rest. I have discussed the relation between diverse devices governing different forms of coordination and translated the economic and distributional goals of insurance law into the language of coordination. The second theme of the chapter has been examining the boundary between market methods of coordination and collective regulation of coordination through legal devices. I explored the connections between these two realms, and their different capacities for emphasizing the economic and distributional goals of coordination. In the course of this exploration I sketched the outlines of a new conception of insurance that is beginning to emerge.

The criticisms and recommendations contained in this chapter do not propose adopting a single theory of coordinated coverage. Rather, they are designed to show that instead of being the result of accidental consistencies or conflicts between coverage, coordination should be a purposive activity that is very much a conscious and calculated feature of the insurance system. Recognizing the capacities of coordination will take the system a long way toward this goal.

7

Translating Insurance Rights into Remedies: The Claims Process

The preceding chapters have examined the many different methods that insurance and insurance law use to allocate and distribute risk. I have paid little attention thus far, however, to the ways in which insurance arrangements are implemented in practice. Until now I have asssumed that policy obligations are fulfilled and that insurance benefits are paid when an insured suffers a compensable loss. But the obligations provided for in insurance policies are not always performed, and valid claims are not always paid. The law is then faced with a dilemma: how should the insurance rights that are set out on paper be implemented in practice? This chapter explores that dilemma.

Until recently there was little law specially applicable to the insurance claims process. The many features that distinguish the insurance claims process from relations between contracting parties in other settings were legally unaccounted for. Insurance claims were simply subject to the ordinary rules of contract performance and breach. The major result was that insurers were insulated from liability for special damages resulting from their failure to settle or defend claims in accordance with policy obligations. That is, in a suit against the insurer for breach of a policy obligation, the insured was entitled only to have the obligation performed. This remedy gave the insured no compensation for any losses he suffered as a result of breach, and it provided the insurer with little additional incentive to perform. The insurer therefore possessed a tremendous strategic advantage in its dealings with insureds. It could refuse to perform its obligations and incur few legal penalties. A successful suit against it would simply yield an order to pay the claim it had originally refused.

In the past few decades, however, the body of law governing claim settlement and defense has been undergoing something of a revolution. Judicial and legislative action on several fronts has created new obligations where none previously existed and has put teeth into longstanding rules by creating new remedies for the failure to comply with policy provisions. The primary effect of these developments has been to realign the balance of advantages enjoyed by insurers and insureds during the claims process. By threatening insurers with additional liability for failing to pay claims or perform other policy obligations, the new rules create stronger incentives for insurers to comply with these duties. Yet the rules also have interesting side effects. Sometimes they encourage insurers to pay invalid claims or to take actions on behalf of insureds that are not required. And in certain cases they create what amounts to a de facto and seemingly paradoxical form of coverage: insurance against the risk of not being insured.

Three major areas of insurance claims law reflect these developments: the new extra-contact liability for an insurer's failure to pay a first-party claim; the rise of a duty to settle liability claims; and the elaboration and regulation of the insurer's traditional duty to defend a liability insured. These three sets of rules have been subjected to much criticism for the extra burdens they impose on insurance companies. I want to defend the rules against this criticism by explaining what they accomplish and how they serve the purposes of insurance law. Although on occasion they have gone too far, for the most part the new rules have positive effects on the claims process. These effects deserve isolation and explanation.

My argument is that two distinct problems run through each of the very different features of the claims process that the new rules address. The first is the problem of contractual specificity: as detailed as they are, insurance policies often are not specific enough to make the rights and obligations of the parties during the claims process crystal clear. The first function of a body of law regulating the claims process should be to specify these rights.

The second problem is the result of contractual discretion. Because of both insufficient specificity and because the insurer is in a position of strategic advantage in its relations with individual insureds, insurers have vast amounts of discretion in determining whether to pay claims and how to perform policy obligations. Rules governing the claims process should constrain this discretion in accordance with the economic, equitable, and distributional purposes of insurance law.

The following pages examine the body of law that has grown up to regulate the claims process, and they analyze the paradoxical form of insurance that often is its by-product. I first explore the connections between the general purposes of insurance law discussed in earlier chapters and the claims process. I then analyze the three major developments in the field in light of these connections. In the final portion of the chapter I synthesize the analysis by scrutinizing the ways in which the balance of advantages in the claims process has been realigned by this new body of legal doctrine.

THE PURPOSES OF REGULATING THE CLAIMS PROCESS

The situations in which the law is called upon to regulate the claims process are fairly simple ones. In the case of first-party, or non-liability, insurance—health, fire, or disability insurance, for example—the insured suffers a loss and files a claim for payment with his insurer. If the insurer pays the claim, there is no reason for legal attention. But if the claim is not paid, the resulting dispute must be resolved. Similarly, when an insured covered by third-party, or liability, insurance (called third-party because the insured is not paid the proceeds) is sued, he gives the insurer notice of the suit. If the insurer does not comply with its obligation to defend the insured, legal intervention is required. And if the insurer refuses an offer of settlement and the suit eventuates in a judgment against the insured in excess of the policy limits, a method of allocating responsibility for the judgment is required.

However, recognizing the need for legal intervention of some sort in each of these situations does not provide a detailed prescription of the form of intervention. Under what conditions should the law intervene, and what remedies should be available when legal assistance can be invoked? The answers should depend on the purposes behind legal regulation. As seen in earlier chapters, three general purposes serve as the foundation for much of insurance law. The connections between these economic, equitable, and distributional purposes and the insurance claims process are the starting point for our analysis of the law regulating that process.

Economic Efficiency

Two separate notions can shed light on the relation between claims regulation and economic efficiency. The first is the contention, advanced by Professors Goetz and Scott,[1] that rules governing contract enforcement can be designed to promote optimal levels of promise making. This notion suggests that insurance claims law can play a role in optimizing the combination of insurance and loss prevention that is one of the purposes of insurance law. The second relevant idea is the theory of efficient breach of contract. This theory holds that the law should encourage contract performance when performance would be efficient, but that it should encourage breach of contract when breach would be the more efficient alternative.[2]

Both notions suggest factors that should be considered in structuring an efficient insurance claims process.

Optimal Levels of Promise Making

Individuals and enterprises purchase insurance when the protection against loss they desire costs less to obtain through insuring than the equivalent protection that can be obtained through investing in loss prevention or self-protection. Ideally, insureds compare these costs in deciding whether to purchase insurance and how much to purchase. However, the attractiveness of insuring against risk also depends, among other things, on the reliability of the coverage the insured may purchase. The more certain the insured is of recovering his insurance proceeds if he suffers an insured loss, the more attractive this form of protection is. The less reliable the insurance, the less attractive it is, and the more desirable are other methods of risk reduction.

Under some circumstances buyers of products can shop or bargain for reliability. For several reasons, however, shopping or bargaining for reliability is likely to be much more difficult in the insurance market than in many others. Information about the reliability of different insurers is hard to come by; the quality of insurance coverage is almost impossible to assess without an expert; there is no feasible way for an insurer to warrant or guarantee the quality of coverage; and negotiating individualized liquidated damage provisions to provide assurance of reliability would be prohibitively expensive. In short, insureds cannot effectively monitor the precautions insurers take to assure the reliability of coverage, and contractual forms of controlling reliability are costly or not feasible. It is hard to know in advance whether one really is "in good hands with All-State." The insurer therefore has relatively uncontrolled discretion to perform in substandard fashion or not to perform at all. Interestingly, the reverse of the moral hazard problem that normally plagues insurance arises out of this discretion: because the insurer has an incentive to underallocate resources to reliability, the insured may be encouraged to overallocate resources to loss prevention as compared to insurance.

The law can mitigate this reverse moral hazard and assist the parties in allocating their resources more efficiently by substituting legal assurance of reliability for the less effective voluntary forms of assurance. The availability of legal sanctions for breach of insurance contracts thereby increases the attractiveness of coverage by making it more reliable. At the same time, however, insurers react to the threat of legal sanctions for breach by making downward adjustments in the quality and quantity of the coverage they offer and the prices they charge. Because of these adjustments, more legal sanctions are not always efficient. Rather, their use is economically warranted up to a point: where the marginal cost of assuring the reliability of coverage through legal remedies for breach equals but does not exceed the marginal cost of providing for reliable protection against risk through additional loss prevention, comparison shopping, and contractual reassurance of the reliability of insurance coverage.

When legal sanctions are provided at this level (other things being equal), an optimal amount of insurance is purchased, and the reverse moral hazard of uncontrolled insurer discretion is reduced as much as it is worth reducing. Any additional legal sanctions would not be worth their cost since they would overassure and encourage the purchase of too much insurance. Fewer sanctions also would sacrifice efficiency because insureds would be investing in loss prevention, self-protection, and contractual assurance of reliability when legal sanctions could provide such assurance at a lower cost.

The parties themselves would agree on an optimal level of legal sanctions if it cost nothing to negotiate about and specify their rights and remedies upon breach. By prescribing these sanctions, the law can save the costs that would be invested in reaching such agreements and can promote optimal levels of insurance and safety when these costs would be too high to warrant reaching agreement on such matters. From an economic standpoint, then, the important question is not the cost of expanded liability for breach of insurance contracts—a factor the insurance industry understandably underscores in analyzing the issue—but how that cost compares to the cost of the reliability assurance devices it replaces.[3] This is a schematic question, and arriving at a quantitative comparison of the costs the question indicates are important will almost always be very difficult. Nevertheless, the theory makes one point of great relevance here. The rules governing breach of insurance contracts not only affect breach of and compliance with the terms of such contracts; the rules also affect the amount of insurance that is purchased and sold. Because achieving an efficient combination of loss prevention and insurance is one of the goals of insurance law, the way rules governing breach are constructed is a central issue for this entire body of law.

Optimal Levels of Promise Breaking

The second economic influence of legal rules regulating the claims process is their effect on the level of promise breaking that occurs. In a competitive market, legal rules governing damages for breach simply serve as timesavers and transaction cost avoiders. Instead of paying the cost of negotiating and specifying their agreements regarding the consequences of breach, the parties can rely on legal rules governing damages. When the rules are unsuitable, often they can be altered by agreement. As long as the aggregate cost of opting out of legal rules is less than the cost that would be incurred by the parties to fashion their own rules, legal sanctions serve an economic purpose.

The theory of efficient breach builds on this picture. The theory holds that awarding damages for breach of contract promotes efficiency by encouraging promisors to breach when breach would produce net gains even after the payment of damages to the promisee. Similarly, the threat of liability encourages performance when the benefits of breaching would be exceeded by the damages suffered by the promisee. The critical element here is the measure of damages awarded upon breach. An excessive measure will overdeter breach; an inadequate measure will underdeter. The normal measure is the promisee's expectation—the monetary value of the contract to him had it been performed.[4] When this legally prescribed measure is unsatisfactory, it is sometimes legally permissible for the parties to contract out of it. In the alternative, they may vary the price of performance to take defects in the legal measure into account. But unless the expectation measure of damages reflects the measure that would most often be adopted by the parties through individual agreements, this measure of damages is inefficient. Either unnecessary costs will be incurred to contract out of the legal measure, or an inefficient number of breaches will occur.

Application of the theory of efficient breach suggests that traditional rules regarding breach of insurance contracts may well be inefficient. First, there is real question whether awarding only expectation damages for breach, at least as such damages are normally calculated, places the insured in the position he or she would have occupied had the contract been performed. Insurance is ordinarily purchased not only to protect against monetary loss. Most people also buy insurance to avoid the worry, anxiety, and suffering resulting from financial uncertainty and insecurity. When an insurance claim is not paid, they not only suffer financially, but emotionally as well. The standard measure of expectation damages—which awards the economic losses caused by breach but does not pay for these emotional, or nonpecuniary damages—may therefore be inadequate. It is likely that if the costs of negotiating an individualized measure of damages were not prohibitive, at least some (though probably not all) of these damages would be made payable in the event of breach.[5]

Yet negotiation of individual agreements about the damages available upon breach—the theory of efficient breach's fail-safe means of assuring efficient levels of promise making and breaking—frequently is not feasible. Sometimes such agreements are legally unenforceable, though the arguments for this prohibition are weak. Even when they are permitted, the costs of individual transactions displacing standard damage rules would often be prohibitively high. And because of the actuarial benefits of standardization, part of the price of individualization would be sacrifice of these benefits. Thus, there is little room for negotiation by the typical consumer; and even commercial insurance that is somewhat more customized requires considerable standardization for it to be actuarially sound. Agreements regarding damages for breach would probably upset actuarial calculations.

Nor is awarding specific performance—a court order that the contract obligation be performed—an adequate alternative to an inefficient measure of damages.[6] Whenever the performance to be ordered is the payment of a certain sum, as it usually is when an insurer breaches, specific performance and the payment of expectation damages are the same remedy: payment of the amount due under the policy. Since there is always a considerable period between breach and the issuance of an order to perform a contract, at least some and perhaps most of the nonpecuniary damages an insured suffers from breach of an insurance contract will occur even if specific performance eventually is granted. For these reasons, the theory of efficient breach suggests that some compensation for the nonpecuniary losses associated with breach of insurance contracts may be appropriate.

The theory also points to a distinction of prime importance for the analysis of insurance claims law. Breaches that do not produce a net social gain, but simply capture a larger share of the gains already allocated under existing contracts are economically wasteful.[7] Such breaches are inefficient because they encourage the insured to take precautions against breach that would not be taken if the insurance coverage in question were completely reliable. For example, the insured may take safety precautions he would not feel the need to take if he perceived his insurance coverage to be more reliable.

Insurance contracts create special opportunities for inefficient breach. Because the insurer is a stakeholder, it has the power simply to refuse to pay a claim when it is presented. Loss of the insured's future business may be a small price to pay if the insured's claim is large. An insurer's failure to pay a claim or perform other policy obligations, therefore, may be nothing more than an attempt by the insurer to capitalize on its strategic advantage and to capture more profit than the policy terms allow it. In addition, because prejudgment interest on the sum due the insured usually is not available as part of the insured's recovery, insurers have an extra incentive to delay payment of claims. The insurer's delay or complete refusal to pay for either of these reasons is inefficient. Many of the cases applying the new rules awarding nonpecuniary damages for bad-faith breaches of insurance contracts appear to involve breaches that are inefficient in this sense.

When insureds are aware of the possibility of such breaches and take precautions against them, the law's failure to provide the necessary assurance of reliability probably is inefficient. When insureds have little such awareness or take no precautions against the insurer's breach, however, the threat of a breach has little impact on efficiency: incentives and behavior are not influenced by matters about which one is ignorant. The more publicity or notoriety that is associated with dealings between insurers and insureds, then, the more effect rules regarding breach may have on efficiency. When breach is not in itself inefficient because of its minimal effect on future incentives, however, it still has equitable and distributional consequences of real significance. We now turn to these consequences.

Equitable Dealings between Insurers and Insureds

Insurance contracts create two kinds of problems for the body of law that regulates the claims process. The first is the problem of contractual specificity. When policy provisions are not drafted in sufficient detail, then greater specificity must be legally supplied. One way to supply it is to fashion terms the parties would have agreed upon had they specified their agreement in more detail. This approach serves the economic goals explored in the previous section. In contrast, the rules can provide that vague or incomplete policy terms mean what one party reasonably expects or, in light of all the circumstances, has a right to expect. The latter is an equitable standard. It dictates an agreement that the parties might not have chosen mutually in order to assure that the insured's expectations are not disappointed. But in achieving equity of this sort, the equitable standard may sacrifice efficiency in the future.

A second problem, though related to the first, is distinct from it. Because of the insurer's strategic advantage, it often has the opportunity to interpret vague or ambiguous policy provisions in its favor. In so doing the insurer may abuse the discretion delegated to it by the policy by taking action that does not accord with the insured's reasonable expectations. Abuse of implicit contractual discretion also has equitable implications since the insurer has contractual responsibility to act for both parties but has acted only for itself.

Both these problems figure in the legal doctrines to be examined shortly. Cutting across the problems, however, is the notion of bad-faith breach of contract often employed in describing insurer behavior. This term seems obviously pejorative, connoting evil intent, deliberate wrongdoing, or at least something more blameworthy than mere carelessness or negligence. Yet the term *bad faith* does not necessarily describe every breach that is caused by the problems of contractual specificity and discretion. For example, initially the insurer may innocently misinterpret a vague policy provision. If it continues to do so in identical cases after the issue has been authoritatively resolved, then it has abused its discretion and acted in bad faith. Similarly, a policy may delegate discretion to the insurer—the right to settle a liability claim, for instance—that the insurer exercises in a manner it believes to be contractually authorized. If that belief is incorrect, contractual discretion has been abused. But the insurer has not acted in bad faith until it has reason to know that its authority to act at its own discretion has been legally constrained. At that point the insurer has deliberately attempted to take advantage of its strategic position by capturing a contractual benefit that is legally allocated to the insured.

Legislation and judicial decisions regulating the claims process have tended to use the term *bad faith* without recognizing that it can have different connotations in different insurance settings. Both abuse of contractual discretion and bad faith have equitable implications, but they are different implications. Abuse of discretion is objectionable on equitable grounds because it contravenes the insured's reasonable expectations. This is in part a circular notion: abuse of discretion is action unfaithful to an insurance policy's purposes, and the purposes of a policy are dependent on what an insured reasonably expects. But the circularity is part of the point. As we saw in examining cases that explicitly employ the expectations principle, from an equitable standpoint the expectations of the parties can help determine the purposes of a policy. This is especially necessary when—by definition—the parties have not specified these purposes by directing in the policy how they shall be implemented.

On the other hand, bad-faith states of mind—what I shall call "subjective" bad faith—are of equitable concern for obvious but different reasons. Deliberately causing injury to another, or acting with disregard of the potential for injury, is inconsistent with the cooperative assumptions of insurance contracts. The insurer-insured relationship is one in which the insured relies on the insurer for protection against harm, and the insurer is paid in part to act as the insured's representative. There is therefore special reason, even apart from the more general demands of contract law and other legal norms, for guarding against bad faith breaches of insurance contracts.

Risk Distribution

Any change in the balance of advantages enjoyed by insurers and insureds during the claims process not only has economic and equitable implications; it has two important risk-distributional effects as well. First, when the rights of insureds are increased, previously undistributed risks are spread among the community of insureds. If insurers must pay claims they previously refused, the risk of suffering the losses in question is thereafter shouldered by all who hold policies. Of course, to the extent that prices increase and insureds reduce their coverage or refrain from purchasing coverage altogether because of the increase, there has been a concomitant decrease in spreading. A choice in favor of a present insured, therefore, may have effects on the future distribution of risk that require consideration. We have seen this effect repeatedly in earlier chapters: mandatory spreading cannot always be achieved without encountering offsetting decreases in forms of spreading that are not mandatory.

Second, altering the balance of advantages between insurers and insureds may also redistribute risk among insureds. If a right to recover damages for the nonpecuniary losses caused by breach is created, then all insureds whose contracts are breached in the manner specified will have that right. But if one class of insureds is disproportionately likely to suffer such damages, then this risk has not been spread evenly and neutrally among all insureds. The new right has actually revised risk-sharing relations among insureds. In order to evaluate this risk-redistributional effect we will look at what I have been calling "the egalitarian standard of risk distribution": the extent to which the insureds being subsidized by the new rules have control over the risk being shifted. For the argument against spreading risks that are within an insured's control is strong, on both moral and economic grounds. As it turns out, although some of the risk redistribution produced by the new rules is justified, other effects are undesirable. They are the price that is paid for the rights created by this new body of law.

THREE DEVELOPMENTS IN CLAIMS REGULATION

The three most important developments in legal doctrine governing insurance claims are: the new rules permitting extra-contract liability for bad-faith refusal to pay first-party claims; the rise of the duty to settle liability claims; and the elaboration and specification of the insurer's duty to defend a liability insured. These are obviously different problems; they are usually considered separately. Yet each development responds to the same phenomenon. By virtue of its position, both as stakeholder of the fund out of which claims are paid and as the contractually designated representative of the insured, the insurer possesses a tremendous strategic advantage when its interests conflict with the insured's. The insurer controls payment, and it controls the other moves that can be taken in the course of a lawsuit to protect the insured from liability. Each of the new developments scrutinized below seems designed in part to counterbalance these strategic advantages. They assure that the discretion delegated to the insurer is not inefficiently abused, that vague policy provisions are interpreted in accordance with the reasonable expectations of the parties, and that the rights specified in policy provisions are implemented.

Bad-Faith Refusal to Pay First-Party Claims

Traditional contract law awarded damages equal only to the insured loss when an insurer wrongfully refused to pay a first-party claim. Prejudgment interest and extra-contract damages such as counsel fees, consequential economic damages, and nonpecuniary emotional losses resulting from the refusal were not compensable.[8] As I explained above, this rule did little to discourage inefficient breaches because a breaching insurer was required to pay only the amount the policy had originally required it to pay. Nor could the rule easily be displaced by individualized terms providing for a more satisfactory measure of damages.

Emergence of the New Cause of Action

Partly as a consequence of these deficiencies, the traditional limitations on damage recoveries are now being relaxed. Courts in many jurisdictions are increasingly awarding aggrieved insurance claimants extra-contract damages for an insurer's refusal to pay first-party claims.[9] Early decisions analogized these awards to such existing causes of action as fraud and intentional infliction of emotional distress. But the shortcomings of these analogies quickly became apparent, and a cause of action for extra-contract damages caused by bad-faith refusals to pay first-party claims has now emerged in independent form. In *Gruenberg v. Aetna Insurance Co.*,[10] the California Supreme Court allowed recovery of compensatory pecuniary and nonpecuniary damages for mental suffering resulting from bad-faith denial of a fire insurance claim. And in *Silberg v. California Life Insurance Co.*,[11] the same court indicated that punitive damages could also be awarded for such a breach, if it was the product of malice, oppression, or intent to vex, harass, or annoy the insured. The courts of many other states are following California's lead, and the independent tort of bad faith seems destined to become well established.

The Economics of the New Right

An important economic assumption underlies the establishment of a cause of action for bad faith. The assumption is that in the absence of transaction costs, the parties to an insurance policy would normally agree to at least some extra-contract damages in the event of breach by the insurer. This assumption seems provisionally acceptable for two reasons. First, part of the risk aversion that accounts for the purchase of insurance is due to the desire to obtain freedom from anxiety as well as to minimize the risk of suffering large losses. Many individuals probably would be willing to pay at least something extra to assure the reliability of their coverage by insuring against the nonpecuniary risks of breach.

Second, because most insureds find it difficult to shop for insurance provid-ing the mixture of reliability, price, and risk that is optimal for them, often it would be cheaper to pay for legal protection against unreliability than to buy it in the market. That is, the costs of the insurer's precautions against liability for breach could be lower than an insured's own search and monitoring costs in the absence of liability. A legal rule increasing the insurer's incentive to take precautions against liability and thereby reassuring insureds of the reliability of coverage therefore would often be efficient.

The facts in the cases employing the bad-faith doctrine support this analysis. The vast majority involve deficient claim investigation followed by improper de-nial of the insured's claim. Consider the two precedent-setting decisions I referred to several paragraphs ago. *Gruenberg* involved an apparently unwarranted suspi-cion of arson by several fire insurers; in *Silberg* the insured was refused payment as a result of a mistaken determination that his medical insurance claim need not be paid because of overlapping workers' compensation coverage. In these cases the insurer abused its discretion and captured a contract benefit that had already been allocated to the insured.

The odds are good that in many such instances the costs of insurer reactions to penalties for this kind of conduct—additional precautions to avoid claim inves-tigation errors, for example—are not as high as the costs of such alternatives as additional self-protection by the insured or negotiating agreements regarding damages for breach. Critics of the new rules have failed to understand this impor-tant point.[12] They have worried about the high cost of liability for bad faith with-out recognizing that the critical issue is not this cost alone. Rather the issue is whether the cost of previous methods of obtaining desired levels of reliable protec-tion against risk exceed the costs of precautions against the new legal liability.

The strongest economic argument against this rationale is that the unavaila-bility of extra-contract damages is a way of guarding against moral hazard. Be-cause insureds are uncertain of the reliability of their coverage, according to this argument, they may invest more heavily in loss prevention, thus neutralizing some of the moral hazard of insurance. But the weakness of this argument is two fold. First, there is no reason to suppose that this approach reduces the inefficiency of moral hazard to a greater extent than awards of extra-contract damages reduce the inefficiencies with which they deal. Second, the impact of moral hazard varies greatly with the form of coverage and the kinds of risk classification it employs. Yet the traditional rule would deny extra-contract damages for breach regardless of the form of coverage in question. Thus, this argument against the new cause of action is not strong.

There is reason to worry, however, that an unlimited right to extra-contract compensatory and punitive damages may produce excessive precautions by insurers. The subjectivity of damages for mental suffering and the lack of real standards in the awarding of punitive damages could create an inefficient *in terrorem* effect: so far there have been quite a number of awards of over a million dollars.[13] A large number of such awards might create an excessive incentive for insurers to pay questionable claims. And in any case some limitation on these awards is probably in order since few people with the opportunity would want to insure themselves for more than $10–20,000 against the risk of suffering nonpecuniary losses from breach of an insurance contract. One such limit might be to eliminate the right to recover punitive damages and to substitute automatic recovery of prejudgment interest.

A stronger alternative would follow the model of the statutes in some states that now allow recovery of attorneys fees for bad-faith refusals in first-party cases and the few that also impose modest punitive damages.[14] More systematic use of legislatively prescribed and legislatively limited penalties for bad faith might make awards more controllable. For example, a statutory penalty for bad-faith refusals, equal to 50 percent of the amount due under the policy, would sacrifice the current rule's capacity to individualize awards of extra-contract damages, but it could have a stabilizing influence worth the sacrifice. Such limitations would tend to shadow the effects that insurance against nonpecuniary losses would produce. Because there would be policy limits on the amount of such coverage if it were available to the insured, he would not be protected against nonpecuniary losses without limit. A statutory limit on penalties would be a rough estimate of the amount of coverage that insureds, on average, would purchase.

Because of the obstacles to bringing suit, however, this form of limitation might not encourage enough insureds to seek legal redress. An alternative might be to pay any punitive damages awarded in excess of a specified sum (for example, everything in excess of $100,000, less counsel fees) to all the insureds who purchased the same kind of policy from the insurer during the same calendar year as the plaintiff. Such awards would retroactively reduce the cost of coverge that had turned out to be unreliable.

The Nature of the Standard

It is now established that punitive damages for bad-faith refusal to pay first-party insurance claims may be recovered only upon proof of intent to harm the insured, or something close to it. But what kind of nonmalicious conduct by the insurer should warrant recovery of extra-contract compensatory damages?

Probably a truly innocent but inaccurate determination of claim ineligibility should not trigger the cause of action. When serious legal issues requiring judicial resolution arise, refusal of payment would not seem to warrant an extra-contract award. Otherwise the insurer would face the prospect of extra-contract liability in a series of cases raising the same issue but might have no opportunity to adjudicate that issue without the threat of extra-contract damages if the result were unfavorable. The very term *bad faith* suggests at least this limitation.

There are two other possible standards.[15] A subjective bad faith standard would make liability turn on the intent of the denial—whether it was made with knowledge of the claim's validity or conscious disregard of the need to investigate the claim. An objective standard would have liability hinge on the reasonableness of the denial and the legitimacy of doubt about the claim's validity based on the facts of the claim and the application of relevant policy provisions.

Although the two standards are quite different in theory, in practice they would often converge. Few of the decided cases involve quiet and considered but merely negligent judgments by claims personnel that the insured's claim is not covered by his policy. Rather, many of the decisions tell the story of repeated attempts by the insured to furnish satisfactory evidence of coverage, and stubborn, vengeful, or blind refusals by insurers to reconsider the denial of payment.[16] Thus, the failure to investigate properly may be only negligent initially but often becomes subjectively in bad faith after the insured's repeated attempts to demonstrate to claims personnel the claim's eligibility.

Another default leading to bad-faith suits involves inaccurate application of policy terms to demonstrated facts. Sometimes this failing parallels what occurs in defective investigations: initial negligence that eventually is transformed into subjective bad faith. I suspect, however, that often such denials are deliberate from the beginning, but not necessarily in bad faith. These denials may well be the result of doubts by claims personnel about the truth of the facts submitted by the insured individual or company filing the claim. Forgery, fraud, and exaggeration by an insured are easy to suspect, but difficult to prove. If, by denying a claim, the insurer calls what it believes is the insured's bluff, the insured may never be heard from again. But some insureds are heard from again, when they file bad-faith suits against the insurer. In such cases what started out as an attempt to discourage pursuit of a falsified claim will sometimes appear to the jury to have been a deliberate and malicious abuse of the insurer's strategic advantage.

These examples illustrate the variety of reasons that may account for an insurer's refusal to pay valid claims. Each refusal involves a different quality or shade of blame. Perhaps because of the law's traditional reluctance to pay consequential damages for breach of contracts, the term *bad faith* has been used to describe each of these different kinds of blameworthy conduct. A bad-faith exception is circumscribed in a way that seems not to threaten these traditional limitations on contract damages. Even a double protection against disregarding these damage limitations has been invoked by describing the cause of action as the tort of bad faith. Then no infringement at all on contract law may seem to be occurring. All this is partly a smoke screen, however, since it is contract law that the rules change, and many of the cases to which the rules apply do not involve bad faith in the ordinary sense of the term.

Regardless of the terminology used, the important issue is not whether the insurer has acted with subjective bad faith; it is whether the insurer has abused its contractual discretion by taking improper advantage of its strategic position. The test for extra-contract liability, therefore, should be whether the insurer's denial of the claim was reasonable, in light of the facts revealed by the insurer's investigation, the specificity of the policy terms, and the coverage expectations of reasonable insureds. Perhaps the term *bad faith* should even be preserved to help mark the point at which the insurer's scrupulous attention to possible defects in the insured's claim most often turns into real abuse of discretion. But if it is retained, we should recognize that the term *bad faith* is a signifier, and that it is not the behavior being signified. The punishment of subjectively wrongful behavior should remain the province of rules governing punitive damages, and compensatory damages should be recoverable regardless of the insurer's state of mind.

Risk-Distribution Effects

The distributional impact of liability for bad faith can be seen best not by looking at the end result—a few recoveries of extra-contract damages—but by looking at the changes in the claims process produced by the threat of such recoveries. The strategic advantage of the insurer in the past meant that the insured had to bear the risk that he would be unable to persuade the insurer of the validity of his claim. Liability for bad-faith denials of valid claims shifts some of this risk of nonpersuasion to the insurer by raising the cost of improper denials. In the past these consisted mainly of the loss of goodwill and the expenses of occasional litigation; and they were partially offset by savings from refusing to pay some valid claims. Under the new rules, liability for extra-contract damages is an added cost of denying some claims. The threat that this liability will be imposed should encourage insurers to pay a higher proportion of doubtful claims than they did in the past. This practice will have the effect of providing coverage against the risk that the insured will not quite be able to prove the validity of his claim. This is de facto insurance.

Two groups are the chief beneficiaries of this new insurance against the risk of not being insured: (1) those who, through no fault of their own, are unable to marshal the previously necessary proof of claim, but who can meet the new, somewhat less demanding threshold of persuasion; and (2) those who know they have ineligible claims but nevertheless file them and are paid because of the threat of extra-contract liability. Since there is little reason to suspect that any particular characteristics are likely to place an individual in the first group, the benefit its members receive seems unobjectionable on distributional grounds. Except for those cases where more careful maintenance of bills or records would have facilitiated proof of a claim, difficulty of proof is probably not a matter within individual control. Such difficulties are fortuitous, depending on coincidences regarding the nature of losses and the availability of information about them. The benefits produced by the threat of extra-contract liability will be extended to all those who randomly find themselves with problems of proof or are subjected to willful refusals by claims personnel to investigate claims effectively. Some of these claimants will actually be entitled to payment, and some will not, but all will receive it.

However, this expansion of coverage may also create a moral hazard that encourages the second group to file claims. The possibility of fraudulent insurance claims is obviously increased by the new cause of action because of the additional potential liability of insurers for wrongful denial of claims. Unwarranted payment to some of those who fraudulently claim coverage (and to a few who innocently claim it when they are not eligible) is thus the price that is paid for protecting deserving claimants against the risk of nonpersuasion.

Settlement of Third-Party Claims

The second new development in claims regulation also involves the settlement of a claim, but not a claim by the insured for payment of his own loss. Rather, another set of rules has developed to govern the insurer's settlement of liability claims against the insured. The typical liability insurance policy appears to leave the insurer complete discretion to settle or litigate suits brought against the insured: " . . . the company *shall* defend any suit alleging . . . bodily injury or property damage and seeking damages which are payable under the terms of this policy, even if the allegations of the suit are groundless, false or fraudulent; but the company *may* make such investigation and settlement of any claim or suit it deems expedient."[17] [Emphasis added.]

The difference between the mandatory "shall" regarding defense and the optional "may" regarding settlement leaves room for little doubt about the meaning of the settlement provision. Insurers are entitled to settle, even against the wishes of the insured, and they are entitled to refuse to settle even if the insured desires the case against him settled.

The Nature of the Problem

This apparently unlimited discretion may lead to conflicts between the interests of insurer and insured when settlement is contemplated. Suppose that Hardy has a policy with Old Reliable, covering him against liability for up to $20,000 for injury to any individual. Laurel sues Hardy, alleging liability that will be covered by Hardy's policy if the allegations prove to be true. Laurel's damages exceed Hardy's policy limits—suppose that these damages are $60,000 in total but that the chances of Laurel's proving liability are only about 50 percent. The claim then has an expected value of $30,000.

Now suppose that Laurel offers to settle for $20,000. Hardy's economic interest favors settlement. He has nothing to gain and everything to lose if Old Reliable refuses to settle. But Old Reliable's interest is not the same as Hardy's. Old Reliable will lose $20,000 if it settles. If it refuses to settle and the case is tried, its expected loss is only $10,000 (50 percent of $20,000) plus its costs of litigation. To put it another way, Old Reliable has a 50 percent chance of saving $20,000 by refusing to settle (less litigation costs, which I will not consider here since they would have only a quantitative, not a qualitative, impact on the problem). Old Reliable's interests, therefore, conflict with Hardy's. If Old Reliable refuses to settle, it risks a net judgment against Hardy for $40,000 ($60,000 less $20,000 coverage).

An insurer's exercise of discretion in this fashion is questionable on both equitable and economic grounds. From the insured's standpoint, the settlement provision is incompletely specified. The insured has a reasonable expectation that, at the least, his interests will not be completely ignored when the insurer makes settlement decisions. Yet that is what the typical settlement provision purports to allow. The insurer's policy right to control defense and settlement is designed to prevent the insured's interest in settling claims instead of litigating them from driving up the average cost of settlements. But it does not follow that this right of control authorizes complete disregard of the insured's interests. Under modern liability policies the insurer does not simply indemnify the insured; it acts as his representative by defending him and entertaining offers of settlement. A liability insurer is certainly more than a mere guarantor of the insured's obligations despite the apparently unconstrained discretion to settle delegated to it by the policy. The insurer need not be regarded as a full-fledged fiduciary for the law to conclude that as a representative of the insured an insurer may not wholly ignore its principal's interests.

If the insured can legitimately expect that whatever the exact scope of the insurer's settlement obligation, the insurer cannot completely ignore the insured's interests, then this responsibility has already been allocated by the contract. The insured has paid for at least some consideration of his interests when settlement is contemplated. Settlement decisions that completely ignore the insured's interest attempt to reallocate this already allocated contractual advantage. They are abuses of contractual discretion.

These equitable concerns take more concrete form when the issue is analyzed in economic terms. If the insurer is allowed to consider only its own interests in deciding when to settle, there will be an inefficiently low number of settlements. *Laurel v. Hardy* illustrates why. Laurel's claim has an expected value of $30,000 (50 percent of $60,000).[18] Therefore, it would make economic sense for the claim to be settled by Hardy and Old Reliable for any amount less than $30,000. To try the case when Laurel would accept less than $30,000 in settlement would waste the costs of litigation—for in the long run the price of doing so in such cases would be $30,000 *plus* litigation costs.

Because the overall expected value of the claim has two components, however, such efficient settlements often will not be reached. The expected value of Old Reliable's exposure is $10,000 (50 percent of $20,000); the expected value of Hardy's exposure is $20,000 (50 percent of the remaining $40,000 of Laurel's damages). Neither Hardy nor Old Reliable, acting with unconstrained discretion, would settle often enough because neither would be fully responsible for all that is risked whenever a proposed settlement is rejected. When Old Reliable refuses to settle the claim for $20,000, it externalizes part of the risk of refusal to Hardy. Although the insurer's incentive to externalize in this way will vary with the expected value of the claim and the insured's policy limits, its interests and that of the insured will never completely coincide.

This analysis holds true regardless of the state of mind of Old Reliable's claims personnel because the issue concerns abuse of contractual discretion, not bad faith. Old Reliable's reasons for refusing to settle are largely irrelevant. It makes no economic difference whether Old Reliable's decision is considered to be a simple departure from the underlying but incompletely specified purpose of the policy or to be an evil and deliberate misuse of its power to the detriment of Hardy. If Laurel and other plaintiffs like him would settle for less than $30,000, then in the long run litigation costs are wasted by refusing to settle. And this is also true even when Old Reliable doubts its own ultimate obligations to Hardy under the policy—perhaps because Hardy has injured Laurel intentionally—but that issue has not yet been resolved. Insurers sometimes have argued that reasonable doubts about their ultimate liability under the policy terms should justify a decision to offer less in settlement than they otherwise would offer.[19] But in an economic sense this poses the same problem as the hypothetical *Laurel v. Hardy*. If Old Reliable is allowed to discount its expected exposure by the probabilty that it will not ultimately have to pay for any of Hardy's liability—for whatever reason—then even fewer settlements will be reached, and even more litigation costs will be inefficiently incurred.

The insurer might even have quite understandable reasons for refusing to settle, such as its desire to protect the long-term interests of all its policyholders. For example, sometimes the insurer's refusal to settle is caused by what one court has called "institutional considerations."[20] An insurer might refuse an otherwise acceptable settlement offer in order to create a reputation for stinginess that will result in lower future settlements or to create an opportunity to appeal a judgment that could establish a favorable precedent. The insured who is exposed to the risk of a judgment above his policy limits in such a case is used to benefit the insurer and the entire community of other insureds. At first glance this practice might appear efficient. But because of the reverse moral hazard it creates, few insureds should agree to it in advance, even though it might seem to serve their interests *ex ante*. Distinguishing an insurer's refusal to settle for legitimate institutional reasons from its naked attempt to externalize the risk of refusing to settle would be very difficult. An insurer authorized to take only the former action often would be tempted to take the latter as well, but there would be no effective way for the insured or a court to second-guess or to regulate such decisions by the insurer.

The Judicial Solution: A Duty of Settlement

Although the courts' reaction to these problems has now evolved to the point where it is reasonably effective, they have had difficulty providing satisfactory explanations for their actions. The settlement problem was first described as bad-faith resolution of a conflict of interest.[21] This label led naturally to a formula designed to avoid the dangers of subjective bad faith. Insurers were said to owe the insured's interests equal consideration to their own.[22] Unfortunately, although an insurer following this standard may have neutralized its improper state of mind, it still will be unable to act neutrally. The standard describes a stalemate, not a method of reaching results. When conflicting interests are given equal consideration, the party with responsibility for action faces an unresolvable dilemma.

Many courts have turned, therefore, to a more concrete formula to implement the sentiment behind the equal consideration notion. They have created a duty of settlement. Under this formula a liabilty insurer must consider settlement offers as though its policy has no limits—as though it would be liable for the entire amount of any judgment that ensued if it did not settle.[23] An insurer must accept any offer within the limits of coverage that a reasonable party responsible for the entire amount of any subsequent judgment would accept. If the insurer rejects such an offer, then it is liable for the full amount of any subsequent judgment including any excess above its policy limits. In our example, if Old Reliable rejected Laurel's offer to accept $20,000 in settlement, and Laurel was later awarded $60,000, Old Reliable would be liable for this entire judgment if its rejection of Laurel's offer were found to be unreasonable.

This reasonable-offer test gives insurers the incentive to act in an economically efficient manner. The insurer is still entitled to risk the insured's assets by refusing to settle, but only when the potential benefits of rejection outweigh the potential risks. The test requires the insurer to internalize the risks of rejecting a reasonable offer to settle instead of externalizing some of these risks to the insured. Whether the insurer's additional liability is conceived simply as expectation damages, or as consequential damages from breach, the incentive this liability creates is the same. The insurer is encouraged to settle when that course would be most efficient and to refuse settlement when that alternative is economically preferable.

Although the reasonable-offer test as it is currently formulated does not impose liability on the insurer for nonpecuniary losses suffered by the insured as a result of a refusal to settle, this was not always the case. The courts originally holding that refusal of a reasonable settlement offer constitutes bad faith also held that damages for mental suffering could be awarded for breach.[24] This logically followed from the label attached to the insurer's behavior. Today, however, the insured hardly ever recovers nonpecuniary damages when a reasonable offer is rejected and a judgment above policy limits is entered against him. He is entitled only to have the entire judgment paid. In fewer than ten of the hundreds of reported cases on settlement over the last fifteen years have such damages been awarded, and in those cases the egregious conduct of the insurer actually deserved the label bad faith.[25]

Although the unavailability of nonpecuniary damages here may appear to be inconsistent with the treatment of first-party bad-faith cases, in fact the difference is probably appropriate. In the first-party cases the insurer risks little by abusing its discretion unless nonpecuniary damages for such abuse are available. This is because the traditional award of expectation damages merely required payment of the amount that was due under the policy in the first place. In contrast, even if a liability insurer is liable only for pecuniary losses resulting from breach of the duty to settle, it has a strong incentive not to breach. Breach results in liability for the amount originally covered by the policy *plus* any excess above the policy limits awarded in the suit against the insured.

Furthermore, it is less clear in the liability insurance setting than in the first-party cases that an award of nonpecuniary damages would shadow what the parties would have agreed to in the absence of transactions costs. The amount of liability insurance that an insured has chosen to buy reflects the point at which the costs of further protection exceed the benefits of the additional security and freedom from anxiety he would derive from that protection. An award of nonpecuniary damages for the insurer's refusal to settle would protect the insured against the very insecurity he had already deliberately chosen to bear. Although insureds undoubtedly expect some protection against above-policy-limits exposure (through settlements by the insurer), they also expect a good deal of this form of exposure in the event they are sued. In light of this expectation, the notion that an insured would desire very much insurance against the nonpecuniary consequences of an insurer's refusal to settle is implausible.

Nonetheless, like the first-party bad-faith rule, the duty to settle does create insurance against the risk of not being insured. The insurer's duty requires it to settle claims that it would not otherwise settle, in order to protect the insured against the risk of a judgment above policy limits. Although the insurer need not accept all offers of settlement within policy limits, when the offer is reasonable as defined by the cases creating the duty, the insured not only has coverage up to his policy limits; he also has some protection against the risk of liability for amounts that exceed those limits. Although by definition a policy provides no coverage against judgments above the policy's limits, the duty to settle creates some insurance against that very risk.

Strict Liability for Refusal to Settle

The reasonable-offer rule places a heavier burden on the insurer than the policy terms themselves, but it does not hold the insurer to a nonfault standard. The insurer is liable only for judgments resulting from rejection of reasonable settlement offers; the insured remains liable for judgments above his policy limits that are entered after the insurer's rejection of unreasonable offers. An alternative sometimes proposed is strict, or nonfault, liability: the insurer is liable for the entire judgment when it rejects any offer of settlement within policy limits, reasonable or not.[26] However, in theory the insurer's conduct under either standard will be the same. It will reject settlement offers that exceed the expected value of a claim and accept offers that are less than that value. It would make no sense for an insurer to accept unreasonable offers even under a strict liability standard. Since by definition unreasonable offers exceed the expected value of the claims they are intended to settle, in the long run the insurer's cost of accepting such offers would exceed the amount of its liability for rejecting them.

Nevertheless, a strict liability standard might have certain advantages over the reasonable-offer rule. First, although the reasonable-offer rule is efficient in theory, it could be inefficient in practice. Because estimates about the expected value of a claim are judgmental, the reasonable-offer rule must grant the insurer considerable latitude to determine whether to accept or reject offers. Only if an offer were clearly reasonable is liability for rejection certain to be imposed. As a consequence, insurers may reject with impunity some offers that they actually would have accepted were there no policy limits. A strict liability standard would hold the insurer liable for all above-policy-limits judgments that could have been avoided by settlement, in order to neutralize the insurer's power to circumvent the demands of the reasonable-offer rule in this fashion.

A second advantage of a strict liability standard is that it would eliminate an anomaly produced by the reasonable-offer test. Under that test, an insured who is severely blameworthy and has caused considerable loss is likely to receive more protection against a judgment above his policy limits than an insured whose liability is questionable.[27] The insurer's incentive and obligation to settle suits against blameworthy insureds is greater because offers to settle suits against them for amounts within policy limits are more reasonable. Other things being equal, the expected value of a claim against a very negligent defendant is high, whereas the expected value of a claim against a defendant who may not have been negligent is lower. Therefore, the least blameworthy defendants will receive the least protection against above-policy-limits judgments under the reasonable-offer test. A strict liability standard, in contrast, would provide equal protection to both classes of insureds.

On the other hand, a strict liability standard might have undesirable equitable and distributional consequences. Insureds can reasonably expect some protection, by way of settlement, against the risk of suffering judgments above their policy limits. This expectation is what justifies imposing a duty of settlement, rather than leaving legally unregulated the discretion purportedly delegated to insurers by the settlement provisions of liability insurance policies. But the expectation of protection through settlement by the insurer certainly does not extend indiscriminately to the risk of all above-policy-limits judgments. The insured cannot reasonably expect the insurer to accept every offer to settle within policy limits, no matter how groundless, false, or fraudulent the claim. Yet that is very nearly what a strict liability standard would require the insurer to do on pain of being automatically liable for any ensuing judgment. Some have even suggested that there be a duty on the insurer's part to make offers of settlement when it has received none.[28] Creating such a duty would be tantamount to abolishing the very practice of having policy limits, except in cases where the plaintiff refuses an insurer's offer to pay the entire amount of the insured's coverage in settlement. This approach certainly would provide the insured with far more coverage than his reasonable expectations would require.

One possible distributional consequence of a strict liability standard is that it could decrease insureds' incentives to purchase high-limits coverage because it would increase insurers' responsibility for above-policy-limits judgments. This would produce initially a subsidy running from those with high-limits coverage to those with lower limits. Adverse selection probably also would occur since a disproportionate number of insureds with potential above-limits exposure would take advantage of the new standard by purchasing low-limits coverage. This effect could compound the subsidy problem.

After a time, however, it should be possible to set rates to counteract these effects by increasing premiums for low-limits coverage enough to offset any increased exposure to above-policy-limits judgments. This might render higher-limits coverage marginally more in demand than it is at present since the price differences between the two would be reduced. At this point it might even make sense to offer insureds a choice between the reasonable offer and strict liability duties of settlement and to price policies for the latter in accordance with their extra value.[29]

Defense of Liability Claims

I shall now take a second look at a problem covered briefly in chapter 5: the scope of a liability insurer's responsibility for defending suits brought against its insured. The issue arises in the following way. The standard liability policy provides that the insurer "shall defend any suit" alleging liability that would be covered by the policy if the suit proved successful, even if the suit is "groundless, false, or fraudulent." This is important protection since an insured whose insurer does not provide a required defense has won only a Pyrrhic victory: regardless of whether his own defense prevails, the costs of defense can be high.

Even under traditional rules insurers fortunately have much less incentive to breach the duty to defend than to deny first-party claims or to refuse reasonable offers of settlement. First, an insurer found liable for breach must reimburse the insured his or her costs of defense. Those costs may exceed what the insurer itself would have spent in defending. Second, if the insured's own defense fails when the insurer has breached its duty to defend, the insurer also must pay any judgment covered by the policy. Such judgments might have been avoided or their size reduced had the insurer supplied a defense more effective than the one mounted by the insured. Economies of scale and the insurer's expertise are likely to give it a comparative advantage in this respect. Third, an insurer which has wrongfully refused to defend normally is liable for reasonable settlements paid by an insured in cases alleging liability covered by the policy. The insurer might have settled for less or defeated the suit altogether had it defended. All these possibilities threaten the insurer with greater liability for refusing to defend than for undertaking this responsibility.

Nevertheless, the duty to defend sometimes is breached. As in the case of settlement of suits against the insured, however, the reason generally is not subjective bad faith, but contractually unregulated discretion. The problem is that policies provide for a duty to defend whenever a judgment against the insured in the suit in question would be payable under the policy. But if at the outset of a suit against the insured the ultimate coverage responsibility of the insurer under the policy is uncertain, then it is also unclear whether the duty to defend has been triggered. The language of the standard liability policy provides almost no guidance. *

The courts are therefore called upon to determine whether and how the insurer's apparent discretion regarding its defense responsibilities should be limited. Three competing principles bear on this question. First, if a suit against the insured turns out to have been covered by the policy, then the insured can reasonably expect to have been defended. On the other hand, the insurer should not have to pay the costs of defense if, in fact, it has no liability under the policy. Finally, when the insurer's ultimate liability under the policy is in doubt, its interests may conflict with the insured's (in ways to be described) if it does defend him. These potential conflicts of interest make requiring the insurer to defend a questionable solution in some cases.

The tensions between these principles must be resolved if the duty of defense is to be implemented. Assuring the reliability of defense insurance is desirable; other things being equal, it is preferable that the insurer not be forced to defend when it ultimately has no coverage responsibility under its policy; avoiding conflicts between the interests of insurers and insureds also is impor-

---

*Three distinct kinds of doubts about when the duty of defense attaches arise because of this incompleteness of policy language. In each instance the insurer questions whether it ultimately has liability under the policy, and therefore also questions its duty to defend. The insurer may have a *policy defense* because of the inapplicability of the policy to the loss in question; it may have an *enforceability defense* because of some conduct of the insured after loss that contravenes conditions of coverage; or the insurer may have a *coverage defense* against someone claiming to be an unnamed but additional insured under the policy—an alleged resident of the household of a named auto liability insured, for example.

tant. These tensions can be resolved in different ways. One way is to strike a compromise between the three principles. A second is to avoid the conflict of interest problem by sacrificing broad,defense coverage. And a third is to strike a different balance, favoring broad defense coverage, but only by exposing the insured to possible conflicts of interest and requiring a defense in some circumstances where in fact the policy provides no coverage. Each alternative is analyzed below.

The Traditional Approach

There are two ways to implement a duty of defense. The insurer can defend, or the insured can defend himself and be reimbursed the costs of defense by the insurer. A direct defense protects the insured's finances but risks conflicts of interest; self-defense avoids conflicts but financially burdens the insured. The traditional approach allows the insurer an option when it doubts its ultimate coverage responsiblity under the policy.[30] The insurer may offer to defend, subject to a reservation of the right to contest coverge in a subsequent legal proceeding. If the insured accepts this reservation of rights, then the defense goes forward, but the coverage question is reserved for later determination. On the other hand, if the insured rejects the insurer's proposed reservation of rights, the insurer must either defend unconditionally or withdraw entirely. If it defends unconditionally, it is liable for coverage unconditionally; if it withdraws, it can contest coverage later in a separate proceeding, as if it had defended under a reservation. The insurer is liable for any judgment within policy limits and for the costs of defense if the policy is later found to cover the suit in question.

Each approach has advantages and disadvantages for the insurer. Suppose the insurer defends subject to a reservation. If the defense succeeds entirely, there is nothing to contest in the later proceeding. If the defense fails, the insurer still may avoid liability, by contesting coverage and proving its lack of responsibility under the policy. Under this option, the insurer has retained control of the defense, but it automatically incurs the costs of defending even if it is later found to have had no such obligation. On the other hand, if the insured rejects the proposed reservation of rights, the insurer still has a choice. It can defend unconditionally, in which case it pays for a defense, but by defending effectively it may avoid the costs of coverage. But if the liability suit is lost, the insurer is unconditionally liable for coverage.

The insurer's last alternative is to withdraw entirely. By withdrawing the insurer may be able to avoid all costs; but it obtains this opportunity only by surrendering control of the defense and thereby risking liability for comparatively higher defense costs and a settlement or judgment against the insured that might have been avoided had it provided a more effective defense than the insured mounted.

The consequences of these different options also provide some, though not complete, protection of the insured's interests. The potentially severe consequences of withdrawing entirely give the insurer some incentive to defend even when its obligation to do so is in doubt. The insured's interest in being defended is served in this way by the traditional approach. But this interest is not served without qualification. Because the insurer must defend unconditionally if at all when the insured rejects a proposed reservation of rights, the insurer may choose not to defend. The insured in such a case must either finance his own defense or discover an attorney willing to finance both the defense and a later suit against the insurer, in the hope of ultimately prevailing in the latter and obtaining a judgment out of which the insured will be able to pay counsel fees. It is not too uncharitable to the legal profession to suggest that it will sometimes be difficult to find such an attorney. So the impecunious insured may be forced to accept the insurer's reservation of rights.

Yet a defense provided under a reservation may not be conducted entirely in the insured's interest. In some jurisdictions determinations made at trial may be subject to the doctrine of collateral estoppel. For example, if the insured has been sued for both battery and negligence and the policy excludes coverage of liability for intentionally caused harm, a finding at trial against the insured on this battery issue may be dispositive of the coverage question and estop, or prevent, the insured from contesting it in the later, or collateral, proceeding. The insurer therefore has an interest in conducting the defense in ways that may prejudice the insured's position in a later proceeding on the coverage issue.[31] Because the insurer's interest is to defeat the suit entirely or to see the insured held liable for behavior not covered by the policy, it may conduct a defense in a manner that is likely to result in one of these alternatives rather than in a judgment of negligence, which would be covered.

Moreover, even apart from taking anticipatory advantage of collateral estoppel, there are other ways in which the insurer's conduct of a defense may prejudice the insured. The insurer defending under a reservation has less incentive to defend vigorously, because it may discount its own expected loss by the probability that it has no liability under its policy at all. The amount worth investing to defeat the suit is correspondingly lower than in an unconditional defense. In addition, the insurer may be able to press the insured to reveal information that will assist the defense, but which could also work to the advantage of the insurer in its later coverage proceeding against the insured.

A partial solution to some of these problems would allow either of the parties to institute a declaratory judgment proceeding to resolve the coverage issue before trial of the tort claim against the insured. But this solution is no cure-all. Since the insured may later prevail in the tort suit, the costs of resolving the coverge question in advance sometimes would be wasted. And even if the issue does have to be resolved eventually, this approach simply forces insureds to finance the legal costs of declaratory judgment proceedings instead of subsequent proceedings on the coverage issue. It shifts costs chronologically; it does not save or redistribute them.

In sum, the traditional approach compromises the three important interests at stake in duty of defense controversies: the desirability of broad defense coverage, the need to avoid conflicts of interest between insurer and insured when the insurer does defend, and the insurer's interest in saving the cost of defense when it has no obligation to provide coverage. The next approach reaches for a different accommodation.

Burd v. Sussex Mutual Insurance Co.

Originating in the New Jersey case of Burd v. Sussex Mutual Insurance Co.,[32] the second approach interprets the insurer's duty of defense differently. Burd allows an insurer with a potential conflict of interest to defend only if the insured consents to the insurer's reservation of the right to contest coverage. Otherwise the insurer may not defend. The insured then mounts his own defense, and is entitled to reimbursement if the defense is successful or if the damages for which the insured is held liable are found to be payable under the policy.

The opinion in Burd is replete with references to the need to protect insureds from conflicts of interests when they are defended by insurers intending to contest coverage later. But Burd differs from the traditional approach only under unusual circumstances, and its emphasis on protecting insureds from conflicts of interest hides its restriction of an extensive right to a defense. In fact, Burd's major protection is extended to insurers.

The logic underlying Burd assumes that under the traditional approach, an insurer can be collaterally estopped to contest coverage in a later proceeding even if it refuses to defend. Under this view, determinations made in the course of the insured's self-defense may be binding on the insurer in the subsequent coverage proceeding, despite the insurer's absence from the case. This is an unlikely assumption, but let us accept it anyway.[33] In jurisdictions where this assumption is correct, before Burd the insurer had some incentive to defend unconditionally and attempt to defeat the suit entirely. Burd eliminates that incentive. If the insurer's interests might conflict with the insured's, the insurer may not defend unless the insured consents; in such cases, *Burd* holds, collateral estoppel does not apply. In this way the insurer is not put in an impossible position—waiving the right to contest coverage if it defends and subjecting itself to possible collateral estoppel if it does not. It is given an unconstrained opportunity to contest coverage at a later time.

But all this depends on the assumption that collateral estoppel can apply against an insurer that does not defend. If we no longer accept this questionable assumption, the effects of *Burd* look a bit different. *Burd* reduces the risk of conflicts of interest,* but only by decreasing the insured's chances of being defended by the insurer. *Burd* therefore improves on the traditional approach only if it is read as requiring the insured's informed consent to the insurer's providing a defense in the face of a conflict of interest. Yet the opinion in *Burd* says nothing about obtaining the insured's informed consent to the insurer's defending even when there may be conflicts between its own interests and the insured's. Though *Burd* eliminates the conflict arising from the threat of collateral estoppel, other conflicts remain: the insurer's diminished incentive to defend vigorously and the possibility that it will obtain information from the insured that can later be used against him in the coverage proceeding. Very few insureds consenting to a reservation of the insurer's right to contest coverage will have any awareness of such possibilities. A reservation of rights merely protects against the insurer's waiver of its rights; it does not purport to inform the insured of potential conflicts. Nevertheless, *Burd* speaks only of consent to the reservation, not of informed consent to these conflicts.

In short, despite their minor differences, both *Burd* and the traditional approach give the insurer a series of options—it may defend subject to a reservation, defend unconditionally, or withdraw entirely—each with different consequences. The insured receives some protection against conflicts of interest (though not

---

*Burd talks as though it protects the insured, by holding that an insurer with a conflict may only defend if the insured consents to a reservation of the right to contest coverage. Yet this prohibition would be necessary only in jurisdictions where an insurer defending without a reservation may nevertheless contest coverage. For if an insurer so defending has waived its right to contest coverage, then it has no conflict because it will be liable for any judgment entered against the insured. Yet the opinion in *Burd* itself acknowledges the traditional rule that an insurer defending without a reservation may not deny coverage later. And if this is so, then there is little reason to prohibit the insurer from defending without a reservation since by doing so the insurer has agreed to defend unconditionally.

complete protection), but he may be left without a defense and may not have the means to finance an effective defense of his own.

Gray v. Zurich Insurance Co.

The last approach to these problems rejects the others: it chooses to risk conflicts of interest in order to assure the insured a defense. But in so doing it almost completely ignores the insurer's interest in not defending when it has no ultimate coverage responsibility. Originating in the California case of *Gray v. Zurich Insurance Co.*,[34] this approach requires the insurer to defend as long as the suit against the insured might result in a judgment covered by the policy. Failure to defend in any such case automatically subjects the insurer to liability both for the costs of the defense and for the judgment in the underlying suit. The insurer may later contest coverage in cases that might be covered by the prolicy only if it povides the insured a defense.

Gray assures the insured a defense in almost any case where a defense might be expected. But it tends to disregard serious conflict of interest problems with the simple prescription that the defending insurer must always conduct litigation only in the interests of the insured. This is too facile a dismissal of the problem. The conflicts that arise when there is a possiblity that the insurer will not be liable on the policy are not entirely extinguished merely by precluding any collateral estoppel, as we saw in discussing the traditional approach and *Burd*. The insurer in such a position may defend less vigorously or be made privy to confidential information that it can later use to the insured's disadvantage in contesting coverage responsibility. The temptation to take advantage in one or more of these ways will not disappear on its own. Moreover, in assuring that there will be a defense of every covered claim, *Gray* pays a risk-distributional price: it also supplies a defense for more claims that turn out not to have been covered than the other two approaches.[35]

This group is composed of two different sets of claimants, for one of which coverage of defense costs is desirable and for one of which it is not. *Gray* requires a defense of insureds accused of causing intentional injury because they might be found liable only for negligence. There is little reason to be concerned that insureds who ultimately are exonerated altogether (or found liable for negligence only) receive such a defense. After all, this group of insureds is found innocent of any deliberate wrongdoing, and coverage of the costs of defense against such claims is not independently available. The desirability of assuring a defense for this group, as we saw in chapter 5, seems to be what motivated the *Gray* court to invoke the expectations principle in the group's behalf.

But a second group—those who are found liable for committing intentional torts—also receives an insured defense under *Gray*. There is no reason to favor this group with such a benefit. Indeed, a policy provision doing so explicitly would probably be held against public policy in most states and declared invalid. This undesirable by-product of *Gray* could be avoided only by requiring the insured to reimburse the insurer the costs of defense in such cases. And even then the insurer would bear the risk of the insured's inability to reimburse these costs—a very real risk since the insured will already have suffered a judgment for which he is individually liable and which is not dischargeable in bankruptcy.

Comparison of the Approaches

The traditional, *Burd*, and *Gray* approaches each must strike a trade-off among three values: avoiding conflicts, assuring a defense, and protecting the insurer against the cost of a defense that the policy does not require it to provide. The need to make these trade-offs inevitably has an impact on the efficiency of the system. Under all three approaches, the party with initial responsibility for defense and settlement will not always have to bear the ultimate cost of its decisions. The possibility that this party, whether insurer or insured, will be able to externalize these costs reduces its incentive to make efficient decisions. Equitable and distributional goals may justify some of this sacrifice of efficiency, though it is a different sacrifice under each approach.

Under the traditional approach and *Burd*, the insurer defending under a reservation of rights agreement may be unwilling to settle a claim that it would otherwise settle or to defend the claim as vigorously as it would were it certain as to its liability under the policy. Only when the insurer finds it desirable to defend unconditionally will it internalize all the costs of its litigation strategies. Because *Burd* makes it easiest for the insurer to avoid defending unconditionally, this approach most strongly promotes the externalization that results from conditional representation. *Gray* probably follows the more efficient course. *Gray* produces less externalization than the other approaches by compelling the insurer to defend even in doubtful cases.

Gray seems superior for several other reasons as well. First, insurers are likely in general to have more ability than insureds to assess the qualifications of defense attorneys and to supervise the conduct of a defense economically. They are less likely to waste defense costs and more likely to take advantage of economies of scale than individual insureds who secure their own defenses. Second, insureds would have to spend more time and energy in searching for credit to finance a defense than insurers, who have ready access to capital. Finally, assuming that a duty to settle exists in all jurisdictions, *Gray* would more often place the insurer, which is legally obligated to make efficient settlement decisions, in a position to do so. *Gray* tends to avoid oversettlement by the insured but shares with the other approaches the risk of underinvestment in a defense whenever the insurer intends to contest coverage in a subsequent proceeding. And because *Gray* more often extends a free defense to those who are later found liable for committing intentional torts, it creates a moral hazard that is itself inefficient.

THE NEW BALANCE OF ADVANTAGES

The new rules regarding bad faith, settlement, and defense have realigned the balance of advantages enjoyed by insurers and insureds in the claims process. These rules recognize that relations between insurers and insureds are not always entirely cooperative. Because the parties can become adversaries once an insurance claim is made, some legal regulation of their relations is required. No adversarial system can be entirely neutral; of necessity an insurance claims system allocates some advantages to insurers and some to insureds.

The following pages step back from the details of the legal doctrines we have been studying in order to examine the more general patterns that the new balance of advantages exhibits. The purpose here is to understand how this body of law has gone about translating the rights it has created into remedies that make these rights real for the parties the rights serve. As in all translation, the source and the product influence each other. As the attempt to translate rights into remedies proceeds, rights are modified and transformed, and existing remedies are reshaped to serve the rights they reflect.

We have seen three different ways in which legal rules governing the claims process realign the balance of advantages we have been examining: (1) they limit insurer discretion by specifying the insurer's obligations under incomplete or vague policy provisions; (2) they counterbalance that discretion by penalizing its abuse; and (3) they reallocate the risk of uncertainty as to the scope of coverage.

Specification

Liability insurance policies often create obligations that are insufficiently detailed to govern insurer conduct completely. They appear to grant the insurer the privilege to settle claims but impose no obligation to do so, and they create a duty to defend the insured without specifying its breadth or limits. If we look at the discretion created by the policy alone, the insurer in these situations is in a particularly advantageous position. Because the insurer controls the fund out of which settlements are paid, it can make decisions with little or no regard for the insured's interests and exclusive regard for its own. Similarly, it can refuse to defend liability claims, or it can defend under circumstances that may prejudice the insured's position in any later dispute over coverage.

These are considerable advantages, neutralized under traditional doctrine mainly by the courts' long-standing tendency to favor insureds in disputes over coverage, administrative regulation of the cost of insurance, and insurers' own long-term interest in maintaining goodwill. Part of the function of the new rules governing claims is to narrow the discretion apparently left to insurers under standard policies by specifying insurers' obligations under vague or incomplete policy provisions. Interpretation of the settlement provisions of the standard liability policy to require that the insured's interests be given consideration is one example. *Gray's* mandate that a defense be provided for any suit that might be covered under a liability policy is another.

These efforts to narrow or limit insurers' discretion, however, only create new rights on paper. These new rights are no more self-enforcing than the insured's right to payment of a valid first-party claim or to a properly conducted defense. It takes a second step in the realignment of advantages to give these rights force.

Counterbalancing Discretion and Penalizing Bad Faith

The second step in the process of legal realignment counterbalances the insurer's strategic position by creating remedies for denying the insured both his traditional policy-based rights, and the newer discretion-limiting rights that have been produced by recent developments in legal doctrine. Extra-contract liability for bad-faith refusal to pay first-party claims is designed to induce greater care by the insurer in its review of claims. The threat of liability for above-policy-limits judgments constrains the insurer's discretion to risk the insured's assets by litigating a case to a verdict instead of settling it. And the various rules governing the duty of defense give insurers an incentive to consider the interests of insureds in deciding how to implement that duty.

Notice, however, that these adjustments do not create mandatory obligations; they merely impose liabilities. They change the stakes in the claims process by making the insurer's exercise of discretion, or its conduct in bad faith, potentially more expensive than either would have been in the past. The insurer still is free to deny first-party claims; but the possible cost of denial has been increased in the event the claim is in fact valid. The insurer still may serve its own interests exclusively in considering settlement offers. It simply risks greater liability by doing so. And in some circumstances the insurer still can breach the spirit of its duty to defend; but it cannot breach without risking liability for much more than the cost of supplying a defense.

The availability of each of these new remedies makes it much more likely that the parties will reach an accommodation that reflects the purposes of their agreement—even when these purposes have been only incompletely specified. In this sense the new rules are not really intended to create new substantive rights, but to enforce the old ones. In the process, however, they inevitably create new rights—in each case, by creating what amounts to new insurance, through allocation of the risk of uncertainty as to coverage.

Allocating the Risk of Uncertainty

All insurance contracts allocate risks. By making policy obligations more concrete and creating new remedies for breach, rules governing the claims process allocate risks that in the past would have been shouldered by the insured. Paradoxically, in each case at least part of this new coverage is insurance against the risk of not being insured.

In the first-party context the insured traditionally bore the risk that the insurer would make an inaccurate determination and deny his claim. With the rise of extra-contract liability for bad faith, however, part of this risk has been shifted to the insurer. The insurer now has a much greater incentive to make accurate determinations. Further, if the insurer makes the wrong determination, under many circumstances the insured is protected against the nonpecuniary consequences of the insurer's denial. In effect, the insured has insurance against damage resulting from the wrongful denial of coverage. Inevitably some people who actually are not covered against the loss in question will nevertheless receive payment for it. This too creates a kind of coverage—against not quite fitting within the boundaries of coverage.

The duty of settlement also creates insurance against uncertainty. A principal function of the duty is to make settlement decisions serve the joint interests of insurer and insured rather than those of the insurer alone. The duty therefore partially protects the insured against the risk of judgments in excess of policy limits, even when there is no uncertainty as to the scope of coverage. In addition, however, the insurer is required to comply with the duty even when it is uncertain whether its policy covers the suit against its insured. By requiring the insurer to ignore this factor in evaluating settlement offers, the duty of settlement shifts this risk of uncertainty as to coverage to the insurer.

Finally, rules putting teeth into the duty of defense also shift to the insurer some of the risk of uncertainty as to coverage. Insurers rarely refuse to defend when coverage responsibilities are certain. They refrain when they believe there is no coverage or when the question is in doubt. *Gray* shifts much of this risk of uncertainty to the insurer by assuring defense insurance whenever there might be coverage. *Burd* and the traditional approach shift less of this risk to the insurer but still shift some of it. In different ways, each approach tends to protect the insured's right to a defense by constraining the insurer's freedom to avoid its obligations when there are doubts about coverage.

The problems that arise during the insurance claims process call for a diversity of solutions. As the law has come to recognize these problems, adjustments have been made in the advantages enjoyed by insurers and insureds in that process. Most important, the traditional rules governing contract damages and other remedies have been modified to take account of the special character of insurance relations. And that special character has informed efforts to constrain insurers' exercise of discretion so that their conduct meets the demands made on it by the mixed purposes of insurance law. Regulation of the claims process should continue to be a dynamic undertaking. Insurance law rights and the remedies that implement them need to be revised as new problems arise, as remedies prove inadequate or excessive, and as the interaction of both rights and remedies leads to new insights about the proper scope of each.

8 Where Do We Go from Here?

The purpose of this book has been to uncover new ways of thinking about insurance and insurance law. Ideas from economics and philosophy and theories about the legal process can produce valuable insights into issues that long have troubled insurance law. My intention throughout has been to begin rather than to conclude a process of analysis.

Before leaving this subject I want to generalize from the analysis in earlier chapters and indicate some of the problems that are raised by that kind of analysis. Three issues can provide a focus for discussion of these general insights and the problems they raise. The first is what might be called the question of "multiple justification." I have isolated three purposes of insurance law—economic, risk-distributional, and equitable—and traced the operation of these purposes through a series of different legal doctrines and issues. But what is the relation between these purposes and the trade-offs that insurance law makes among them?

The second question concerns the role of insurance law in promoting risk distribution and redistribution. Insurance law is one of many devices whose effect sometimes is to redistribute wealth. What can be said—again, in general—about the proper role of insurance law in this respect?

Finally, as insurance becomes a more and more important device for distributing risk, what does this increased importance say about the rest of public affairs? Many names have been given to the kind of society we maintain—postindustrial, welfare-capitalist, postmodern, and so forth. What more can we learn about the kind of society we are becoming by examining more carefully the functions of insurance and the burdens we place on it in the future?

I do not propose to address these questions at length here. Rather I want to show how they naturally arise from the problems surveyed in preceding chapters and to note the kinds of issues that need to be resolved in order to answer them at greater length and in more detail. Once we understand that insurance law can be structured to accord with our complicated attitudes toward the distribution of risk, these questions arise almost automatically. They raise issues that should be high on any agenda for research into the functions of insurance in our legal and economic system.

MULTIPLE JUSTIFICATION

The dominant message of this book is that insurance law can best be understood by examining the economic, distributional, and equitable purposes that it serves. Assessing the influence of each of these purposes on the bodies of law examined was an important part of every chapter. Yet each analysis was somewhat ad hoc and intuitive. There was no calculus that determined the weight of each purpose or the proper priorities among them when they came into conflict.

Is there a formalizable relation among these purposes? I doubt that there is, although I will try to show in a moment that my analysis has suggested some regularities in the relation among the purposes. But in my view there is no deeper formal structure beyond the purposes. The relations between them reflects the position of the intuitive pragmatist that was described in chapter 2. The answers and insights that we can gain about the fundamentals of insurance law are contextual and prudential, not formulaic. The purposes we isolated and the analytical elaboration of them we achieved are as close to a hard bottom as we are likely to get in understanding this body of law. Still, it may be useful to see what a general statement of the relation among the purposes of insurance law would look like, if only to see how far we are from having a satisfactory one.

One interpretation of this relation would be that the goals of insurance law are each the expression of a single, overriding principle. There would, however, be deep disagreement about the identity of that principle. It might resemble Ronald Dworkin's egalitarian thesis that everyone is entitled to equal concern and respect[1] or the cluster of libertarian values reflected in Robert Nozick's *Anarchy, State, and Utopia*.[2] Depending on the constitutive principle chosen, the power and application of the three subsidiary goals of insurance law would differ. For example, Dworkin's principle might allow a great deal of room for risk-distributional considerations; Nozick's would allow almost none. The point is that the primary principle would help shape the three subsidiary goals of insurance law.

I do not believe, however, that any single principle, even a complex and rich one, can explain most of insurance law. As a consequence I doubt that any particular conception of equality or liberty could do so. In fact, any attempt to explain insurance law by reference to one of these two principles alone would not really constitute an explanation. It would instead be an argument for substantially modifying this body of law to accord with a single principle, for majestic notions like equality and liberty are much more normative than they are descriptive of actual legal regimes in our system.

A second view, at the other extreme, is that there can be no systematic relation among the purposes of insurance law. According to this view, any attempt to describe such a relation would be silly because the accommodation of purposes reached in any given domain of insurance law simply reflects the arbitrary combination of values in ascendancy at the time. No neutral principle for adjudicating among the purposes is available because that principle itself would reflect a bias in favor of one or more of its subsidiary purposes. If this is true, then neutral principles are not neutral because they have no objective status; and they are not principled because they are shot through with contradictions.[3]

This kind of attack on the attempt to develop theory in insurance law perhaps is ultimately irrefutable, as it is when it is levelled against the attempt to develop a theory of any human activity. The way we behave and ought to behave is responsive to values, values are subject to change, and different people or groups hold different values at any given time. Admittedly any theory that totally ignored this metaphysical fact of life would be naive. But law and theories about it are designed to stand between us and this metaphysical nightmare—to help construct something that makes social life under the threat of meaninglessness worthwhile.

Even if it is only the existence of shared values that makes legal theory possible, complete skepticism about the possibility of theory is not warranted. We are not totally lacking in community; we speak, reason together, and agree on a great deal. Individuals' values do overlap. For example, most people can recognize the sentiment that is implicit in the notion of economic efficiency without ignoring the counterbalancing importance of fairness in the distribution of value. People want to economize and they care about waste; but they care about a fair distribution of advantages and opportunities as well, even if they cannot agree entirely on how to define that criterion or measure results. How we go about accommodating these competing values is the important question. Ambivalence about the choice among goals that are not entirely compatible is not necessarily evidence of contradiction; it can represent instead a sophisticated recognition of the complexity of the world and of its imperfections.

This recognition should lead, therefore, to the last interpretation of the rela-

tion among the purposes of insurance law. Under this interpretation these purposes are semi-autonomous. They are not each responsible to a single overriding
principle. At times these goals are inconsistent, and some reconciliation or accommodation among them must be reached. But this does not mean that the reconciliation is unprincipled or unsystematic. Rather, the process occurs in specific
contexts, where reasons for any determined weighting of purposes can be articulated, examined, and criticized. In fact, as experience in articulating the strength
of each purpose in particular settings accumulates, regularities begin to emerge.

The first and most important regularity we have observed is the logical priority of economic goals throughout insurance law. This dominance is reflected in
the very existence of a private insurance market. The law makes incursions into
that market, both to facilitate the market's operation and to impose noneconomic
purposes on it. But private incentives are allowed to operate in the absence of specific and deliberate legal intervention. The result is that freedom of contract and
the pursuit of economic efficiency automatically prevail unless a specific legal decision to alter this arrangement is made. Thus, insurers are generally entitled not
to offer pollution liability insurance when it is too difficult to price, just as they are
permitted to divide insureds into risk classes, to coordinate coverage by contract,
and otherwise to seek their own advantage in ways that often work to the benefit of
the community at large as well.

On the other hand, sometimes this pursuit of economic self-interest is counterproductive; then the law may intervene. For instance, part of the idea behind
both the expectations principle and the new rules governing the claims process is
that the threat of liability will cause adjustments in the behavior of insurers that
will be more conducive to overall efficiency than the practices that occur in the
absence of such threats. Judicial and legislative approaches to the coordination of
coverage deal with inefficiency in a different way. Like so many legal rules, legally
prescribed coordination strategies save the costs of reaching individual agreements
providing for coordination.

Furthermore, even when legal intervention is designed to achieve distributional or equitable aims, as opposed to efficiency, the power and legal status of the
private market must be reckoned with. The operation of private incentives may
confound the law's attempt to achieve such aims even after a decision that they
should take precedence over economic values. The decision to sacrifice efficiency
in favor of these other goals therefore cannot be made only in the abstract; the
method used to implement the sacrifice must also be considered because the most
straightforward method may not always be the most effective. Examples of this
phenomenon abound: if the law demands that occurence as well as claims-made
coverage be offered by liability insurers, less insurance may be sold; and if certain

forms of risk classification are prohibited, surrogate forms with very similar draw-backs may emerge.

Even when concurrent private incentives do not prevent legal rules from achieving desired results, the operation of these incentives may have undesirable side effects. For example, the cost of coverage may rise when the reasonable expectations of insureds are honored, pricing some potential purchasers out of the market; or the law's effort to assure that the rights expressed in insurance policies actually are implemented may in practice extend coverage to those who have no actual right to it. These side effects have deficiencies that are often worth tolerating in order to obtain the direct effects that accompany them. But decision makers need to anticipate these effects when they evalute alternative approaches to intervention.

These potential difficulties also suggest the importance of selecting the proper legal institution to do the job in question, especially when the job involves a partial "taming" of the market. As we saw in examining the expectations principle, different legal institutions have very different strengths in this regard. By imposing liability rules, the courts can alter the economic incentives of both insurers and insureds. But they cannot mandate particular actions through such rules because enterprises in the market are still legally free to act in their own economic interests by incurring the cost of liability instead of altering their behavior. In contrast, administrative regulation and legislation have a greater capacity to control activity directly. When there is collective certainty about the economically desirable course, or an intention to redistribute or spread risk systematically, these two approaches are likely to be superior to the less systematic capacities of adjudication. But the courts have the ability to be selective in their application of general rules and, therefore, can individualize their equitable determinations. Although legislative or regulatory rules also can strive to encourage equitable dealing between insurers and insureds, they risk elevating form over substance because of the distance of general rules from the cutting edge of individual transactions.

Further, when more than one legal institution has authority to take legal action, these institutions should be cognizant both of the flexibility of the market and of their relations to each other. We saw in chapter 6 that the courts could not and should not avoid resolving coordination conflicts; but to be effective, they should recognize that the most valuable contribution they can make to the coordination process is to provide clarity and predictability of result. Similarly, legislatures and regulators are in a much better position to influence the distributional impact of various coordination schemes. Their position does not require action; but if action is to be effective, it should come from one of these two institutions in most instances.

Two other insights generated in earlier chapters also bear on the problem of multiple justification. In building a theory of coordinated coverage we saw that a new conception of insurance may be starting to emerge. This conception views insurance as a multilateral risk-sharing arrangement rather than exclusively as the sum of a series of bilateral contracts. Further, in exploring the new rules governing the claims process, we saw that the level and form of insurance activity *ab initio* is in part determined by the legal rules that govern it, including the rules that implement policy rights in practice. Both these analyses suggest a sense in which legal rules do not simply stand outside a field of activity—in this case insurance— and operate upon it. The rules that are producing a new conception of insurance and the legal regime that governs the claims process are also parts of the fields they regulate. These legal and nonlegal realms permeate each other.

Thus, what seemed at first to be a paradoxical form of insurance—coverage against the absence of insurance—was only superficially paradoxical. The legal actions and economic reactions that produced this unusual form of coverage were as natural as any other legal or economic event. Thinking of rules about insurance claims as having economic intentions and distributional side effects, or distributional aims and economic consequences, was simply a convenient way of distinguishing categories that aid analysis.

In short, it makes sense to talk of separate economic, equitable, and risk-distributional purposes of insurance law because isolating purposes in this way helps to clarify both what we are doing and what else we might do with insurance law. But there is a misleading feature to the question, "How are the goals related?" The question excessively reifies these three categories. The notion that legal and economic activity are analytically independent is, similarly, slightly misleading. The purposes of insurance law represent different matters of importance and, in this sense, have a separate status. But they arise out of concrete issues; their relation to each other in general is simply the sum of their relations in particular settings. That relation is generalizable as far as we have gone and undoubtedly a bit further in the future. But the sum of what has been done to accommodate the three purposes in individual cases and subfields is all that there is to their relation. This is the sense in which insurance law reflects a pragmatic vision of risk-distributional justice.

In saying this I am not suggesting that there is never any conflict among the purposes of insurance law. As we saw almost continually in the preceding pages, there are consistent tensions among all the things we want, ideally, to do with insurance law and the things that it is possible to do. Because our values are "fragmented," to use Thomas Nagel's term,[4] the purposes of insurance law that reflect these values are fragmented as well. There is probably no way to specify in advance a method of resolving these tensions or, failing that, of devising a general formula for choosing one value over another. But we can try continually to articulate the bases of our intuitions about the proper way to accommodate the tensions among our goals in particular settings. Creating categories that help to analyze these goals is a useful method of articulating these intuitions.

RISK REDISTRIBUTION

Proposals to use individual bodies of law—like torts, or contracts, or insurance law—to redistribute wealth are typically met with a trio of criticisms. This form of redistribution is said to be inefficient, inequitable, and undemocratic. It is inefficient because there are likely to be cheaper ways of transferring wealth and because the transfers tend to be in kind and therefore do not necessarily reflect the uses that would be preferred by recipients if they were entitled to choose how to spend their redistributed wealth. Such redistribution is thought to be inequitable because it mainly burdens participants in the tort, contract, or insurance systems and therefore does not systematically allocate burdens in accordance with ability to pay. And such redistribution is said to be undemocratic because it is fashioned by unelected institutions or takes place in ways that are camouflaged because of their complex effects.

Certainly in comparison to a global decision to redistribute wealth, perhaps through a highly progressive negative income tax or some similar device, these criticisms of local redistribution through particular legal doctrines have force. Local risk redistribution may be less effective than a global form, especially if a global system of risk allocation could be operated efficiently. It is less clear, however, that local redistribution would be any less effective than an inefficiently operating global system. And the latter is what would probably result, if we were to have a global system.

If in fact global redistribution is not feasible or not desired, then there may be as much justification for sacrificing efficiency to advance risk-distributional goals as there is for making the opposite sacrifice. Seeking efficiency in insurance law can be just as antidistributional as promoting risk distribution through this body of law can be inefficient. What we need is a reason for choosing one or the other goal or some combination of the two that is an acceptable compromise. Certainly no compromise can be achieved if efficiency is made a criterion that risk-distribution efforts must satisfy before they can be considered legitimate. If we start by accepting a given distribution of wealth, as welfare economics must do in order to proceed, then attempting to satisfy distributional goals often will be inefficient because it will not maximize the value of resources in the hands of those who possess them. But if the existing distribution is open to question, then redistributing efficiently is only a value other things equal. Efficiency under such circumstances is not necessarily to be valued above other goods, although we saw frequently in our analyses that the criterion of efficiency, other things being equal, provided one method of assessing alternative rules for preferability.

Despite this general justification for local forms of risk distribution, legal institutions have not always been sensitive to the nuances of their risk-distributional efforts. The courts have shown a decided tendency to overlook two important distinctions: between short and long-term distributional effects and between risk spreading in general and specific risk redistributions. Since the courts are not effectively positioned to control the side effects of their distributional efforts, they should be especially careful to anticipate these effects when contemplating legal intervention in the private market. The positive effects of short-term risk spreading may be outweighted by disadvantages in the long run; and a decision to extend coverage will not always spread risk broadly and evenly over the entire community of risk sharers. When distributional interventions fail even to take account of all their distributional implications, they are most susceptible to criticism on economic grounds.

The charge that risk redistribution through insurance law is inequitable and undemocratic requires a different kind of answer. Whereas very few individual redistributional legal actions receive anything like express popular consent, that is also true of the vast majority of political and legal decisions our institutions make. Moreover, the less direct the political check on attempts at risk redistribution, the more likely popular preferences expressed in market decisions will be able to exercise an indirect check.

This is because the market itself produces a form of economic checks and balances against unacceptable redistribution. The kinds of programs that are capable of withstanding market attempts at circumventing redistribution—mandatory rules regarding risk classification linked with minimum insurance requirements, for example—usually are legislative. These must command considerable popular support to be enacted. But redistributional actions taken by legal institutions that are not as politically accountable as legislatures—an insurance commissioner's prohibition of age or sex as rating variables or a court's extension of the right to extra-contract damages for bad-faith breach of an insurance contract—are much more subject to market reaction or neutralization. Those who are burdened more than they are benefited by such redistributional moves can vote against them with their wallets by purchasing less insurance and investing the money saved in other forms of protection. I am not suggesting that this opportunity eliminates all the inequities that otherwise inhere in such redistributional moves. But the opportunity to vote economically does afford a kind of safety value that protects against unanticipated pressures arising out of redistributional experiments.

In the end, it seems to me, local redistributional experiments must prove themselves to be acceptable over the long run, or market and political forces will combine to eliminate them. Therefore, their undemocratic character need not be a major worry. The danger of local redistributional efforts lies not in their long-run effect on the majority, which ultimately will have its way. Rather, any dangers they entail lie in the adverse short-run effects of misguided experiments, and in the inability of small minorities who happen to be specially disadvantaged by these experiments to avoid suffering because of them. The rare teenager who lives with his grandmother and wants to drive a car only a few miles a week to take her to the grocery store may have to pay half the price of the car for mandatory liability insurance. In short, to remedy one risk-distributional unfairness, another may have to be tolerated.

INSURANCE IN THE FUTURE

One of the many clues to the kind of society we are becoming is the role that insurance now plays and the role that it may play in the society of the future. We have seen that insurance law helps mediate between two very different approaches to the management of risk: individual risk bearing and collective risk sharing. In our economy this is an important task since a host of controversial political and legal questions turn on the relative importance of these two realms. We have a heavily managed economy in which the state, through law, is intimately involved. But a great deal of authority is still left to individual decisions in the marketplace. Individual responsibility is encouraged, but a variety of safety nets, some universally available and some privately purchased, are also prevalent. There is no very accurate name to be used in describing this state of affairs. It is a combination of two contradictions in terms: welfare capitalism and free-market socialism.

Regardless of its name, two points can be made about the kind of society we live in now and the one we are becoming. Insurance plays a significant role in that society, and law—in this case insurance law—is an important device for marking the boundary between the public and private domains of influence over insurance. For instance, there is now heavy emphasis in our system on privately financed, legally supervised protection against risk, much of it in the form of insurance. Private automobile insurance is required and homeowner's coverage

nearly so. Health and life insurance cover vast numbers of people. First-party accident and disability insurance are growing forms of coverage. More public devices for distributing risk—such as workers' compensation, unemployment
insurance, and Social Security—are almost universal. Businesses also make heavy
use of insurance. They often have general liability insurance, specific liability
coverage tailored to their individual needs, business interruption and contingent
business interruption coverage, and fire insurance.

Even if all this coverage were miraculously priced in accordance with each
individual's and business's expected loss, in the aggregate it would amount to a
startling accumulation of protection against the random misfortunes of life and
commerce. When we add to the simple existence of all this coverage the inevitable inefficiencies of classification and pricing, the implication is all the more clear.
Our society has constructed a massive set of insurance arrangements to protect
against risk and has broadly distributed the burden of this protection.

However much we still rely on entrepreneurship and risk taking to serve other
social goals, it is obvious that there is now great stress on avoiding risk by distributing it broadly. In contrast to what might have been said fifty or even thirty years
ago, there is now a widespread and decided preference for security over speculation. And there seems little reason to doubt that this trend will continue. Moreover, the legal rules, the legislation, and the regulatory standards surveyed
throughout this book are part of this trend. To be sure, these sources of law recognize other goals besides promoting broader risk distribution—that recognition
is what makes insurance law complex and worth studying. But we saw the law make
persistent attempts to reconcile the goals, or at least to allow them each space to
operate, instead of systematically subordinating one to the other. Consequently,
broad risk distribution is being encouraged on a variety of fronts.

What can we look for in future insurance developments to provide clues concerning the direction we are heading? I would monitor three separate phenomena
for evidence of trends: the nature of any growth in insurance coverage, the relative
stress placed on loss prevention by this new or increased coverage, and the role
played by public insurance markets in remedying the deficiencies of the private
sector.

The Growth of Coverage

Growth in the amount and kinds of insurance purchased could be significant evidence of the shape our social institutions will take in the future. Growth in the
amount of coverage people buy could be some indication of a shift toward protection against catastrophic losses—a form of loss against which there is compara-

tively little protection at present. Insurance is widespread, but it is purchased at low limits. At present, insurance is used more to provide minimal or modest protection against misfortune than to guard against catastrophe. Individuals are still bearing the risk of great loss, although government benefits and the right to discharge debts in bankruptcy are available as protection against certain forms of catastrophic loss. This is one reason that coordination of multiple sources of coverage is likely to become an increasingly prominent legal problem as coverage proliferates. Legal strategies of coordination permitting or encouraging stacking insurance policies together would reflect greater emphasis on protection against catastrophic loss.

Not only would growth in aggregate levels of insurance protection be significant; an increase in the portion of the population covered by certain forms of insurance would indicate greater social stress on the benefits of risk distribution. For example, at present disability insurance is much less widespread than medical insurance. Social Security and veterans' benefits provide the only substantial protection against disability for most people. Families and social service agencies are therefore called on to nurture and provide a large share of the support received by the disabled. The scope and extensiveness of disability insurance and the role of families and social service agencies in supporting the disabled may thus be linked or at least mutually influential. Change in the nature of any one of these endeavors might make change in the others worth anticipating.

This potential relation betwen disability insurance and noninsurance forms of protection is really an example of a broader point: the advent of new forms of insurance coverage can provide evidence of evolving attitudes toward risk in general and toward the specific risks against which the new forms of coverage protect. For instance, for some ten years now there has been growing ferment about the incidence of medical malpractice and products liability lawsuits. There are new proposals on the table to abolish or limit legal liability for losses arising out of medical care and the use of such dangerous products as prescription drugs. First-party insurance coverage would be substituted for legal liability as a method of providing compensation for these losses. In chapter 3 we examined slightly different but related proposals for compensating the victims of exposure to asbestos and other toxic chemicals. The evolution of all these proposals has been stalled not only by technical difficulties, but also by principled objections. The major such objection concerns the undesirability of relieving those responsible for these losses—health care personnel, pharmaceutical manufacturers, or the chemical industry—of legal liability for their actions.

Renewed consideration or implementation of such systems could signal an important change in our attitudes toward the nature of the risks these activities pose. At present, medical malpractice, product-related losses, and environmental injuries tend to be regarded as exceptional occurrences in otherwise relatively safe activities. When such injuries are suffered, the normal assumption is that there is a potential defendant in a lawsuit who is to blame for the injuries. A shift toward first-party insurance plans—even a slow, evolutionary shift—might well suggest that medical, product, or environmental injuries had come to be perceived in a new way: as part of the normal risk of being a patient, a consumer, or a citizen, and worth compensating without the careful attention to individual causal responsibility that inheres in compensation based on standards of tort liability. The rise of similar forms of coverage against other kinds of losses might signal analogous changes in social perceptions of the causes of those losses and the controllability of the risks that give rise to them.

Relative Stress on Loss Prevention

The tension between loss prevention and the broad distribution of risk runs through all the subjects analyzed in this book. The shape of future reconciliations of this tension within insurance law could reveal much about our potentially changing attitudes toward individual risk bearing and more collective responsibility for misfortune and loss.

Stress on loss prevention in insurance obviously tends to reflect a focus on individual responsibility. In contrast, emphasis on risk distribution underscores the social consequences of loss. Both loss prevention and loss distribution, of course, are methods of avoiding the effects of injury and loss. But they do so from very different perspectives. Increased stress in the future on risk distribution could indicate an evolving recognition of the inevitability of a certain amount of injury in a society as technological and industrial as ours. At some point it would symbolize a very significant change in social perceptions: a collective acceptance of the current—and perhaps ultimate—imperfectability of our world. Increased stress on loss prevention, on the other hand, would reflect the dominance of more traditional ideas about individual responsibility for loss and a continuing belief in the possibility of progress toward a safer, more secure world. Stress on loss prevention through insurance devices might indicate as well that more public forms of loss prevention, such as direct regulation and the promulgation of mandatory safety standards, had failed to live up to their promise. If these public forms of controlling dangerous activities reach the limits of their effectiveness before they prove satisfactory, we may have no choice but to make heavier use of insurance and civil liability systems to promote the safety and risk reduction we desire.

The Role of Public Insurance Markets

Whatever the shape of our risk-bearing future, it is likely to rely heavily on market forces to supply the insurance coverage that distributes risk. Yet there are limits on the capacity of legal institutions to make use of competitive insurance markets in achieving all the goals of insurance law. The market does not always function effectively enough; and when it does function effectively, often it is sufficiently flexible to defeat, neutralize, or at least partially circumvent the purposes of legal intervention. Partial regulation sometimes is less effective than no regulation at all. Achieving greater risk spreading or specific forms of risk redistribution through the use of legal doctrines, therefore, is likely to continue to be difficult.

As a consequence, we may see increased governmental maintenance of separate insurance markets to assure that public policies regarding risk distribution reach all whom they are designed to benefit. Residual insurance markets maintained or created by government to offer coverage for those who cannot obtain it at a reasonable price are a matter of intense interest to the insurance industry. But, except at rare moments of controversy, the creation and operation of such public markets does not capture much popular attention. Nevertheless, it is easy to envision the proliferation of government-operated markets as an alternative to traditional forms of regulating the private market. In addition, compromises between complete public takeover of specific insuring functions and regulation in the classic manner may well be more common as the years go by. Publicly created and supervised residual markets such as the assigned-risk pools described in chapter 4 can serve this purpose by requiring insurers collectively to bear the cost of insuring the otherwise uninsurable applicant.

In the future, public and residual insurance markets may be even more active in filling vacuums left by the private market, perhaps because of excess uncertainty in the private sector about the scope of the risks these secondary markets are created to cover. The problems handled through governmentally managed insurance or mandatory residual markets could provide a helpful clue about the risks that have been transformed in public perception from individual options to social necessities. Certainly the current emphasis on various kinds of residual markets in the automobile insurance field reveals a great deal about the centrality of the automobile in our culture. The use of an automobile at a tolerable cost has become almost a fundamental right; the maintenance of residual markets that assure all drivers minimum insurance coverage follows from and reflects this development. The rise of similar markets in other fields would be an equally revealing manifestation of the egalitarian, risk-sharing point of view noted throughout the book.

Finally, public or residual markets might come to be used to compete with private markets by demonstrating the inadequacy or overcautiousness of private enterprise decisions about marketing and insurability. The use of government power to keep the private insurance market operating efficiently, not through regulating it but by competing against it, would offer still further evidence of the transformation of our attitudes toward the way we distribute risk. It may well be that the best way to regulate, at least under certain circumstances, is by competing with the industry being regulated. Where the private market is insufficiently bold, public markets may show the way by operating in the desired fashion. If the public approach proves to be competitive, it will be imitated. And if this approach is not competitive, it may at least supply risk-distributional benefits that can collaterally justify its adoption.

Predicting the future is of course a dangerous undertaking. The analysis and predictions I have engaged in here are not intended as a comprehensive guide to the future, but only as a brief sketch of the kinds of problems to be kept in mind and the inferences that might be drawn from future developments. Attempts to understand and shape the nature of insurance law will have a better chance of succeeding if we anticipate the mutual influence of legal and social change on each other. As we move toward these changes our understanding of the larger implications of where we have been and where we are going can only help to improve our ability to control our course.

Notes

CHAPTER 1

1. In 1982, health insurance premiums in the United States totalled $99 billion; Health Insurance Association of America, *Source Book of Health Insurance Data* 13 (1982–83). In the same year, property/casualty insurance premiums (excluding accident and health insurance) exceeded $99 billion; Insurance Information Institute, *Insurance Facts* 24 (1981–82). Life insurance premiums that year were $50 billion; *see* American Council of Life Insurance, *Life Insurance Fact Book* 5 (1984).

2. *See* J. Appleman, *Insurance Law and Practice* (rev. ed. 1981); G. Couch, *Cyclopedia of Insurance Law* (2d ed. R. Anderson 1966).

3. *See*, e.g., R. Keeton, *Basic Text on Insurance Law* (1971); A. Widiss, *A Guide to Uninsured Motorist Coverage* (1969).

4. *See*, e.g., G. Calabresi, *The Costs of Accidents* (1970); R. Keeton, *Basic Text on Insurance Law* (1971); S. Kimball and H. Denenberg (eds.), *Insurance, Government, and Social Policy* (1969); J. O'Connell, *Ending Insult to Injury* (1975); W. Young and E. Holmes, *Cases and Materials on the Law of Insurance* (2d ed. 1985).

5. For examples of analysts working within the movement, *see* G. Calabresi, *The Costs of Accidents* (1970); R. Posner, *Economic Analysis of Law* (2d ed. 1977); Coase, "The Problem of Social Cost," 3 *J. of Law and Econ.* 1 (1960); Goetz and Scott, "Enforcing Promises: An Examination of the Basis of Contract," 89 *Yale L.J.* 1261 (1980); Priest, "A Theory of the Consumer Product Warranty," 90 *Yale, L.J.* 1297 (1981).

6. Three very different works in this tradition are R. Dworkin, *Taking Rights Seriously* (1977); R. Nozick, *Anarchy, State, and Utopia* (1974); and J. Rawls, *A Theory of Justice* (1971).

7. By far the leading work is H. Hart and A. Sacks, *The Legal Process: Basic Problems in the Making and Application of Law* (tentative ed. 1958), a work that has influenced thousands of law students since it became available as a teaching tool.

CHAPTER 2

1. *See* J. Appleman, *Insurance Law and Practice* (rev. ed. 1981); G. Couch, *Cyclopedia of Insurance Law* (2d ed. R. Anderson 1966).

2. Two fine single-volume works are R. Keeton, *Basic Text on Insurance Law* (1971); and W. Young and E. Holmes, *Cases and Materials on the Law of Insurance* (2d ed. 1985).

3. This threefold division is similar to and in part derived from Calabresi and Melamed, "Property Rules, Liability Rules, and Inalienability: One View of the Cathedral," 85 *Harv. L. Rev.* 1089 (1972).

4. Because this definition is intended to be simple and nontechnical, it necessarily oversimplifies. In fact, economists employ at least four efficiency-related notions. See Coleman, "Efficiency, Utility, and Wealth Maximization," 8 *Hofstra L. Rev.* 509, 512–20 (1980).

5. This formulation is of course a paraphrase of Guido Calabresi's famous statement of the function of accident law. *See* G. Calabresi, *The Costs of Accidents* 26 (1970). Technical application of the notion described in the text to insurance can be found in Erlich and Becker, "Market Insurance, Self-Insurance, and Self-Protection," 80 *J. Pol. Econ.* 623 (1972).

6. For example, people are not necessarily equally averse to different kinds of risk. Some may fear an occasional large loss more than several moderate-sized losses. The effects of loss prevention may also vary. Some safety precautions reduce the possibility of very large losses but not of small ones; other precautions reduce all risk proportionately. The combination of insurance and loss prevention purchased will depend on preferences for and aversion to those different levels of risk.

7. For a more technical discussion of the factors that may impede the operation of perfectly competitive markets, *see* J. Hirshleifer, *Price Theory and Application* 446–58 (1976).

8. I discuss moral hazard in more detail in chapter 4. For discussions of the economics of moral hazard, *see* Erlich and Becker, "Market Insurance, Self-Insurance, and Self-Protection," 80 *J. Pol. Econ.* 623 (1972); Holmstrom, "Moral Hazard and Observability," 10 *Bell J. Econ.* 74 (1970); Shavell, "On Moral Hazard and Insurance," 93 *Quart. J. Econ.* 541 (1979).

9. *See* R. Keeton, *Basic Text on Insurance Law*, 268–88 (1971).

10. *See id.* at 288–301.

11. Under a coinsurance provision, the insurer pays only a percentage of an insured loss, and the policyholder bears the remainder. *See id.* at 137–40.

12. Under a deductible provision, a specified sum is deducted from the amount of the loss that the insurer would otherwise be obligated to pay the insured. *See* 15 G. Couch, *Cyclopedia of Insurance* § 54:100 (2d ed. R. Anderson 1966).

13. *See* Coase, "The Problem of Social Cost," 3 *J. of Law and Econ.* 1 (1960).

14. *See*, e.g., G. Calabresi, *The Costs of Accidents* 26 (1970); R. Posner, "A Theory of Negligence," 1 *J. Legal Stud.* 29, 33 (1972).

15. For example, *compare* J. Rawls, *A Theory of Justice* (1971) (liberal theory of justice) *with* R. Nozick, *Anarchy, State, and Utopia* (1974) (libertarian theory). In

addition, contemporary popular beliefs about distributive justice are characterized by a considerable amount of ambivalence. For an interesting study of popular attitudes, *see* J. Hochschild, *What's Fair* (1981).

16. *See generally* R. Nozick, *Anarchy, State, and Utopia* (1974).

17. *See* A. Sen and B. Williams, *Utilitarianism and Beyond* (1982); J. Smart and B. Williams, *Utilitarianism: For and Against* 12–27 (1973).

18. For instance, neither the Pareto-optimality measure of efficiency nor the Kaldor-Hicks measure necessarily maximizes utility. *See generally* Coleman, "Efficiency, Utility, and Wealth Maximization," 8 *Hofstra L. Rev.* 509 (1981).

19. *See* D. Kahneman, P. Slovic, and A. Tversky (eds.), *Judgment under Uncertainty: Heuristics and Biases* 1–20 (1982); Kahneman and Tversky, "Prospect Theory: An Analysis of Decisions under Risk," 47 *Econometrica* 263 (1979); Shoemaker and Kunreuther, "An Experimental Study of Insurance Decisions," 46 *J. Risk and Ins.* 603 (1979).

20. *See* Kelman, "Choice and Utility," 1979 *Wisc. L. Rev.* 769.

21. *See* G. Calabresi, *The Costs of Accidents* 64 (1970).

22. There are, however, a number of other possible explanations of this phenomenon that would not make use of the diminishing marginal utility theory of money.

23. *See* R. Keeton, *Basic Text on Insurance Law* 341–439 (1971) (rights at variance with policy provisions).

24. For discussion of the different forms and measures of equality, *see generally* D. Rae et al., *Equalities* (1981).

25. *See* J. Rawls, *A Theory of Justice* (1971).

26. *See* Dworkin, "What Is Equality? Part 2: Equality of Resources," 10 *Phil. and Pub. Aff.* 283 (1981).

27. Both Rawls and Dworkin begin by hypothesizing a contract between potential members of a society desiring to arrive at principles governing the distribution of wealth. The device aids in exploring the terms to which people treating each other as equals might agree in that situation. The distribution each theory arrives at, however, cannot be translated into an egalitarian remedy of existing inequality in any simple way. The terms of hypothetical social contracts tend to govern the basic structure of society rather than the rules constituting subsystems within it, such as insurance law. *See* Rawls, "The Basic Structure as Subject," in *Values and Morals* 47 (A. Goldman and J. Kim eds. 1978). But the themes that are emphasized at the hypothetical contract level can help make the ideal of equality more concrete, and thereby reveal the implications of egalitarian values.

The typical contracting procedure is to rule out consideration of matters thought to be morally irrelevant to distributive justice. John Rawls, for example, rules out any knowledge by the contracting parties about their individual circumstances. All that is known in his original position is known about society, not about one's own position or prospects. *See* J. Rawls, *A Theory of Justice* 137 (1971). In this position, he argues, people would be very risk averse and would agree to principles protecting those who are worst off from any distribution working to their disadvantage. This society would have very strong egalitarian tendencies because only inequalities working to the advantage of the worst off would be permitted. In contrast, Ronald Dworkin conceives a distributional scheme that allows some knowledge about individual characteristics to be taken into account. His fundamental principle that people should be treated as equals would allow a distribution that is ambition sensitive but not endowment sensitive. *See* Dworkin, "What Is Equality? Part 2: Equality of Resources," 10 *Phil. and Pub. Aff.* 283, 311 (1981). Aspects of individual tastes and desires would be allowed to affect wealth and prospects, but physical and mental powers would not. All would start out with an equal distribution of resources. But those willing to take risks might eventually have more or less wealth than those who are risk averse. The result would still be an egalitarian society, but possibly one with greater differences in wealth than that envisioned by Rawls.

These hypothetical distributions move from initial positions of equality (conceived a bit differently in each theory) to a limited amount of inequality, depending on how much potential for inequality is embedded in each initial position. Thus, if we were to begin with an equal distribution of resources, then individuals could use those resources to insure against the risk that their skills and abilities would be below average, or they could take this risk and use their resources for other things. Any resulting inequality would be fair because it would be the result of treating people as equals. Yet because in this book I am addressing the problem from a starting point of inequality, the best approach would seem to be to derive egalitarian values from the work of such theorists as Rawls and Dworkin without attempting to apply their schemes to insurance law in any more direct way.

28. *See* M. Sandel, *Liberalism and the Limits of Justice* 70–79 (1982).

29. *See*, e.g., City of Los Angeles Dep't of Water & Power v. Manhart, 435 U.S. 702 (1977) (sex-based pension contribution rates in city-run pension plan violates Title VII of the Civil Rights Act of 1964); Arizona Governing Co. v. Norris, 436 U.S. 7073 (1983) (sex-based pension benefit differential in state-run pension system violates Title VII); Division of Insurance, Commonwealth of Massachusetts, *Automobile Insurance Risk Classification: Equity and Accuracy* 145 (1978) (decision by state insurance commissioner prohibiting sex-based automobile insurance classification).

30. Consider the 1970 Department of Transportation study that called the notion of the avoidability of automobile accidents into question with the results of its survey of ordinary driving habits. Drivers were covertly observed during one to two miles of city driving. Of the group, 48 percent were judged entirely safe, 41 percent committed more safe driving acts than unsafe ones, 9 percent committed an equal number, and 1 percent drove unsafely more than safely. In total, then, 52 percent committed at least one unsafe act in less than two miles of driving. *See* D. Klein and J. A. Waller, "Causation, Culpability, and Deterrence in Highway Crashes," in Department of Transportation, *Automobile Insurance and Compensation Study* 64 (1970).

31. For a more detailed discussion of this point, *see* R. Dworkin, *supra* note 26.

32. I acknowledge two key influences on my thinking about pragmatism. The first is Knapp and Michaels, "Against Theory," 9 *Critical Inquiry* 790 (June 1983); the second is R. Rorty, *Philosophy and the Mirror of Nature* (1979). *See also* M. Waltzer, *Spheres of Justice* (1983) (different spheres of activity subject to different norms of distributive justice).

33. For a different, though not entirely inconsistent classification in a more general vein, *see* Eisenberg, "The Bargain Principle and Its Limits," 95 *Harv. L. Rev.* 741 (1982) (bargains may be invalidated in certain cases of distress, transactional incapacity, unfair persuasion, or price ignorance).

34. For a contrasting view of the function of disclosure requirements in contractual settings, see Kronman, "Mistake, Disclosing Information, and the Law of Contracts," 7 J. Legal Stud. 1 (1978) (any duty to disclose information relevant to a contract should depend on the efficiency of information-gathering incentives created by the duty).

35. Legal theorists have disagreed about whether it is sensible to regulate the substance of contracts between parties with unequal bargaining power simply because of that inequality. Compare Leff, "Unconscionability and the Code: The Emperor's New Clause," 115 U. Pa. L. Rev. 485 (1967) and R. Posner, The Economic Analysis of Law 84 (2d ed. 1977) with Ellinghaus, "In Defense of Unconscionability," 78 Yale L. J. 757 (1969).

36. For such an argument, see Schwartz, "Seller Unequal Bargaining Power and the Judicial Process," 49 Ind. L. J. 367 (1974).

37. These rules prevent a harmless misrepresentation of fact by the insured from invalidating an entire policy. See R. Keeton, Basic Text on Insurance Law 369–93 (1971).

38. These rules avoid penalizing the insured for possessing overlapping coverage. See id. at 170–73. They are discussed in detail in chapter 6.

39. These rules invalidate provisions that unduly restrict coverage in light of the price charged for it. See id. at 348–49.

40. See, e.g., Gruenberg v. Aetna Ins. Co., 108 Cal. Rptr. 480, 510 P.2d 1032 (1973); United States Fed. & Guar. Co. v. Peterson, 540 P.2d 1070 (S. Ct. Nev. 1975).

41. See, e.g., Crisci v. Security Ins. Co., 66 Cal. 2d 425, 426 P.2d 173 (1967).

42. See, e.g., Gray v. Zurich Mut. Ins. Co., 65 Cal. 2d 263, 419 P.2d 168, 54 Cal. Rptr. 104 (1966); Burd v. Sussex Mut. Ins. Co., 56 N.J. 383, 247 A.2d 7 (1970).

43. See generally H. Hart and A. Sacks, The Legal Process: Basic Problems in the Making and Application of Law (tentative ed. 1958); J. Landis, The Administrative Process (1938); J. Mashaw and R. Merrill, Administrative Law: The American Public Law System (1985); G. Robinson, E. Gellhorn, and H. Bruff, The Administrative Process (2d ed. 1980); Diver, "Policymaking Paradigms in Administrative Law," 95 Harv. L. Rev. 393 (1981); Stewart, "The Reform of American Administrative Law," 88 Harv. L. Rev. 1667 (1975).

44. See Paul v. Virginia, 9 Wall. 168, 19 L. Ed. 357 (1869).

45. See United States v. South-Eastern Underwriters Ass'n, 322 U.S. 533, 64 S. Ct. 1162, 88 L. Ed. 1440 (1944).

46. 15 U.S.C.A. § 1012–14 (1945).

47. Id. at § 1013(a).

48. See R. Keeton, Basic Text on Insurance Law 538 (1971). For discussion of what constitutes regulation for the purpose of exemption from federal antitrust law under McCarran-Ferguson, see Kimball and Boyce, "The Adequacy of State Rate-Regulation: The McCarran-Ferguson Act in Historical Perspective," 56 Mich. L. Rev. 545, 566–76 (1958).

49. See P. MacAvoy (ed.), Federal-State Regulation of the Pricing and Marketing of Insurance (1977) (recommending optional reallocation of regulatory jurisdiction).

50. For a survey and analysis of the range of issues involved in the legislative and administrative regulation of insurance, see S. Kimball and H. Denenberg (eds.), Insurance, Government, and Social Policy (1969).

51. *See* Kimball, "The Unfinished Business in Insurance Regulation," 1969 *Wisc. L. Rev.* 1019.

52. The 1943 New York Standard Fire Insurance Policy, now used in many states, is perhaps the most famous example of legislative prescription of an entire policy. *See* N.Y. Ins. L. § 168 (McKinney 1966 and Supp. 1983–84).

53. *See generally* Kimball and Pfennigstorf, "Legislative and Judicial Control of the Terms of Insurance Contracts: A Comparative Study of American and European Practice," 39 *Ind. L. J.* 675 (1964).

54. *See id.* at 698.

55. *See* Pfennigstorf, "The Enforcement of Insurance Laws," 1969 *Wisc. L. Rev.* 1026.

56. For discussion of the reasons existing firms may actually favor regulation of their industry, *see* Stigler, "The Theory of Economic Regulation," 2 *Bell J. Econ.* 3 (1971).

57. Often consumer groups even at the federal level also are at a financial disadvantage when lobbying in opposition to corporate interests. *See* Robinson, "The Federal Communications Commission: An Essay on Regulatory Watchdogs," 126 *U. Pa. L. Rev.* 169, 231 (1978).

58. *See* Stigler, "The Theory of Economic Regulation," 2 *Bell J. Econ.* 3 (1971).

59. *See* R. Keeton, *Basic Text on Insurance Law* 557 (1971).

60. Both California and New York, for example, have moved away from the older system of prior approval of rates and toward more open competition in rate setting. *See* P. MacAvoy (ed.), *Federal-State Regulation of the Pricing and Marketing of Insurance* 20–22 (1977).

61. *See* Rodis, "Limited Omnipotence: The Bases and Limitations of the Powers of Insurance Regulators," 13 *Forum* 386, 390 (1978).

62. *See* Kimball, "An Approach to a General Theory of Insurance Regulation," in *Insurance, Government, and Social Policy* 4 (S. Kimball and H. Denenberg eds. 1969); Kimball, "The Purpose of Insurance Regulation: A Preliminary Inquiry in the Theory of Insurance Law," 45 *Minn. L. Rev.* 471 (1961).

63. *See* Kimball, "An Approach to a General Theory of Insurance Regulation," in *Insurance, Government, and Social Policy* 3–16 (S. Kimball and H. Denenberg eds. 1969). Richard Stewart, former Commissioner of Insurance of New York, has proposed three goals: assuring the availability, quality, and affordability of insurance coverage. *See id.* at 24–27.

64. *See* Diver, "Policymaking Paradigms in Administrative Law," 95 *Harv. L. Rev.* 393, 433 (1981).

65. Some of the more recent examples of challenges to the constitutionality of insurance statutes involve no-fault automobile insurance plans. *See*, e.g., Pinnick v. Cleary, 360 Mass. 1, 271 N.E.2d 592 (1971); Montgomery v. Daniels, 38 N.Y.2d 41, 340 N.E.2d 444, 378 N.Y.S.2d 1 (1975). Most such challenges have been rejected.

66. *See* R. Keeton, *Basic Text on Insurance Law* 341–439 (1971).

67. *See* Stewart and Sunstein, "Public Programs and Private Rights," 95 *Harv. L. Rev.* 1193 (1982).

68. *See*, e.g., Royal Globe Ins. Co. v. Superior Ct., 153 Cal. Rptr. 842, 592 P.2d 329 (1979).

CHAPTER 3

1. For example, the relatively early observations of Fleming James, Jr., have not been built upon as much as might have been expected. *See* James and Thorton, "The Impact of Insurance on the Law of Torts," 15 *Law & Contemp. Probs.* 431, 440–42 (1950); James, "Accident Liability Reconsidered: The Impact of Liability Insurance," 57 *Yale L.J.* 549 (1948) [hereinafter cited as "Accident Liability Reconsidered"]; James, "Contribution among Joint Tortfeasors: A Pragmatic Criticism," 54 *Harv. L. Rev.* 1156 (1941). The most important and detailed subsequent discussion can be found in G. Calabresi, *The Costs of Accidents* (1970).

2. *See* United States v. Carroll Towing Co., 159 F.2d 169, 173 (2d Cir. 1947) (Hand, J.); Conway v. O'Brien, 111 F.2d 611, 612 (2d Cir. 1940) rev. on other grounds, 312 U.S. 492 (1941); *see also* Calabresi and Hirschoff, "Toward a Test for Strict Liability in Torts," 81 *Yale L.J.* 1055, 1057 (1972); Posner, "A Theory of Negligence," 1 *J. Legal Stud.* 29 (1972).

3. *See generally*, Office of Technology Assessment, *Technologies for Determining Cancer Risks from the Environment* (1981).

4. S. Epstein, *The Politics of Cancer* 39 (1978) (latency period for cancer induced by smoking may be twenty to forty years; similar latency period for asbestosis); Comment, "Liability Insurance for Insidious Disease: Who Picks Up the Tab?," 48 *Fordham L. Rev.* 657–59 and nn. 6, 7 (1980).

5. This dangerous tendency is obviously one of the factors that has prompted financial responsibility requirements in environmental legislation. *See*, e.g., Comprehensive Environmental Response, Liability and Compensation Act, § 108(a)(1), (b)(1), 42 U.S.C. §§ 9608(a)(1), (b)(1) (1982) (requiring insurance, guarantee, surety bonding, or qualification as self-insurer for vessels that carry hazardous substances; similar requirements may be imposed on other facilities beginning in 1985) [hereinafter cited as "Superfund Act"]. *See also* Resource Conservation and Recovery Act of 1976 § 7(b), 42 U.S.C. § 6925(a) (1982) (requiring permit for owner or operator of facility for the treatment, storage, or disposal of hazardous waste, as defined in the act, for operators of chemical facilities).

6. For a discussion of the different incentives of management and the effects of civil liability on firms, *see* Stone, "The Place of Enterprise Liability in the Control of Corporate Conduct," 90 *Yale L.J.* 1 (1980).

7. *See* L. Cheek, "Hazardous Substance Liability Insurance for Vessels and Facilities" 17 (1981) (unpublished manuscript on file with the author) (At present, premiums "are based on a combination of judgment, guesswork, prayer, and the ancient principle of charging what the traffic will bear."); Comment, "Compensating Hazardous Waste Victims: RCRA Insurance Regulations and a Not So 'Super' Superfund Act," 11 *Envtl. L.* 689, 710 n. 144 (1981) (Premiums may be based on a combination of factors including hazard potential of the waste, characteristics of population at risk, site characteristics, and the insured's waste management policies and safety record).

8. *See*, e.g., Keene Corp. v. Ins. Corp. of N. America, 667 F.2d 1034, 1052 (D.C. Cir. 1981), *cert. denied*, 455 U.S. 1007 (1982); Borel v. Fibreboard Paper Prods. Corp., 493 F.2d 1076, 1095 (5th Cir. 1973), *cert. denied*, 419 U.S. 869 (1974); Summers

v. Tice, 33 Cal. 2d 80, 86, 199 P.2d 1, 4–5 (1948) (establishing alternative liability); Hall v. E.I. DuPont de Nemours & Co., 345 F. Supp. 353 (E.D.N.Y. 1972). *See also,* Note, "Tort Actions for Cancer: Deterrence, Compensation, and Environmental Carcinogenesis," 90 *Yale L.J.* 840, 855–59 (1981) (recommending that once victim proves that defendant is responsible for an exposure to a carcinogen the burden shift to defendant to rebut the presumption that such exposure caused the plaintiff's cancer).

9. *See,* e.g., Michie v. Great Lakes Steel Div., 495 F.2d 213, 216 (6th Cir.), *cert. denied,* 419 U.S. 997 (1974).

10. *See* Sindell v. Abbott Laboratories, 26 Cal. 3d 588, 612, 607 P.2d 924, 937, 163 Cal. Rptr. 132, 145, *cert. denied,* 449 U.S. 912 (1980) (cancer victim may sue group of DES manufacturers that comprised 90 percent of the DES market); *see also* Robinson, "Multiple Causation in Tort Law: Reflections on the DES Cases," 68 *Va. L. Rev.* 713 (1982); Case Comment, "Refining Market Share Liability: Sindell v. Abbott Laboratories," 33 *Stan. L. Rev.* 937 (1981); Note, "Market Share Liability: An Answer to the DES Causation Problem," 94 *Harv. L. Rev.* 668 (1981). *But see* Ryan v. Eli Lilly & Co., 514 F. Supp. 1004, 1007–08, 1018 (D.S.C. 1981) (rejecting the Sindell market share theory and granting defendant's motion for summary judgment because plaintiff failed to identify the particular manufacturer of the suspected carcinogenic drug); Mizell v. Eli Lilly & Co., 526 F. Supp. 587, 595–96 (D.S.C. 1981) (rejecting the Sindell test).

11. *See* Hall v. E.I. DuPont de Nemours & Co., Inc., 345 F. Supp. 353, 376–77 (E.D.N.Y. 1972); Moses v. Town of Morgantown, 192 N.C. 102, 133 S.E. 421 (1926); *see also* Superfund Act § 101(32), 42 U.S.C. § 9601(32) (1982).

12. *Cf.* Landes and Posner, "Joint and Multiple Tortfeasors: An Economic Analysis," 9 *J. Legal Stud.* 517, 540–41 (1980) (market share liability may have misallocative effects); Comment, "Market Share Liability for Defective Products: An Ill-Advised Remedy for the Problem of Identification," 76 *Nw. U. L. Rev.* 300, 311–12 (1981) (Market share liability may impose liability "on defendants who are wholly innocent of any wrongdoing towards plaintiff.").

13. *See* Superfund Section 301(e) Study Group, Senate Comm. on the Environmental Public Works, 97th Cong. 2d Sess., *Injuries and Damages from Hazardous Waste—Analysis and Improvement of Legal Remedies* 262 (1982) (recommending against wholesale adoption of burden-shifting devices in toxics cases) [hereinafter cited as *Superfund Compensation Study*]; *cf.* Calabresi, "Concerning Cause and the Law of Torts: An Essay for Harry Kalven, Jr.," 43 *U. Chi. L. Rev.* 69, 85 (1975) (cause in fact requirement for imposition of tort liability simply serves as a useful way of calculating some of the costs that should be considered when making risk/safety tradeoffs).

14. *See,* e.g., Insurance Services Office, "1981 Pollution Liability Policy," in Pollution Liability Insurance Association (PLIA), *Pollution Liability Insurance: Its History, Its Opportunity, and Its Present Status* (1981). One version of the history behind the move from occurrence to claims-made coverage is described in Light, "The Long Tail of Liability: Hazardous Waste Disposal Insurance and the Superfund Act's Post–Closure Liability Trust Fund," 2 *Va. J. Nat. Res. L.* 179 (1982).

15. How long coverage extends after the expiration of the policy period depends on whether the policy covers only manifestations of disease during the policy period, exposures during the period regardless of when injury from exposure is manifested, or wrongful acts during the policy period regardless of when the exposure or manifestation

they cause occurs. *See*, e.g., Keene Corp. v. Ins. Co. of N. America, 667 F.2d 1034, 1046–47 (D.C. Cir. 1981), *cert. denied*, 455 U.S. 1007 (1982); Ins. Co. of N. America v. Forty-Eight Insulations, Inc., 451 F. Supp. 1230 (E.D. Mich. 1978), *aff'd*, 633 F.2d 1212 (6th Cir. 1980), *cert. denied*, 454 U.S. 1109 (1981).

16. Typically the first claims-made policy purchased by the insured contains a retroactive date and covers only claims arising out of activities occurring after that date. *See* "Pollution Liability Policy," *supra* note 14. As subsequent policies are purchased, however, the length of the covered period increases.

17. *See*, e.g., Federal Coal Mine Health and Safety Act of 1969, § 424(b), as amended by Black Lung Benefits Revenue Act of 1977, § 3(d), 30 U.S.C. § 934(b) (1982); Deepwater Port Act of 1974 § 18(f)(3), 33 U.S.C. § 1517(f)(3) (1982); Superfund Act §§ 221(a), (b), 42 U.S.C. §§ 9631(a), (b) (1982) and 26 U.S.C. §§ 4611, 4661 (1982); Trans-Alaska Pipeline Authorization Act § 204(c)(5), 43 U.S.C. § 1653(c)(5) (1982); Outer Continental Shelf Lands Act Amendments of 1978 § 302(d), 43 U.S.C. § 1812(d) (1982); Fla. Stat. Ann. § 376.11(4) (West 1975) (pollution spill fund); Me. Rev. Stat. Ann. tit. 38 § 551 (1978 and Supp. 1979–84) (oil spill fund); N.J. Stat. Ann. § 58:10–23.11(h) (West 1982) (hazardous waste control and compensation fund); N.C. Gen. Stat. § 143–215.87 (Supp. 1983) (oil and hazardous waste spill fund); Wash. Rev. Code Ann. § 90.48.390 (Supp. 1984) (oil spill fund). *See also* Trauberman, "Compensating Victims of Toxic Substances Pollution: An Analysis of Existing Federal Statutes," 5 *Harv. Envtl. L. Rev.* 1, 18–28 (1981). Creation of a new fund is proposed in *Superfund Compensation Study*, *supra* note 13. For a proposed comprehensive scheme, *see* Soble, "A Proposal for the Administrative Compensation of Victims of Toxic Substance Pollution: A Model Act," 14 *Harv. J. on Legis.* 683 (1977).

18. *See*, e.g., Deepwater Port Act of 1974 § 18(c)(1), (f)(2), 33 U.S.C. § 1517(c)(1), (f)(2) (1982); Superfund Act § 111(a), 42 U.S.C. § 9611(a) (1982).

19. *See*, e.g., Federal Coal Mine Health and Safety Act of 1969 §§ 411–26, 30 U.S.C. §§ 921–36 (1982). Toxic tort victims may be entitled to compensation from a fund under less demanding burdens of proof or more liberal rights of recovery than would be applied in tort actions brought directly against the culpable enterprise itself. For such a proposal, *see Superfund Compensation Study*, *supra* note 13 at 209–19.

20. *See*, e.g., Trans-Alaska Pipeline Authorization Act § 204(c)(1), 43 U.S.C § 1653(c)(1) (1982); Outer Continental Shelf Lands Act Amendments of 1978 §§ 101(12), 303(a), 43 U.S.C. §§ 1801(12), 1813(a) (1982); N.J. Stat. Ann. §§ 58:10–23.11(g) (West 1982) (attaching liability for cleanup and removal costs and direct and indirect costs, no matter by whom sustained). *Cf.* Superfund Act § 111(a), (c), 42 U.S.C. § 9611(a), (c) (1982) (reimbursement only to federal or state governments for damaged natural resources).

21. *See*, e.g., Trans-Alaska Pipeline Authorization Act § 204(a)(1), 43 U.S.C. § 1653(a)(1) (1982); Superfund Act § 107(a), 42 U.S.C. § 9607(a) (1982).

22. Social Security is one example of the many public approaches to compensation. For a delineation of the various sources of compensation available to those injured by exposure to toxic substances, *see* Pfennigstorf, "Environment, Damages, and Compensation," 1979 *Am. Bar Found. Research J.* 347. *See also* Trauberman, "Compensating Victims of Toxic Substance Pollution: An Analysis of Existing Federal Statutes," 5 *Harv. Envtl. L. Rev.* 1 (1981).

23. *See*, e.g., Resource Conservation and Recovery Act of 1976, 42 U.S.C. §§

6910–87 (1982); Federal Water Pollution Control Act, 33 U.S.C. §§ 1251–376 (1982); Safe Drinking Water Act, 42 U.S.C. §§ 300f to 300j–9 (1982); Toxic Substances Control Act, 15 U.S.C. §§ 2601–29 (1982). For a discussion of public controls at the state level, see Currie, "State Pollution Statutes," 48 *U. Chi. L. Rev.* 27 (1981); Cohen, "New Developments in State Hazardous Waste Legislation," 9 *Cap. U.L. Rev.* 489 (1980). Environmental protection statutes are by no means the only direct approach to the regulation of dangerous chemicals. For discussion of two others, see Merrill, "CPSC Regulation of Cancer Risks in Consumer Products: 1972–1981," 67 *Va. L. Rev.* 1261 (1981); Merrill and Schewel, "FDA Regulation of Environmental Contaminants of Food," 66 *Va. L. Rev.* 1357 (1980).

24. The description here is simplified for the purpose of analysis. Funds might actually mix subrogation and nonsubrogation features. For example, a fund might have subrogation rights only against enterprises guilty of negligence or only against those guilty of reckless disregard of dangers they pose. It should also be stressed that neither subrogated nor nonsubrogated funds necessarily makes recovery from the fund the victim's sole avenue of recovery; the victim's cause of action against the responsible party can be preserved and exercised if the victim is willing to forego recovery from the fund or, under some proposals, even if he has recovered from the fund. For instance, one proposal advocates a two-tiered approach in which some victims would be entitled to recover on a nonduplicative basis from both the fund and the responsible party, with the first recovery deducted from the second. See *Superfund Compensation Study, supra* note 13, at 158–283. Thus, not even a nonsubrogated fund automatically insulates responsible parties from liability. But if recovery from the fund is more quickly and easily obtained, it may be the preferred approach and have the effect of reducing responsible parties' exposure. In any case, much of what I say in the text about the effect of subrogation actions applies as well to actions by the claimant whose tort rights are not fully extinguished after recovery from a fund.

25. Creating a compensation fund, of course, is not the only or necessarily the most efficient way to facilitate settlement of claims and swift compensation. For instance, Professor Jeffrey O'Connell's proposals for achieving these goals would not require the creation of new institutions or bureaucracies. See O'Connell, "Foreclosing Claims for Personal Injury from Toxic Substances by Defendants' Tender of Economic Losses," 2 *Va. J. Nat. Res. L.* 203 (1982); O'Connell, "A Proposal to Abolish Defendants' Payment for Pain and Suffering in Return for Payment of Claimants Attorneys' Fees," 1981 *U. Ill. L. Forum* 333.

26. For discussions of the problem in more general terms, see Fleming, "The Collateral Source Rule and Loss Allocation in Tort Law," 54 *Calif. L. Rev.* 1478 (1966); James, "Social Insurance and Tort Liability: The Problem of Alternative Remedies," 27 *N.Y.U.L. Rev.* 537 (1952); O'Connell, "A Proposal to Abolish Contributory and Comparative Fault, with Compensatory Savings by also Abolishing the Collateral Source Rule," 1979 *Ill. L. Forum* 591.

27. For a proposal that grants the fund subrogation rights only for exposures occurring after the fund's enactment, see *Superfund Compensation Study, supra* note 13 at 245–51.

28. See J. Feinberg, *Doing and Deserving: Essays in the Theory of Responsibility* 95–118 (1970) (discussing the expressive function of punishment).

29. *See*, e.g., Resource Conservation and Recovery Act of 1976, 42 U.S.C. § 6910–87 (1982).

30. *See* Cheek, "Risk-Spreaders or Risk-Eliminators? An Insurer's Perspective on the Liability and Financial Responsibility of RCRA and the Superfund Act," 2 *Va. J. Nat. Res. L.* 149 (1982).

31. *See* R. Keeton, *Basic Text on Insurance Law* 5 (1971); *but see* J. O'Connell, *Ending Insult to Injury* 22–24 (1973) (insurance industry has not been heavily involved in safety research).

32. *See* Ingram, "Insurance Coverage for Problems in Latent Disease and Injury Cases," 12 *Envtl. L.* 317–18 (1982); Mehaffy, "Asbestos-Related Lung Disease," 16 *Forum* 341 (1981).

33. *See* R. Keeton, *Basic Text on Insurance Law* 581–82 (1971).

34. *See* Superfund Act § 108, 42 U.S.C. § 9608. This also seems to be the intention of the EPA regulations implementing the financial responsibility requirements of the Resource Conservation and Recovery Act, *supra* note 23. Insurers are required to provide first-dollar coverage, even where a policy is issued subject to a deductible, but are entitled to reimbursement from the insured where the liability in question is excluded in the policy. 47 Fed. Reg. 16,548 (1982). This also has been the effect of certification of automobile liability insurance as meeting state and financial responsibility requirements. *See* R. Keeton, *Basic Text on Insurance Law* 235 (1971). Since most financial responsibility laws require only $20,000 of automobile liability coverage, the insurer's risk that it will not be reimbursed in any single case is not as great as it could be in the toxics field where financial responsibility requirements will sometimes be in the millions.

35. For analogues, *see* Connor v. Great Western Sav. and Loan Ass'n, 69 Cal. 2d 850, 447 P.2d 609, 73 Cal. Rptr. 369 (1968) (savings and loan held liable for personal injuries caused by breach of duty to supervise construction of housing development it financed); Nelson v. Wire Rope Corp., 311 Ill. 2d 69, 199 N.E.2d 769 (1964) (workers' compensation insurer may be held liable to employee of its insured for negligently conducted safety inspection).

36. Detailing the possible forms of such compensation is far beyond the scope of this chapter. One avenue that might be explored is equity participation. *Cf.* Coffey, " 'No Soul to Damn; No Body to Kick': An Unscandalized Inquiry into the Problem of Corporate Punishment," 79 *Mich. L. Rev.* 386, 413–24 (1981).

CHAPTER 4

1. The vast majority have focused on sex discrimination. *See*, e.g., Benston, "The Economics of Gender Discrimination in Employee Fringe Benefit Plans: *Manhart* Revisited," 49 *U. Chi. L. Rev.* 489 (1982); Bernstein and Williams, "Title VII and the Problem of Sex Classification in Pension Programs," 74 *Colum. L. Rev.* 1203 (1974); Brilmayer, Hekeler, Laycock, and Sullivan, "Sex Discrimination in Employer-Sponsored Pension Plans: A Legal and Demographic Analysis," 47 *U. Chi. L. Rev.* 505 (1980); Kimball, "Reverse Sex Discrimination: *Manhart*," 1980 *Am. B. Found. Research J.* 915; Rutherglen, "Sexual Equality in Fringe-Benefit Plans," 65 *Va. L. Rev.* 199 (1979).

2. *See* Arizona Governing Comm. v. Norris, 463 U.S. 1073 (1983).

3. *See*, e.g., H.R. 100, 98th Cong., 1st Sess. (proposed prohibition of discrimi-

nation in insurance on the basis of race, color, religion, sex, or national origin); S. 372, 98th Cong., 1st Sess. (same).

4. *See* R. Keeton, *Basic Text on Insurance Law* 557–67 (1971); Kimball, "The Purpose of Insurance Regulation: A Preliminary Inquiry in the Theory of Insurance Law," 45 *Minn. L. Rev.* 471 (1961).

5. *See* City of Los Angeles, Dep't of Water and Power v. Manhart, 435 U.S. 702 (1978) (interpreting the act as prohibiting use of sex in determining rates of an employer-sponsored pension plan).

6. *See* Arizona Governing Comm. v. Norris, 463 U.S. 1073 (1983).

7. *See*, e.g., Cal. Ins. Code § 1852 (West 1972); Ga. Code Ann. § 33–9–4; R. Keeton, *Basic Text on Insurance* 565 (1971).

8. *See*, e.g., Shavers v. Kelley, 402 Mich. 554, 267 N.W.2d 72 (1978) (statutory mandate that rates not be excessive, inadequate, or unfairly discriminatory is insufficiently specific to meet constitutional demands of due process of law as applied to mandatory no-fault automobile coverage); State *ex rel.* Comm'n of Ins. v. N.C. Rate Bureau, 300 N.C. 381, 269 S.E.2d 547 (1980) (overturning insurance commissioner's regulation of process by which insurers ceded risks to an involuntary reinsurance facility).

9. *See* Erlich and Becker, "Market Insurance, Self-Insurance, and Self-Protection," 80 *J. Pol. Econ.* 623 (1972).

10. *See* L. Freifelder, *A Decision Theoretic Approach to Insurance Ratemaking* 124 (1976).

11. The creation of insurance classes produces only comparative risk predictions, also known as risk relativities. Once the classes are fixed, decision makers know how the expected losses of one class compare with the expected losses of others. But they have not yet set premiums—they have only fixed the proper ratio of the premiums to be charged each class.

In order to set actual prices, cost calculations must be made. In practice the process is complex, but in schematic terms it is straightforward. Rates are set by adding together expected losses, expenses (commissions, administrative expenses, anticipated costs of litigation, and so forth), a premium to cover the risk of variation from the mean expected loss (if the violation is likely to be volatile), and a margin for profit. *See* H. Denenberg et al., *Risk and Insurance* 516–22 (2d ed. 1974) [hereinafter cited as H. Denenberg]. This is a simple enough calculation, although obtaining accurate data to make it is no easy accomplishment.

The rates charged may be revised in either of two ways. *See generally id.* at 528–30. The loss ratio method compares the actual losses suffered during the policy period to premiums collected and adjusts premiums upward or downward depending on how this ratio compares to the ratio of expected losses to premiums. If expected losses were projected to be 60 percent of premiums, but the actual loss ratio turned out to be 80 percent, then the loss ratio method would suggest a rate increase of 33⅓ percent since actual losses had been one-third higher than expected. In taking this approach the loss ratio method makes no change in the composition of risk classes. It merely revises rates from a preexisting base.

In contrast, the pure premium method actually is a way of calculating rates anew rather than revising them. The pure premium is the ratio of actual dollar loss to the total number of exposure units, or units of risk. In workers' compensation, for example, an exposure unit is one hundred dollars of salary; so the pure premium for workers' compensation insurance is a rate per one hundred dollars of salary paid. The pure premium method yields a new rate to be charged, if past loss experience is completely credible, rather than a percentage change in the previous rate.

Since past loss experience is not completely credible, however, the loss ratio and pure premium methods count both actual losses and expected losses in adjusting premiums, thus discounting the predictive value of actual loss experience to some extent. But the pure premium method suggests a new premium, whereas the loss ratio method suggests only a percentage change in the old premium. The pure premium method therefore makes assigning insureds to new classes more feasible. See Kulp, "The Rate-Making Process in Property and Casualty Insurance—Goals, Techniques, and Limits," 15 *Law and Contemp. Prob.* 493, 500 (1950). When there is no reason to think that the variables supporting existing classifications have become less reliable or that use of more powerful variables has become feasible, the two methods of rate revision may be equally satisfactory. But where such changes are possible, the pure premium method of revision makes it easier to recognize any increasing heterogeneity in existing classes.

12. *See* National Association of Insurance Commissioners, D–3 Advisory Committee, *Private Passenger Automobile Insurance Risk Classification* 326 (1979) [hereinafter cited as *NAIC Study*]; S. Rea, Jr., and M. Trebilcock, *Rate Determination in the Automobile Insurance Industry in Ontario: The Use of Age, Sex, and Marital Status as Rating Variables* 40–41 (1981) [hereinafter cited as Rea and Trebilcock]; Shayer, "Driver Classification in Automobile Insurance," in Massachusetts Division of Insurance, *Automobile Insurance Risk Classification: Equity and Accuracy* 3–6 (1978) [hereinafter cited as *Equity and Accuracy*].

13. *See* Stanford Research Institute, *The Role of Risk Classifications in Property and Casualty Insurance: A Study of the Risk Assessment Process* 50–51 (Final Report 1976) [hereinafter cited as *SRI Report*].

14. *See id.*, Supplement at 78.

15. *See* O'Hare, "Information Strategies as Regulatory Surrogates," in E. Bardach and R. Kagan (eds.), *Social Regulation: Strategies for Reform* 232 (1982).

16. This form of classification is sometimes also called loss rating. For a discussion, see N. Doherty, *Insurance Pricing and Loss Prevention* 48–53 (1976).

17. I use the term *hunch* deliberately. Sometimes fairly refined categories are used without much data to back them up. Little statistical support seems to exist, for example, for many of the credits and charges made for the supposedly good and bad features of a fire risk. *See* H. Denenberg, *supra* note 11 at 533.

18. *See* Shavell, "On Moral Hazard and Insurance," 93 *Quart. J. Econ.* 541, 551 (1979) (*ex ante* rating may be optimal where expenditures on risk-posing assets are fixed over a period, *ex post* rating preferable where risk-reducing activity can be varied).

19. In a sense, then, the differences in the incentive effects of feature and experience rating in insurance resemble certain differences between negligence and strict liability in the law of torts. Like negligence liability, feature rating imposes a cost on the insured for characteristics that are correlated with the occurrence of losses. The insured then decides whether changing those characteristics that can be changed will be worth the reductions in feature rates these changes would produce. Experience rating, on the other hand, imposes a cost on the insured that is dependent only on the occurrence of a loss.

In this sense it resembles strict liability. For a theory of the difference between negligence and strict liability, *See* Calabresi and Hirschoff, "Toward a Test for Strict Liability in Torts," 81 *Yale L.J.* 1055 (1972). Another parallel is that experience rating, like strict liability, may have more impact on activity levels than fault-based liability or feature-based risk classification. *See* Shavell, "Strict Liability Versus Negligence," 9 *J. Legal Stud.* 1 (1980).

20. *See* H. Denenberg, *supra* note 11 at 516; N. Doherty, *Insurance Pricing and Loss Prevention* 54–55 (1976).

21. *See* U.S. Dep't of Commerce, *Intra-Agency Task Force on Products Liability* VI–18 (Final Report 1977).

22. For a discussion of the costs of consuming information, *see* O'Hare, "Information Strategies as Regulatory Surrogates," in F. Bardach and R. Kagan (eds.), *Social Regulation: Strategies for Reform* 229 (1982).

23. *See*, e.g., "Excerpt from the Opinion, Findings, and Decision on 1978 Automobile Insurance Rates by James M. Stone, Commissioner of Insurance," in *Equity and Accuracy, supra* note 12 at 180–81.

24. Certain kinds of age discrimination, for example, may be acceptable because the elderly benefit from their classification. If elderly drivers and their passengers have below-average losses when they are involved in automobile accidents because their incomes are below average, then charging them less for first-party no-fault insurance may be quite acceptable. In this setting, age is an admissible variable. But charging the elderly higher rates for liability insurance (assuming that their loss experience would warrant higher charges) might well be unacceptable.

25. For a discussion of the different senses in which the concept of efficiency can be employed, *see* Coleman, "Efficiency, Utility and Wealth Maximization," 8 *Hofstra L. Rev.* 509, 512–20 (1980).

26. Technically speaking, an efficient system would charge in accordance with marginal costs—the additional cost added by each insured purchasing coverage. But since most costs in this context are in fact marginal costs—the amount of the loss an insured suffers, the costs of defending him against suit, and so forth, the simplification seems warranted. *See* Williams, "Price Discrimination in Property and Liability Insurance," in S. Kimball and H. Denenberg (eds.), *Insurance, Government, and Social Policy* 210–12 (1969).

27. *See* L. Freifelder, *A Decision Theoretic Approach to Insurance Ratemaking* 70 (1976); *NAIC Study, supra* note 12 at 178.

28. *See* Rea and Trebilcock, *supra* note 12 at 41.

29. *See SRI Report, supra* note 13 at 49–50 (risk assessment processes in effect in 1976 explained only 30 percent of the variance of expected loss distribution among drivers).

30. *See* Rothschild and Stiglitz, "Equilibrium in Competitive Insurance Markets: An Essay on the Economics of Imperfect Information," 90 *Quart. J. of Econ.* 629 (1976).

31. The prevalent technique is use of the Poisson model, which helps predict accident likelihood variability. *See SRI Report, supra* note 13, Supplement at 175–79.

32. *See NAIC Study, supra* note 12 at 44.

33. *See NAIC Study, supra* note 12 at 16.

34. *See* Rea and Trebilcock, *supra* note 12 at 66.

35. *See* Posner, "A Theory of Negligence," 1 *J. Legal Stud.* 29 (1972).

36. This notion might be considered an application of Rawls's difference principle to insurance. *See* J. Rawls, A *Theory of Justice* 75–83 (1971).

37. The insurance industry position, unsurprisingly, is that there is no basis for choosing between alternatives that involve the same aggregate amounts of overcharging or undercharging. The industry's position is essentially utilitarian. The utility or disutility resulting from such inaccuracy, in the industry's view, is simply a function of the total amount of inaccuracy and not at all related to the way the inaccuracy is distributed. *See NAIC Study, supra* note 12 at 155–74.

38. This might be described as an egalitarian classification scheme. For a version of this approach, *see* Ferrera, "Identifying Equitable Insurance Premiums for Risk Classes: An Alternative to the Classical Approach," in *Equity and Accuracy, supra* note 12 at 74–110.

39. For a table of life expectancies, *see* U.S. Dep't of Commerce, Bureau of the Census, *Statistical Abstract of the United States* 72 (1982–83).

40. *See generally* Underwood, "Law and the Crystal Ball: Predicting Behavior with Statistical Inference and Individualized Judgment," 88 *Yale L.J.* 1408 (1979).

41. For discussion of the natural lottery, *see* J. Rawls, A *Theory of Justice* 12, 72 (1971).

42. *See*, e.g., Austin, "The Insurance Classification Controversy," 131 *U. Pa. L. Rev.* 517 (1983) for discussion from a critical-legal-studies viewpoint.

43. *See NAIC Study, supra* note 12 at 142.

44. *See id.* at 19.

45. *See* Kimball, "Reverse Sex Discrimination: *Manhart,*" 1979 *Amer. Bar F. Res. J.* 83, 119–122.

46. *See* Rutherglen, "Sexual Equality in Fringe-Benefit Plans," 65 *Va. L. Rev.* 199 (1979). *Compare* Brilmayer, Hekeler, Laycock, and Sullivan, "Sex Discrimination in Employer-Sponsored Insurance Plans: A Legal and Demographic Analysis," 47 *U. Chi. L. Rev.* 505 (1980).

47. *See* Ferrerra, "Identifying Equitable Insurance Premiums for Risk Classes: An Alternative to the Classical Approach," in *Equity and Accuracy, supra* note 12 at 74.

48. *See NAIC Study, supra* note 12 at 16.

49. For a catalog and analysis of these devices, *see* VII U.S. Dep't of Commerce, *Intra-Agency Task Force on Products Liability* (Legal Study 1977).

CHAPTER 5

1. *See* R. Keeton, *Basic Text on Insurance Law* 350–57 (1971).

2. *See* Kievet v. Loyal Protective Life Ins. Co., 34 N.J. 475, 170 A.2d 22 (1961).

3. *See* Ransom v. Penn. Mut. Life Ins. Co., 43 Cal. 2d 420, 274 P.2d 633 (1954).

4. *See* Gray v. Zurich Mut. Ins. Co., 65 Cal. 2d 263, 419 P.2d 168, 54 Cal. Rptr. 104 (1966).

5. *See* Keeton, "Insurance Law Rights at Variance with Policy Provisions," 83 *Harv. L. Rev.* 961, 967 (1970).

6. Several years ago my own count yielded decisions voicing the expectations principle in over a hundred cases, decided both before and after Professor Keeton's article.

See, e.g., cases compiled in Note, "A Reasonable Approach to the Doctrine of Reasonable Expectations as Applied to Insurance Contracts," 13 *U. Mich. J.L. Ref.* 603 (1980).

7. *See* e.g., Kievet v. Loyal Protective Life Ins. Co., 34 N.J. 475, 170 A.2d 22 (1961).

8. *See*, e.g., Smith v. Westland Life Ins. Co., 15 Cal. 3d 111, 539 P.2d 433, 123 Cal. Rptr. 649 (1975).

9. *See*, e.g., Gray v. Zurich Mut. Ins. Co., 65 Cal. 2d 263, 419 P.2d 168, 54 Cal. Rptr. 104 (1966).

10. In many cases the courts have noted specifically the significance of the insurer's misleading conduct to the decision to honor the insured's expectations. *See*, e.g., Smith v. Westland Life Ins. Co., 15 Cal. 3d 111, 122, 539 P.2d 433, 442, 123 Cal. Rptr. 649, 657 (1975); INA Life Ins. Co. v. Brundin, 533 P.2d 236, 242 (Alaska 1975); Prudential Ins. Co. v. Lamme, 83 Nev. 146, 149, 425 P.2d 346, 348 (1967). In other cases, the influence of that conduct on the court's decision is more speculative. *See*, e.g., Thompson v. Occidental Life Ins. Co., 9 Cal. 3d 904, 513 P.2d 353, 109 Cal. Rptr. 473 (1973).

11. 306 N.Y. 357, 118 N.E.2d 555 (1954). For a more recent case applying the Lacks rule, *see* Riordan v. Auto. Club, 422 N.Y.S.2d 811, 814 (1979).

12. 58 Cal. 2d 862, 377 P.2d 284, 27 Cal. Rptr. 172 (1962).

13. 55 N.J. 117, 259 A.2d 889 (1969).

14. *See also* Providential Life Ins. Co. v. Clem, 240 Ark. 922, 403 S.W.2d 68 (1966) (upholding insureds' right to rely on group accident insurance application and holding insureds were not bound by the terms of a policy they had no opportunity to read); Lawrence v. Providential Life Ins. Co., 238 Ark. 981, 385 S.W.2d 936 (1965) (same); INA Life Ins. Co. v. Brundin, 533 P.2d 236, 242 (Alaska 1975) (expectations of purchaser of accident coverage were influenced by advertising literature).

15. 354 F. Supp. 514 (S.D. Tex. 1973).

16. Earlier accident cases had also held for the insured but without articulating a rationale resting on expectations. *See*, e.g., Silverstein v. Metropolitan Life Ins. Co., 254 N.Y. 81, 85, 171 N.E. 914, 915 (1930) (holding that "thin skulled" plaintiffs can recover for accidents they suffer because "[a]ny different construction would reduce the policy and its coverage to contradiction and absurdity") (Cardozo, C.J.).

17. 34 N.J. 475, 170 A.2d 22 (1961).

18. This theory of liability is similar to the English contract law doctrine of fundamental breach, under which provisions denying the buyer the essence of what he agreed to purchase are invalid. *See* Meyer, "Contracts of Adhesion and the Doctrine of Fundamental Breach," 50 *Va. L. Rev.* 1178, 1198 (1964). *Cf.* Llewellyn, "Book Review," 52 *Harv. L. Rev.* 700, 702–03 (1937) (discussing the need to mark out, for given transactions, the "minimum decencies" a court will insist upon).

19. Cases involving other kinds of insurance have adopted similar rationales. *See*, e.g., C. & J. Fertilizer, Inc. v. Allied Mut. Ins. Co., 227 N.W.2d 169 (Iowa 1975) (burglary and robbery policy could not condition coverage on proof of visible marks of entry); Foremost Life Ins. Co. v. Water, 88 Mich. App. 599, 278 N.W.2d 688 (1979) (refusal to enforce a subrogation clause that would defeat the primary purpose of a disability policy); Lariviere v. New Hampshire Ins. Group, 120 N.H. 168, 413 A.2d 309 (1980) (liability policy covering insured's building and moving business could not exclude cov-

erage for damage occurring during the movement of any building because such exclusion would defeat the reasonable expectations of the insured).

Most of the accident cases following Kievet, however, have relied only on the reasonableness of an assumption that accident coverage would include the injury at issue and not on whether literal application of the policy would emasculate coverage. *See*, e.g., Corgatelli v. Globe Life & Accident Ins. Co., 96 Idaho 616, 533 P.2d 737 (1975); Perrine v. Prudential Ins. Co., 56 N.J. 120, 265 A.2d 521 (1970). The policy in Kievet extended coverage to all "accidental bodily injuries," but many policies, such as the one in Perrine, limit the right of recovery to injuries due to "accidental means." The distinction between accidental means and accidental results has sometimes affected the reasoning and decision in accident insurance cases. *See*, e.g., Landress v. Phoenix Mut. Ins. Co., 291 U.S. 491 (1934) (distinction drawn); Gottfried v. Prudential Ins. Co., 82 N.J. 478, 414 A.2d 544 (1980) (distinction drawn, but if policy insures against accidental bodily injury it is an accidental result policy). *But see* Burr v. Commercial Travellers Mut. Accident Ass'n, 295 N.Y. 294, 67 N.E.2d 248 (1946) (distinction collapsed).

20. 15 Cal. 3d 111, 539 P.2d 433, 123 Cal. Rptr. 649 (1975).

21. The earlier cases adopting this rule had relied more directly on the ambiguity of the receipt than on the expectations of the insured. *See*, e.g., Gaunt v. John Hancock Mut. Life Ins. Co., 160 F.2d 599, 601 (2d Cir. 1947), *cert. denied*, 331 U.S. 849 (1947); Ransom v. Penn Mut. Life Ins. Co., 43 Cal. 2d 420, 425, 274 P.2d 633, 636 (1954). In those cases, although probably not technically ambiguous, the receipts were complex and convoluted. In Smith, the language of the receipt was much less convoluted, and the court put less stress on ambiguity than on the expectation created by payment of a first premium.

22. The courts may also be concerned with the difficulty of proving expectations, although they generally do not specify this concern. The applicant is deceased, and normally the only testimony about what he expected comes from the insurer's soliciting agent. Courts may therefore place the burden of proving the absence of an expectation of coverage on the insurer. *See* Collister v. Nationwide Life Ins. Co., 479 Pa. 579, 595, 388 A.2d 1346, 1354 (1978) (insurer failed to establish by clear and convincing evidence that deceased could not have entertained reasonable expectations of coverage).

23. Date 2 varies from receipt to receipt, but the principle is the same: no one has coverage for the period between application (date 1) and satisfaction of whatever condition precedent is imposed (date 2). This argument admittedly is a bit exaggerated since there are some advantages that will accrue to an insured who lives past date 2 and is therefore covered "from the date of application." For example, the policy may be incontestable sooner, and there may be accelerated cash surrender value. *See* Gaunt v. John Hancock Mut. Life Ins. Co., 160 F.2d 599, 601 (2d Cir. 1947), *cert. denied*, 331 U.S. 849 (1947). But these benefits are slim in comparison to the main advantage of having life insurance and the applicant's main purpose in purchasing it—insurance in the event of death.

24. *See* R. Keeton, *supra* note 1, at 286. The exclusionary provision usually is worded in one of two ways: (1) "This policy does not apply to bodily injury or property damage which is either expected or intended from the standpoint of the insured," or (2) "This policy does not apply:... to bodily injury... caused intentionally by or at the direction of the insured." *See* State Farm Fire & Cas. Co. v. Muth, 190 Neb. 248, 249,

252, 207 N.W.2d 364, 365, 366 (1973) (providing examples of policies employing both provisions).

25. *See, e.g.,* Lamb v. Belt Cas. Co., 3 Cal. App. 2d 624, 630, 40 P.2d 311, 314 (1935). Other courts have recognized that the pleadings may not be an accurate indication of the merits of the case. They have looked beyond the pleadings, and have required a defense if the suit potentially seeks damage covered by the policy. *See, e.g.,* Columbia S. Chem. Corp. v. Manufacturers & Wholesalers Indem. Exch., 190 Cal. App. 2d 194, 200, 11 Cal. Rptr. 762, 766 (1961); Ritchie v. Anchor Cas. Co., 135 Cal. App. 2d 245, 251, 286 P.2d 1000, 1004 (1955).

26. 65 Cal. 2d 263, 419 P.2d 168, 54 Cal. Rptr. 104 (1966). *See also* Nat'l Indem. Co. v. Fleisher, 469 P.2d 360 (Alaska 1970); Hogan v. Midland Nat'l Ins. Co., 3 Cal. 3d 553, 476 P.2d 825, 91 Cal. Rptr. 153 (1970); Lowell v. Maryland Cas. Co., 65 Cal. 2d 298, 419 P.2d 180, 54 Cal. Rptr. 116 (1966); Zurich Ins. Co. v. Rombaugh, 384 Mich. 228, 180 N.W.2d 775 (1970).

27. Under the clause, the insurer agreed:

[t]o pay on behalf of the insured all sums which the insured shall become legally obligated to pay as damages because of bodily injury or property damage, and the company shall defend any suit against the insured alleging such bodily injury or property damage and seeking damages which are payable under the term of this endorsement, even if any of the allegations are groundless, false or fraudulent.

28. The court stated: "The basic promise [the insuring clause] would support the insured's reasonable expectation that he had bought the rendition of legal services to defend against a suit for bodily injury which alleged he had caused it, negligently, nonintentionally, intentionally or in any other manner." 65 Cal. 2d at 273, 419 P.2d at 174, 54 Cal. Rptr. at 110. The court's use of the word *support* certainly implies that it believed the insured's expectation would exist independently of his reading of the policy; otherwise the basic promise could hardly be said to support that expectation.

29. *See, e.g.,* Kievet v. Loyal Protective Life Ins. Co., 34 N.J. 475, 170 A.2d 22 (1961).

30. *See, e.g.,* cases cited at note 26 *supra. See also* St. Paul Fire & Marine Ins. Co. v. Weiner, 606 F.2d 864 (9th Cir. 1979); United States v. United States Fidelity & Guar. Co., 601 F.2d 1136 (10th Cir. 1979); Gowing v. Great Plains Mut. Ins. Co., 207 Kan. 78, 483 P.2d 1072 (1971). Contra, Chipokas v. Travelers Indem. Co., 267 N.W.2d 393 (Iowa 1978); Hins v. Heer, 259 N.W.2d 38, 40 (N.D. 1977).

31. 10 Cal. 3d 216, 514 P.2d 1219, 110 Cal. Rptr. 139 (1973).

32. The court said, "An attorney ordinarily buys malpractice insurance only during the time he is in practice. But because his liability for malpractice insurance may continue long after his negligent act and injury . . . he would . . . reasonably expect coverage against liability for negligent acts occurring during the policy period so as to be protected against claims asserted during retirement."

33. *Compare* Goldberg, "Institutional Change and the Quasi-Invisible Hand," 17 J. *of Law and Econ.* 461 (1974) (suggesting that intervention to effect allocation of resources can be effective) *with* Coase, "The Choice of the Institutional Framework: A Comment," 17 J. *of Law and Econ.* 493 (1974) (arguing that regulation is likely to be anticompetitive).

34. Payment of a first premium is thought to reduce the likelihood that the insured will withdraw from the transaction. *See* Prudential Ins. Co. v. Lamme, 83 Nev. 146, 149, 425 P.2d 346, 347 (1967).

35. Not all those who reasonably expect coverage will bring suit, and not all meritorious claims will succeed. In addition, the courts are limited by the remedy they can impose. For arguments that remedies in some insurance cases should include additional damages in order to assure compliance with liability rules, *see* Holmes, "Is There Life after Gilmore's Death of Contract?—Inductions from a Study of Commercial Good Faith in First-Party Insurance Contracts," 65 *Cornell L. Rev.* 330, 353–88 (1980); Slawson, "Mass Contracts: Lawful Fraud in California," 48 *S. Cal. L. Rev.* 1, 26–28 (1975). *See also* my discussion of this position and the cases adopting it in chapter 7.

36. *See* Hill, "Damages for Innocent Misrepresentation," 73 *Colum. L. Rev.* 679, 686–88 (1973).

37. Only when the plaintiff and defendant have a relationship of trust and confidence or where the defendant is an expert whose product is information is such a recovery permitted. *See* James and Gray, "Misrepresentation (Pt. 1)," 37 *Md. L. Rev.* 286, 308 (1977).

An exception to the rule that fraud or negligence is required, and one that provides some analogical support for the expectations decisions, is found in the law of warranty. Warranty law holds a seller responsible for his express and implied representations concerning the quality of his product, regardless of his blameworthiness or his intent to deceive. Warranty law, however, has been confined mainly to sales of goods. A seller of goods may be held responsible for the expectations of a buyer if he had reason to know that the buyer was relying on his skill or judgment to fulfill those expectations. *See* U.C.C. § 2–315.

38. 3 J. Pomeroy, *Equity Jurisprudence* § 870 (2d ed. 1982).

39. *Id. See also* Restatement (Second) of Contracts § 20 (1979).

40. "Knowledge by one party of the other's mistake regarding the expression of the contract is equivalent to mutual mistake." S. Williston, *Contracts* § 1548, at 125 (3d ed. 1970). The Restatement adopts a similar rule: when one party knows or has reason to know the meaning the second party attaches to the contract, then the contract has that meaning, unless the second party also knows or has reason to know the meaning attributed to it by the first party. Restatement (Second) of Contracts § 20 (1979). *See also* 3 A. Corbin, *Contracts* § 357 (rev. ed. 1960).

41. *See, e.g.,* D. Dobbs, *Handbook on the Law of Remedies* §§ 9.5, 11.6 n. 20 (1973); G. Palmer, *Mistake and Unjust Enrichment* 75 (1962) (inequitable conduct usually involves knowledge of the other person's mistake).

42. One obvious difference between estoppel and the expectations principle is that the former requires detrimental reliance. For a discussion of the justifications for dispensing with a reliance requirement in expectations cases, *see* R. Keeton, *supra* note 1 at 977–79.

43. *See* Williston, "Liability for Honest Misrepresentation," 24 *Harv. L. Rev.* 415, 424 (1911).

44. *See* 1 G. Couch, *Cyclopedia of Insurance Law* § 15.73 (2d ed. R. Anderson 1966). Absent ambiguity, the logic of freedom of contract supports a presumption that the parties actually assented to the written agreement, and only a strong showing that

one of the elements necessary to contract formation is missing will invalidate that agreement. *See* Murray, "Unconscionability: Unconscionability," 31 *U. Pitt. L. Rev.* 1, 20–21 (1969); Slawson, "Standard Term Contracts and Democratic Control of Lawmaking Power," 84 *Harv. L. Rev.* 529, 539–47 (1971). It is therefore not surprising that in almost all of the expectations cases, the courts attempt to ground their decisions at least in part on the ambiguity of policy language.

45. For examples of this principle applied in the insurance context, *see* Herzog v. Nat'l Am. Ins. Co., 2 Cal. 3d 192, 198–99, 465 P.2d 841, 844, 84 Cal. Rptr. 705, 709 (1970); Sorensen v. Farmers Ins. Exch., 56 Cal. App. 3d 328, 128 Cal. Rptr. 400 (1976); Commercial Union Assurance v. Gollan, 118 N.H. 744, 394 A.2d 839 (1978).

46. The relationship between the expectations principle and the doctrine of unconscionability has never been entirely clear. The remedy granted in the expectations cases goes beyond that normally available for unconscionability. U.C.C. § 2–302 provides that upon finding a contract or provision unconscionable, the court may refuse to enforce the contract, enforce the contract without the unconscionable clause, or so limit the unconscionable clause as to avoid an unconscionable result. *See* U.C.C. § 2–302. The expectations principle, by contrast, does not limit itself to declaring exclusions from coverage invalid; it also broadens unexpectedly narrow insuring clauses. For example, consider a policy insuring against all injuries "caused solely and exclusively by external, violent, and accidental means." *See* Burr v. Commercial Travellers Mut. Accident Ass'n, 295 N.Y. 294, 67 N.E.2d 248 (1946). A court finding the clause unconscionable could rescind the contract and return the insured's premium. The court would also have authority under U.C.C. § 2–302 to limit application of the clause. But there is no way to limit the clause so as to expand coverage. The expectations principle, on the other hand, would not merely invalidate the clause; it would reform it to supply the expected coverage.

47. *See*, e.g., First Nat'l Bank v. Fidelity & Cas. Co., 428 F.2d 499 (7th Cir. 1970), *cert. denied*, 401 U.S. 912 (1971); Herzog v. Nat'l Am. Ins. Co., 2 Cal. 3d 192, 465 P.2d 841, 84 Cal. Rptr. 705 (1970); Rodman v. State Farm Mut. Auto. Ins. Co., 208 N.W.2d 903 (Iowa 1973).

48. Had agencies made the deliberate decision to refrain from detailed regulation, the argument against judicial involvement would be stronger. *See* Morris, "Waiver and Estoppel in Insurance Policy Litigation," 105 *U. Pa. L. Rev.* 925, 951–52 (1957). Consider one court's assessment of the issue: "In Idaho, as in most states, the consuming public and the public interest is to be guarded by a state insurance commissioner. The policy in question herein is an example that the efforts of the state authority have at times fallen short of adequately discharging that responsibility." Corgatelli v. Globe Life & Accident Ins. Co., 96 Idaho 616, 619, 533 P.2d 737, 740 (1975).

49. *See* R. Dworkin, *Taking Rights Seriously* 84–86 (1977).

50. The seminal article on this problem referred to such issues as polycentric. The article was in circulation for many years before it was published. *See* Fuller, "The Forms and Limits of Adjudication," 92 *Harv. L. Rev.* 353 (1978). For applications of Fuller's notions, *see* Henderson, "Judicial Review of Manufacturer's Conscious Design Choices: The Limits of Adjudication," 73 *Colum. L. Rev.* 1531 (1973); Henderson, "Expanding the Negligence Concept: Retreat from the Rule of Law," 51 *Ind. L.J.* 467 (1976). This point of view has also been disputed. *See*, e.g., Chayes, "The Role of the Judge in Public

Law Litigation," 89 *Yale L. Rev.* 1281 (1976); Fiss, "Foreword: The Supreme Court, 1978 Term—The Forms of Justice," 93 *Harv. L. Rev.* 1 (1979).

51. For other points of view about the proper relation of risk spreading and other distributional concerns to nondistributional goals, *see* Calabresi and Hirschoff, "Toward a Test for Strict Liability in Torts," 81 *Yale L.J.* 1055, 1091–93 (1972) (distributional concerns should rarely be automatically excluded from consideration); Fletcher, "Fairness and Utility in Tort Theory," 85 *Harv. L. Rev.* 537, 547 n. 40 (1972) (just deserts are the only proper distributional consideration in allocating tort liability); Schwartz, "Products Liability and Judicial Wealth Redistributions," 51 *Ind. L.J.* 558 (1976) (action for distributional reasons alone is justified if there is popular agreement that it is proper and application of the resulting rules can be predictable and certain).

52. For an example of the kind of case that can raise this problem, *see* Keene Corp. v. INA, 667 F.2d 1034 (1981) (insured asbestos manufacturer could reasonably expect liability coverage under policies in effect during period of plaintiff's exposure to asbestos, during latency period of plaintiff's disease, and at the time that disease manifested itself). There was no contention in the case that the insurers had misled the plaintiff regarding the scope of coverage, and because the interpretive problem under scrutiny had already been well recognized, there was no information-production justification for invoking the expectations principle. Yet the court did not clearly articulate the only remaining justification for invoking the principle—achieving risk-distributional goals.

53. There are, of course, advantages to retaining more general standards. General standards using indeterminate language leave the courts with considerably more flexibility than more precise rules, which are triggered by specific fact situations. *See* R. Dworkin, *Taking Rights Seriously* 22–28 (1977); H. Hart and A. Sacks, *The Legal Process, Basic Problems in the Making and Application of Law* 155–58 (tentative ed. 1958); Kennedy, "Legal Formality," 2 *J. Legal Stud.* 351 (1973). The more precise the rule, the less room that is left for achieving the purposes underlying the rule, unless its purpose is to provide a clear-cut solution, regardless of the rule's substance. *See* Kennedy, "Form and Substance in Private Law Adjudication," 89 *Harv. L. Rev.* 1685, 1689–90 (1976).

CHAPTER 6

1. *See* note 1, chapter 1.

2. Standard combination automobile policies provide medical expense coverage on a no-fault basis to the named insured, members of his family, permitted users of the vehicle, and passengers. *See, e.g.,* Insurance Information Institute, *Sample Insurance Policies* 16–17 (undated) (Family Combination Automobile Policy). No-fault legislation in a number of states has mandated the expansion of this coverage to include wage loss and other protections. This expanded coverage is often referred to as "personal injury protection," or simple "PIP" coverage.

3. *See generally* A. Widiss, *A Guide to Uninsured Motorist Coverage* (1969).

4. One exception is the work of Jeffrey O'Connell. *See, e.g.,* O'Connell, "Offers That Can't Be Refused: Foreclosure of Personal Injury Claims by Defendants' Prompt Tender of Claimants' Net Economic Losses," 77 *N.W. L. Rev.* 589 (1982); O'Connell, "A Proposal to Abolish Contributory and Comparative Fault, with Compensatory Savings by Also Abolishing the Collateral Source Rule," 1979 *U. Ill. L. Rev.* 591.

5. *See* Fleming, "The Collateral Source Rule and Loss Allocation in Tort Law," 54 *Calif. L. Rev.* 1478 (1966).

6. *See* R. Keeton, *Basic Text on Insurance Law* 88 (1971).

7. *See id.* at 88–90.

8. *See* G. Calabresi, *The Costs of Accidents* 145–47 (1970).

9. *See* D. Kahneman, P. Slovic, and A. Tversky (eds.), *Judgment under Uncertainty: Heuristics and Biases* 3–20 (1982); Kahneman and Tversky, "Prospect Theory: An Analysis of Decisions under Risk," 47 *Econometrica* 263 (1979); Shoemaker and Kunreuther, "An Experimental Study of Insurance Decisions," 46 *J. Risk and Ins.* 603 (1979). Although the conclusions reached about people's statistical intuitions and consequent risk-taking propensities vary in these works, each contradicts to some extent the now-classic expected utility model of decision under uncertainty embodied in Friedman and Savage, "The Utility Analysis of Choices Involving Risk," 56 *J. Pol. Econ.* 279 (1948).

10. *See* e.g., Keene Corp. v. Ins. Co. of N. America, 667 F.2d 1034 (D.C. Cir. 1981), *cert. denied*, 455 U.S. 1007 (1982) (insurers with policies covering period of exposure or manifestation jointly and severally liable); Ins. Co. of N. America v. Forty-Eight Insulations, 633 F.2d 1212 (6th Cir. 1980) (insurers with policies covering period of exposure liable on pro rata basis).

11. *See* 8A J. Appleman, *Insurance Law and Practice* § 4906 (rev. ed. 1981). These three approaches often serve as building blocks in the construction of more complex provisions, yielding what might be called compound excess-escape or pro rata-escape clauses. The purpose of a compound excess-escape clause is to preclude stacking. Such clauses resemble the following: "This insurance shall apply only as excess insurance over any other similar insurance available to the insured as primary insurance, and this insurance shall then apply only in the amount by which the limit of liability of this coverage exceeds the applicable limit of such other insurance." The purpose of compound pro rata-escape clauses is also to preclude stacking coverage, but they designate the insurer as co-primarily liable, rather than as liable only for an excess share: "If the insured has other similar insurance available, the damages shall be deemed not to exceed the higher of the applicable limits of liability of this and such other insurance, and the company shall not be liable for a greater proportion of any loss than the limit of liability hereunder bears to the sum of the applicable limits of liability of this and such other insurance."

12. *See* Alleman, "Resolving the 'Other Insurance' Dilemma: Ordering Disputes among Primary and Excess Insurers," 30 *U. Kan. L. Rev.* 75 (1981); Note, "Concurrent Coverage in Automobile Liability Insurance," 65 *Colum. L. Rev.* 319 (1965); Note, "Automobile Liability Insurance—Effect of Double Coverage and 'Other Insurance' Clauses," 38 *Minn. L. Rev.* 838 (1954); Comment, "'Other Insurance' Clauses: The Lamb-Weston Doctrine," 47 *Ore. L. Rev.* 480 (1968); Comment, "Is There a Solution to the Circular Riddle?," 25 *S.D.L. Rev.* 37 (1980).

13. *See* R. Keeton, *Basic Text on Insurance Law* 147–53 (1971). There are two different kinds of subrogation. A property insurer normally has an equitable right of subrogation even in the absence of a policy provision granting that right. A legal right of subrogation arises only from such a policy provision. *See generally* Kimball and Davis, "The Extension of Insurance Subrogation," 60 *Mich. L. Rev.* 841 (1962).

14. An insurer's right of subrogation may be implemented in any of three ways. First, if the insurer has paid the insured, the insurer is subrogated to the insured's rights against any third party legally responsible for the insured's loss. Derivative recovery by the insurer is then permitted. Second, if the insurer pays the insured and the insured later recovers all or part of the same loss from a third party, the insurer may be entitled to partial or full reimbursement out of that recovery. The much-maligned collateral source rule exists at least in part to make this form of subrogation possible. Third, if the insurer obtains recovery from a third party prior to payment of a claim by his insurer, the latter may not be obligated to make payment under the policy. *See* R. Keeton, *Basic Text on Insurance Law* 158–59 (1971).

15. For discussion of the wisdom of allowing subrogation and the relation of the right to the collateral source rule, *see* 2 F. Harper and F. James, *The Law of Torts* 1343–60 (1956); Fleming, "The Collateral Source Rule and Loss Allocation in Tort Law," 54 *Calif. L. Rev.* 1478 (1966); McCoid, "Allocation of Loss and Property Insurance," 39 *Ind. L.J.* 647 (1964).

16. A typical provision reads as follows:

The limit of liability for uninsured motorists coverage stated in the declarations as applicable to each person is the limit of the company's liability for all damages for care and loss of services because of bodily injury sustained by one person as the result of any one accident and, subject to the above provision respecting each person, the limit of liability stated in the declarations as applicable to each accident is the total limit of the company's liability for all damages, including damages for care and loss of services because of bodily injury sustained by two or more persons as the result of any one accident.

See Sample Insurance Policies, supra note 2 at 18 (Family Combination Automobile Policy).

17. Sometimes a separability clause is included in multivehicle policies, indicating that the provisions of the policy apply separately to each vehicle. Such a clause makes more plausible the argument that stacking is permissible. Insurers in turn have responded by adding language to limit-of-liability clauses, providing that total liability is limited to the sum stated in the policy, "regardless of the number of . . . automobiles or trailers to which this policy applies." In addition to the argument from the language of the separability clause, the claim is often made that acceptance of premiums calculated to cover two or more vehicles, but providing only a single set of coverages, is unconscionable. The ambiguity created by the conjunction of the limits of liability and separability clauses is also sometimes cited in support of the pro-stacking position. *See* Note, "Stacking of Uninsured Motorist and Medical Expense Insurance Coverages in Automobile Insurance Policies," 13 *Ga. L. Rev.* 1014, 1032, (1979).

18. *See* Association of Casualty and Surety Companies, Inland Marine Underwriters Association, National Automobile Underwriters Association, National Board of Fire Underwriters, National Bureau of Casualty Underwriters, and Surety Association of America, *Guiding Principles: Casualty-Fidelity-Fire-Inland Marine First-Party Property Losses and Claims* (1963) [hereinafter referred to as "Guiding Principles"]. Other guiding principles include Claims Executives Council, *Guiding Principles for Primary and Excess Insurance Companies* (1973); Federation of Insurance Counsel and International Association of

Insurance Counsel, *Guiding Principles for Cooperation in the Defense of Multiple Litigation* (1978); National Conference of Lawyers and Liability Insurers, *Guiding Principles* (1969).

19. *See* "Guiding Principles," *supra* note 18 at 3.

20. 667 F.2d 1034 (D.C. Cir. 1981), *cert. denied*, 102 U.S. 1644 (1982).

21. *Id.* at 1045–46.

22. *See* Roe, "Bankruptcy and Mass Tort," 84 *Colum. L. Rev.* 846 (1984); Note, "The Manville Bankruptcy: Treating Mass Tort Claims in Chapter 11 Proceedings," 96 *Harv. L. Rev.* 1121 (1983).

23. *See* Epstein, "The Legal and Insurance Dynamics of Mass Tort Litigation," 13 *J. Legal Stud.* 475 (1984).

24. *See*, e.g., New Amsterdam Cas. Co. v. Hartford Acc. & Ind. Co., 108 F.2d 653 (6th Cir. 1940).

25. *See*, e.g., Trinity Universal Ins. Co. v. Gen. Acc. Fire and Life Assurance Co., 138 Ohio St. 488, 35 N.E.2d 836 (1941). A variation is to honor a policy provision specifically reciting that the premium charge has been reduced because it is intended as secondary whenever there is other insurance available. *See*, e.g., State Farm Mut. Auto Ins. Co. v. W. Cas. & Sur. Co., 477 S.W.2d 421 (Mo. S. Ct. 1972).

26. *See* Lamb-Weston, Inc. v. Ore. Auto Ins. Co., 219 Or. 110, 346 P.2d 643 (1959). An earlier decision in the federal system had reached the same result in the absence of any Oregon law on point. *See* Oregon Auto. Ins. Co. v. United States Fidelity & Guaranty Co., 195 F.2d 958 (9th Cir. 1952).

27. These factors include the apparent intent of the policies, their specificity in designating themselves as secondary, whether the premiums charged reflect the exposure undertaken, and whether either company insured the risk in question as a mere incident of its object. *See* Miller v. Nat'l Farmers Union Property & Cas. Co., 470 F.2d 700 (8th Cir. 1972). *See also* Bettenburg v. Employers Liab. Assurance Corp., 350 F. Supp. 873 (D. Minn. 1972); Auto Owners Ins. Co. v. Northstar Mut. Ins., 281 N.W.2d 700 (Minn. S. Ct. 1979); Sathre v. Brewer, 289 Minn. 424, 184 N.W.2d 668 (1971).

28. The cases are numerous. For a few examples, *see* Billups v. Alabama Farm Bureau Mut. Cas. Ins. Co., 352 So. 2d 1097 (Ala. S. Ct. 1977) (permitted user of vehicle cannot stack uninsured motorist coverage of owners); Cheseroni v. Nationwide Mut. Ins. Co., 410 A.2d 1015 (Del. S. Ct. 1980) (stacking denied); Squire v. Economy Fire and Cas. Co., 69 Ill. 2d 167, 370 N.E.2d 1044 (1977) (stacking permitted); Bradley v. Mid-Century Ins. Co., 409 Mich. 1, 294 N.W.2d 141 (1980) (stacking permitted).

29. *Compare* Allstate Ins. Co. v. Anderson, 87 Mich. App. 539, 274 N.W.2d 66 (1978) (passenger in vehicle can stack uninsured motorist coverage), *with* Travelers Ins. Co. v. Pac, 337 So. 2d 397 (Fla. Dist. Ct. of App. 1976) (employee of fleet owner cannot stack uninsured motorist coverage on other vehicles in the fleet).

30. *See*, e.g., State Farm Mut. Auto Ins. Co. v. Maryland Auto Ins. Fund, 277 Md. 602, 356 A.2d 560 (1976).

31. *See* Welch v. Hartford Cas. Ins. Co., 221 Kan. 344, 559 P.2d 362 (1977); Wasche v. Milbank Mut. Ins. Co., 268 N.W.2d 9, 13 (Minn. S. Ct. 1978); State Farm Mut. Auto Ins. Co. v. Williams, 481 Pa. 130, 392 A.2d 281 (1978).

32. *See* Ray v. State Farm Mut. Auto Ins. Co., 498 F.2d 220 (6th Cir. 1974) (Ohio

law); Menke v. Country Mut. Ins. Co., 78 Ill. 2d 420, 401 N.E.2d 539 (1980); Goodville Mut. Cas. Co. v. Borror, 275 S.E.2d 625 (Va. S. Ct. 1981).

33. *See*, e.g., Fla. Stat. Ann. § 627.4132; Ann. Code of Md. Art. 48A § 543(a).

34. *See*, e.g., Ann. Code of Md. Art. 48A § 540.

35. *See*, e.g., Ann. Code of Md. Art. 48A § 543(d); N.J.S.A. 39: 6A–6; N.Y. Ins. Law § 671.2(b).

36. *See* N.J.S.A. 39: 6A–6; N.Y. Ins. Law § 671(2)(b).

37. *See*, Ann. Code of Md. Art. 48A § 543(d). Add-on no-fault statutes require the purchase of PIP coverage but do not enact any concomitant limitations on victims' right to tort recoveries.

38. *See* R. Keeton, *Basic Text on Insurance Law* 341–49 (1971).

39. For a limited example of a mandatory legislative scheme superseding the effects of other-insurance clauses, *see* Cal. Ins. Code Ann. § 11580.9.

40. *See*, e.g., Ann. Code of Md. Art. 48A § 540 (PIP insurer not entitled to subrogation).

CHAPTER 7

1. *See* Goetz and Scott, "Enforcing Promises: An Examination of the Basic Contract," 89 *Yale L.J.* 1261 (1980).

2. *See*, e.g., Farber, "Reassessing the Economic Efficiency of Compensatory Damages for Contract Breach," 66 *Va. L. Rev.* 1443 (1980); Goetz and Scott, "Liquidated Damages, Penalties, and the Just Compensation Principle: Some Notes on an Enforcement Model and a Theory of Efficient Breach," 77 *Colum. L. Rev.* 554 (1977); Leff, "Injury, Ignorance, and Spite—The Dynamics of Coercive Collection," 80 *Yale L.J.* 1 (1970); Linzer, "On the Amorality of Contract Remedies: Efficiency, Equity, and the Second Restatement," 81 *Colum. L. Rev.* 111 (1981). *But see* McNeil, "Efficient Breach of Contract: Circles in the Sky," 68 *Va. L. Rev.* 947 (1982).

3. *Compare* Goetz and Scott, "Enforcing Promises: An Examination of the Basis of Contract," 89 *Yale L.J.* 1261, 1293 (1980).

4. In some settings, however, a damage rule may encourage efficient breach but have inefficient effects on the promisee's reliance. For a discussion, *see* A. Polinsky, *An Introduction to Law and Economics* 29–36 (1983).

5. For discussion of the reasons contracting parties might want some, but not complete, protection against the nonpecuniary consequences of breach, *see* Rea, "Nonpecuniary Loss and Breach of Contract," 11 *J. Legal Stud.* 35 (1982).

6. *See generally* Kronman, "Specific Performance," 45 *U. Chi. L. Rev.* 351 (1978); Schwartz, "The Case for Specific Performance," 89 *Yale L.J.* 271 (1979).

7. For discussion of the distinction between the two kinds of breach, *see* Burton, "Breach of Contract and the Common Law Duty to Perform in Good Faith," 94 *Harv. L. Rev.* 369 (1980); Goetz and Scott, "Principles of Relational Contracts," 67 *Va. L. Rev.* 1089, 1139 n. 118; Klein, Crawford and Alchian, "Vertical Integration, Appropriable Rents, and the Competitive Contracting Process," 21 *J. of Law and Econ.* 297, 298–307 (1978).

8. *See* 16A J. Appleman, *Insurance Law and Practice* § 8878.15 (rev. ed. 1981).

9. *See* Holmes, "Is There Life after Gilmore's Death of Contract?—Inductions from a Study of Commercial Good Faith in First-Party Insurance Contracts," 65 *Cornell L. Rev.* 330 (1980); Note, "The Availability of Excess Damages for Wrongful Refusal to Honor First Party Insurance Claims—An Emerging Trend," 45 *Fordham L. Rev.* 164 (1976).

10. 9 Cal. 3d 566, 108 Cal. Rptr. 480, 510 P.2d 1032 (1973).

11. 11 Cal. 3d 452, 113 Cal. Rptr. 711, 521 P.2d 1103 (1974).

12. *See*, e.g., Allen, "Insurance Bad Faith Law: The Need for Legislative Intervention," 13 *Pac. L.J.* 833 (1982); Kornblum, "The Defense of the First Party Extra-Contract Case: Strategy in Negotiations and Discovery," 12 *Forum* 721 (1977); Tasi, "Appellate Arguments against Extra-Contractual Damages in First Party Insurance Cases," 47 *Ins. Counsel J.* 188 (1980).

13. For an early report of the amounts of these awards, *see* Kornblum, "The Defense of the First Party Extra-Contract Case: Strategy in Negotiations and Discovery," 12 *Forum* 721, 723 (1977).

14. For a compilation of the provisions of these statutes, *see* Holmes, "A Model First-Party Insurance Excess-Liability Act," 14 *Ga. L. Rev.* 497, 506 n. 34 (1980).

15. *See id.* at 538.

16. *See*, e.g., Anderson v. Continental Ins. Co., 85 Wis. 2d 675, 271 N.W.2d 368 (1978) (repeated refusal of homeowner's insurer to evaluate and consider insured's proof of loss); United States Fidelity & Guar. Co. v. Peterson, 540 P.2d 1070 (Nev. S. Ct. 1975) (aware of insured construction contractor's precarious financial condition, liability insurer received several notices of contractor's valid claims to payment under liquidated damage provisions of construction contract, promised to pay upon completion of repairs under contract, but failed to do so); Gruenberg v. Aetna Ins. Co., 9 Cal. 3d 566, 108 Cal. Rptr. 480, 510 P.2d 1032 (1973) (fire insurers encouraged the bringing of criminal charges against insured, falsely implying that he had a motive to commit arson, knowing that he would fail to appear for deposition during pendency of arson proceeding, and then denied payment for failure to appear).

17. *See* Insurance Information Institute, *Sample Insurance Policies* 16 (undated pamphlet) (Family Combination Automobile Policy).

18. For discussions of the expected value of a lawsuit, *see* Danzon and Lillard, "Settlement Out of Court: The Disposition of Medical Malpractice Claims," 12 *J. Legal Stud.* 345 (1983); Posner, "An Economic Approach to Legal Procedure and Judicial Administration," 2 *J. Legal Stud.* 399, 418 (1973).

19. For discussion of this problem, *see* Johansen v. California State Auto. Ass'n Inter-Ins. Bureau, 15 Cal. 3d 9, 123 Cal. Rptr. 288, 538 P.2d 744 (1975).

20. *See* Rova Farms Resort, Inc. v. Investors Ins. Co., 65 N.J. 474, 499, 323 A.2d 495, 508 (1974).

21. *See*, e.g., Communale v. Traders & Gen. Ins. Co., 50 Cal. 2d 654, 328 P.2d 198 (1958).

22. *See* Keeton, "Liability Insurance and Responsibility for Settlement," 67 *Harv. L. Rev.* 1136, 1145 (1954).

23. *See* R. Keeton, *Basic Text on Insurance Law*, 510–11 (1971).

24. *See*, e.g., Crisci v. Security Ins. Co., 66 Cal. 2d 425, 58 Cal. Rptr. 13, 426

P. 2d 173 (1967). *See also* Holmes, "Third Party Insurance Excess Liability and Its Avoidance," 34 *Ark. L. Rev.* 525 (1981).

25. *See, e.g.*, Crisci v. Security Ins. Co., 66 Cal. 2d 425, 58 Cal. Rptr. 13, 426 P. 2d 173 (1967) (insurer's refusal to settle for more than $3,000 resulted in a judgment of $100,000 against an insured with a $10,000 policy, after a recommendation of settlement by the insurer's attorney. The insured thereafter suffered a decline in physical health, exhibited hysteria, and attempted suicide).

26. *See, e.g.*, Rova Farms Resort, Inc. v. Investors Ins. Co., 65 N.J. 474, 500, 323 A.2d 495, 509 (1974) (dicta); Schwartz, "Statutory Strict Liability for an Insurer's Failure to Settle: A Balanced Plan for an Unresolved Problem," 1975 *Duke L.J.* 901.

27. For discussions of this anomaly, *see* Note, "Insurer's Liability for Refusal to Settle: Beyond Strict Liability," 50 *S. Cal. L. Rev.* 751 (1977); Note, "Excess Liability: Reconsideration of California's Bad Faith Negligence Rule," 18 *Stan. L. Rev.* 475 (1966).

28. *See* Rova Farms Resort, Inc. v. Investors Ins. Co., 65 N.J. 474, 493, 323 A.2d 495, 505 (1974); Note, "Expanding the Insurer's Duty to Attempt Settlement," 49 *U. Colo. L. Rev.* 251 (1978).

29. *See* Schwartz, "Statutory Strict Liability for an Insurer's Failure to Settle: A Balanced Plan for an Unresolved Problem," 1975 *Duke L.J.* 901, 918.

30. *See* Boise Motor Car Co. v. St. Paul Mercury Indem. Co., 62 Idaho 438, 112 P.2d 1011 (1941); R. Keeton, *Basic Text on Insurance Law* 502–08 (1971).

31. *See* Continental Ins. Co. v. Bayliss & Roberts, Inc., 608 P.2d 281 (S. Ct. of Alaska 1980).

32. 56 N.J. 383, 267 A.2d 7 (1970).

33. For discussion of the collateral estoppel issue as it arises in this context, *see* Morris, "Conflicts of Interest in Defending under Liability Insurance Policies: A Proposed Solution," 1981 *Utah L. Rev.* 457; Note, "The Effect of Collateral Estoppel on the Assertion of Coverage Defenses," 69 *Colum. L. Rev.* 1459 (1969). The assumption described in the text is unlikely because collateral estoppel applies against parties not involved in the original case only if they are in "privity of interest" with a party in the case. It would be implausible to conclude that an insurer which had withdrawn from the case because of a conflict of interest with the insured was nevertheless in "privity" with it for this purpose.

34. 65 Cal. 2d 263, 54 Cal. Rptr. 104, 419 P.2d 168 (1966).

35. *See generally* Note, "The Insurer's Duty to Defend Made Absolute, Gray v. Zurich," 14 *U.C.L.A. L. Rev.* 1328 (1967).

CHAPTER 8

1. *See* R. Dworkin, *Taking Rights Seriously* (1977).

2. *See* R. Nozick, *Anarchy, State, and Utopia* (1974).

3. This is very roughly the position of adherents to what has come to be known as the "critical legal studies movement." *See* R. Unger, "The Critical Legal Studies Movement," 96 *Harv. L. Rev.* 561 (1983).

4. *See* his essay, "The Fragmentation of Value," in T. Nagel, *Mortal Questions* 128 (1979).

Index

249